W9-AEF-295

TEACHING READING
TO ENGLISH LANGUAGE LEARNERS

Teaching Reading to English Language Learners

Insights from Linguistics

Kristin Lems
Leah D. Miller
Tenena M. Soro

THE GUILFORD PRESS
New York   London

© 2010 The Guilford Press
A Division of Guilford Publications, Inc.
72 Spring Street, New York, NY 10012
www.guilford.com

All photos © 2010 Kristin Lems

Printed in the United States of America

This book is printed on acid-free paper.

Last digit is print number: 9   8   7   6   5   4   3   2   1

Library of Congress Cataloging-in-Publication Data

Lems, Kristin.
    Teaching reading to English language learners : insights from linguistics /
Kristin Lems, Leah D. Miller, Tenena M. Soro.
        p. cm.
    Includes bibliographical references and index.
    ISBN 978-1-60623-468-6 (pbk.: alk. paper) — ISBN 978-1-60623-469-3
(hardcover: alk. paper)
    1. Language and languages—Study and teaching.   2. Reading.   3. Second
language acquisition.   I. Miller, Leah D.   II. Soro, Tenena M.   III. Title.
    P53.75.L46 2009
    372.41—dc22

                                                                                              2009036414

About the Authors

Kristin Lems, EdD, is Professor in the ESL/Bilingual Education Program at National-Louis University, where she directed a 5-year grant from the U.S. Department of Education in ESL teacher education in DuPage County, Illinois. She pursued her twin interests in reading and ESL through a doctorate in reading and language from National College of Education and a master's degree in TESOL from the University of Illinois at Urbana–Champaign. Her doctoral dissertation on adult ESL oral reading fluency won a finalist award from the International Reading Association for Outstanding Dissertation of the Year. Dr. Lems spent 2 years as a Fulbright Scholar in Algeria doing inservice training of postsecondary EFL teachers, and wrote a book on ESL/EFL methods for the Peace Corps. Her coedited book, *Fluency Instruction: Research-Based Best Practices*, with Timothy Rasinski and Camille Blachowicz, was a finalist for the Frye Book Award of the National Reading Conference. Dr. Lems consults on reading and ESL in the Chicago Public Schools. She is also a professional folk singer and sings for children in schools and libraries in several languages, including Farsi, which she learned teaching in Iran.

Leah D. Miller, MA, is Assistant Professor in the ESL/Bilingual Education Program at National-Louis University, and also teaches graduate linguistics courses at the University of Illinois at Chicago. She has served as coordinator of the ESL/Bilingual Education Program at National-Louis University for the past decade and has taught all of the courses in the program. In addition to doctoral coursework in linguistics at Northwestern University, Ms. Miller has a master's degree in TESOL from Southern Illinois University. She is on the board of Illinois TESOL/BE, where she heads its Awards Committee, and serves as a consultant on issues related to ELL assessment and the WIDA standards. She has presented at TESOL conventions and meetings of the American Educational Research Association, the American Association for Applied Linguistics, the National Council of Teachers of English, and other prestigious venues. She has a keen interest in content-area ESL and linguistics, and, with Kristin Lems, codirected a Department of Education grant in ESL teacher education. Besides reading research, Ms. Miller's passions include spending time with four adopted grandchildren and Jervis the cat, and reading dictionaries.

Tenena M. Soro, PhD, teaches courses in linguistics, cross-cultural education, foundations, and reading for the ESL/Bilingual Education Program at National-Louis University. He has also taught courses in ethics and philosophy, linguistics, and social science at Columbia College, Northeastern Illinois University, and Northwestern University. He has a doctorate in linguistics and a Graduate Certificate in African Studies from Northwestern University, in addition to two undergraduate degrees from Université d'Abidjan, Ivory Coast. Dr. Soro's dissertation included a linguistic analysis of his native language, Cebaari, and he is proficient in six additional languages. He has presented on linguistics and ESL topics at state and national conferences, including TESOL and the American Educational Research Association, and in 2008 he received the Outstanding Adjunct Faculty Award from National-Louis University. In addition to teaching, he is a serious student of yoga and meditation.

Preface

Educators and policymakers agree that there is an urgent need to rethink the assumptions around teaching the increasing numbers of English language learners (ELLs) in the United States. To bring those students to academic success in a limited period of time, educators need a working knowledge of the systems that compose English and how students are expected to use them for success in reading and writing. P. David Pearson (2007) puts it well:

> As a profession, we have not met our responsibilities to ensure that all of us as teachers, whether novice or veteran, possess the very best and most current knowledge available. We have been too ready to dismiss deep disciplinary knowledge—linguistics (from phonology to text structure to pragmatics), language development, psychology of reading and learning, orthography, literature, and culture—as too distant from the concerns of classroom teaching to merit much emphasis in our pre-service and in-service programs.
>
> Both the teaching profession and the profession of teacher educators should redress this wrong by insisting on more rigorous standards for teacher knowledge. (p. 151)

A panel called by the Carnegie Corporation raised a similar list of challenges to improve the teaching of adolescent ELLs. One of the six recommendations was to increase educator capacity for improving literacy in these students (Short & Fitzsimmons, 2007).

Teaching Reading to English Language Learners aims to address precisely these concerns by increasing the knowledge base of educators involved with teaching ELLs.

Teachers in our many classes have overwhelmingly demonstrated to us their interest in obtaining a deeper knowledge of English that includes linguistic elements. Many have indicated to us that the book's chapters have given them many "aha!" moments. Piloting this book over the course of 18 months has shown us that teachers can make immediate use of their new knowledge in a variety of teaching situations, and that they want to.

Our book was written for the following audiences: (1) instructional leaders in English as a second language (ESL) and bilingual education; (2) reading teachers and specialists who need to know more about the processes of ESL reading; (3) current or future ESL teachers who need to develop expertise about reading; and (4) general education teachers at all grade levels who need to know more about both ESL and reading in English for ELL students. This book can be used in reading classes, ESL or applied linguistics classes, elementary or secondary education methods classes, and study groups for practicing teachers or coordinators.

We wrote this book after looking in vain for a text that could be used for a graduate course we teach about reading in English as a new language. Students in our classes are obtaining their state endorsements in teaching ESL and they will be considered the experts in their buildings or districts. Therefore they need to master key concepts related to linguistics as well as those related to reading. Some of the books we considered focused only on ESL students in higher education; others made assumptions about second-language reading that were not validated in second-language acquisition research; and the linguistics-focused books were overly technical, with few applications to life in the classroom. After years of preparing supplementary handouts, we decided it was time to combine our knowledge of research and best practices from the reading and linguistics fields into one place and include suggestions for usable classroom applications. We have tried to present these insights in a manner that is clear, readable, and even enjoyable. You will be the judge of that effort!

Chapter 1 contains an overview of the second-language acquisition field because we want to establish a common set of understandings and terminology for our readers. Chapter 2 is devoted to a subject that is of scholarly interest in several professions but often glossed over: the influence of first language on learning a new language, especially in regard to reading. These two chapters also establish our point of view on some important issues that schools must address when planning programs for their ELLs.

The seven chapters that follow address specific components that must be built into a "syndrome of success" in order for ELLs to enjoy and succeed in reading and writing in English:

- The critical development of oracy.
- Learning successful decoding of the English alphabet.
- Using morpheme study to increase vocabulary.

- Understanding word formation processes, cognates, and collocations in English.
- Developing reading fluency.
- Developing a set of flexible reading strategies.
- Learning to write in the forms school demands, and using writing to learn.

At the beginning of each chapter, we include a list of new vocabulary introduced in the text. The meaning of each term can be looked up in the glossary at the end of the book. Within each chapter, we have interspersed pertinent vignettes from our own experiences and those of ESL practitioners we know. The chapters are followed by a section titled "What Does This Mean in the Classroom?" with practical applications that are consonant with the linguistic insights of the chapter. Some of these are described in detail and can be used right away, whereas others are only sketched briefly. The end of each chapter contains questions for further study. They can be used in a classroom setting, professional development setting, or for self-study.

This book may raise as many questions as it answers for you. However, we are confident that bringing awareness of linguistic features of English will have both immediate and long-term benefits for your classroom teaching or instructional leadership. It is also likely to raise your curiosity about language in general. You will notice things about English and about literacy—your own and that of your students—that have never occurred to you before! And you will undoubtedly find ways to incorporate your new understandings into your educational venue.

The more we have learned about the subject of learning to read in English as a new language, the more exciting the journey has become. Although we are glad to see the book completed and ready to make its contribution to the world, we continue to be captivated by these compelling topics. We are also mindful that these insights can have a huge positive impact on the lives of real learners in the real world. We wish you happy reading!

Acknowledgments

We'd like to thank the following teachers for sharing their professional experiences in the book: Arlene Duval, Beth Bullis Dominguez, Vicki Musial, Janis Mara Michael, Anne Grossmann, Seung Hee Ma, Theresa Kubasak, Kathleen McColaugh, Margarita Jaime, Rob Schoonveld, Reena Patel, Virginia Runge, and Maria Isabel Orescanin. You have given our readers many great ideas!

Many thanks to Kyle Perkins for reading an early draft of the manuscript and providing valuable feedback. We also appreciate the assistance of the following colleagues who made important contributions to the book: Camille Blachowicz, XiuWen Wu, Pauline Wong, Gale Stam, Po Fan Ng, Antonina Lukenchuk, and Matt Granger.

We appreciate the fine support from the team at The Guilford Press— it was a pleasure to work with you every step of the way! Special thanks to Craig Thomas, as well as Anna Nelson, Joi Rowe, Mary Beth Wood, Katherine Lieber, Lauren Foust, and Paul Gordon. Thanks also to indexer Carol Lems-Dworkin and to the authors and artists whose materials we have included in the book.

We appreciate the comments and suggestions of hundreds of students who used piloted versions of the book. Your interactions with the book as it evolved have made it much better!

Most of all, we appreciate the encouragement and support of our families and friends, who endured so much in the past 2 years when we were unavailable—even on weekends and holidays—as we worked on this book. Your belief that we were doing something important and valuable meant everything to us.

Contents

Guide to Pronunciation
in This Book

We have chosen to avoid special symbols in favor of common, simplified forms that can be created on a standard typewriter, with the exception of the schwa sound, /ə/.

Consonants

Sound	as in
Voiced	
/b/	*bad*
/d/	*dog*
/g/	*go*
/j/	*job, fudge*
/l/	*lid*
/m/	*mad*
/n/	*not*
/r/	*red*
/v/	*van*
/w/	*win*
/z/	*zip*
/ng/	*sing*
/th/	*that*
/y/	*young*
/zh/	*measure*

Voiceless

/p/	*pin*
/t/	*tap*
/k/	*kid*
/f/	*fit*
/h/	*hat*
/s/	*sad*
/ch/	*chin*
/sh/	*shell*
/TH/	*think*

Vowels

Sound	as in	commonly called
Short vowels		
/ae/	*had*	short *a*
/e/	*bed*	short *e*
/i/	*bid*	short *i*
/a/	*father, hot*	short *o*
/oo/	*book*	alternate short *u*
/u/	*cut*	short *u*
/ə/	unstressed vowels (*across, zebra*)	schwa sound
Long vowels (all diphthongs in English)		
/ey/	*say*	long *a*
/iy/	*see, happy*	long *e*
/ay/	*I*	long *i*
/ow/	*go*	long *o*
/uw/	*you, food*	long *u*
/aw/	*saw, dog*	open *o*
Additional diphthongs		
/ou/	*house, crowd*	
/oy/	*toy*	
r-controlled vowels		
/ar/	*hard*	
/er/	*hurt*	
/ir/	*fear*	
/eyr/	*care*	
/ayr/	*fire*	
/owr/	*floor*	
/uwr/	*sure*	

CHAPTER ONE

Big Ideas and Research That Guide the Profession

New Vocabulary in This Chapter: English language learners (ELLs), language-based theory of learning, phonology, morphology, syntax, semantics, orthography, syndrome of success, language-specific, second-language acquisition (SLA), balanced literacy, communicative competence, idiom, input hypothesis, comprehensible input, motherese/caretaker speech, output hypothesis, comprehensible output, affect, affective filter, integrative motivation, instrumental motivation, assimilative motivation, intrinsic motivation, resiliency, grammar translation, English as a foreign language (EFL), English as a second language (ESL), audiolingualism, oral proficiency, communicative approach, content-based instruction (CBI), content area, cognitive academic language learning approach (CALLA), specially designed academic instruction in English (SDAIE), sheltered instruction observation protocol (SIOP), sheltered instruction, socially constructed, zone of proximal development (ZPD), instructional conversation, realia

Language is an important part of how humans communicate with each other. It is no small thing! Through language, we learn how to "mean things" (Halliday, 1993) and how to share all of those meanings with others. The story of how those meanings are created and shared is truly the story of the human family. It is our distinctly human endowment.

Being able to share meanings with others in more than one language is an even more remarkable achievement. There is no question about the value of biliteracy and bilingualism both for the individual and society. It opens options for self-expression, economic viability, and common problem solving across language groups. We unequivocally support bilingualism and biliteracy as a core goal for an educated society.

That being said, however, we do not pretend that achieving this goal is easy, fast, or inexpensive! Many program models have been implemented in the United States and around the world to facilitate the development of biliteracy. In this book, our specific goal is to help educators foster the growth of English academic proficiency by *English language learners (ELLs)* in the pre-K–12 learning environment regardless of the program model in which they are situated.

Certain big ideas about learning, literacy, and second language acquisition underlie and inform the rest of the book, so we introduce them briefly in this chapter. In addition, we provide an overview of some of the research-based best practices for teaching English as a new language that emanate from those big ideas.

The Language-Based Theory of Learning

The *language-based theory of learning* (Halliday, 1993) is a good organizing principle for talking about second language acquisition. Halliday considered all learning as a linguistic process taking place in three interconnected areas: learning language, learning content through language, and learning about language. Figure 1.1 shows these three areas of the language-based theory of learning.

Halliday (1993) explains his theory:

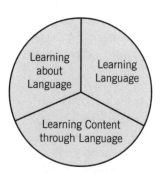

FIGURE 1.1. Three language functions. Based on the language based-model of learning (Halliday, 1993).

With this formulation I was trying to establish two unifying principles: that we should recognize not only a developmental continuity right through from birth to adult life, with language in home, neighborhood, primary school, secondary school, and place of work, but also a structural continuity running through all components and processes of learning. (p. 113)

Halliday recognized that language is more than a skill; it is also a tool for all other learning. Halliday's formulation nicely captures the concept of language both as a means to an end and an end in itself and helps guide our thinking about how teaching English as a new language needs to account for all of those functions. Those who teach English as a new language can structure in activities that help learners learn language, learn content through language, and learn about a language; conversely, learners will struggle if any one of these three functions is neglected.

Universals and Specifics of Language and Literacy

Language is a system that contains small elements that can be combined in an infinite number of ways in order to make larger structures. Human language has four universals: phonology, morphology, syntax, and semantics. The *phonology* of a language is the set of its sound patterns and the rules that govern how they can be combined; these patterns and rules give the language its distinct auditory identity. *Morphology* is the set of units of meaning that make up the words of a language and the ways those units of meaning can be combined. Every language also has *syntax*, the set of rules governing the ways in which words can be combined into phrases and sentences. Finally, the *semantics* of a language are the meanings that emerge from all of the previous three elements: the sounds, word meanings, and word-order patterns. Even though the phonology, morphology, syntax, and semantics of every language differ, all languages have them.

On the other hand, not every language has a writing system, or *orthography*. The first evidence of written records dates back only about 10,000 years; writing systems were invented in the same fashion that early civilizations invented the wheel, glass, and other sociocultural characteristics. Although orthographies also differ according to language, their invention in any society is not inevitable.

This difference is important because the four universals are naturally acquired by native speakers of a language, whereas orthography is a feature of literacy, is not natural, and needs to be taught (Peregoy & Boyle, 2005, p. 164). Pinker (2007) says, "Language is an instinct, but reading is not" (p. 14). If reading and writing were universal and inevitable, no language group would have failed to develop a writing system, but we know that many societies, even some lasting several centuries, have not. The Mississippian peoples living in Cahokia, for example, developed complex dwellings, trade, many tools, and fine works of art, but never developed a writing system. Because reading and writing are not inevitable processes even in a first language, it stands to reason that considerable energy and effort are needed to learn to do them in a new language.

Interaction of Two Developing Systems

When ELLs achieve literacy in a new language, there are two large-scale, long-term developmental processes going on at the same time. One is the learning of literacy, and the other is the learning of the new language. The two metaprocesses develop, overlap, and interact in many complex ways. Their successful dual outcomes can be thought of almost as a kind of "syndrome." Normally a syndrome is thought of as a group of factors which, taken together, form a pattern that accompanies a disease or disorder. However, we'd like to flip that definition to describe a positive pattern. A positive syndrome for literacy in a new language, which we will call a *syndrome of success*, can be thought of as a situation in which the presence of seemingly disconnected factors working in combination make success more likely. Because they are complex, researchers do not know all of the necessary ingredients or proportions thereof, but we do know that a certain number of characteristics need to be "in the mix," and that some cannot be missing.

Some key features for the syndrome of success in building first language literacy include: listening comprehension, phonological and phonemic awareness, oral language production, the concept of word, sound–symbol matching (phonics), word recognition, ability to construct meaning from print, fluent decoding, fluency, recognition of grammar and syntax patterns, vocabulary knowledge, knowledge of the function of punctuation, ability to spell, awareness of the diverse purposes of print, the ability to relate new information to prior experiences, writing for different purposes, and many other skills. In school settings, these are often classified into the five-part framework developed by the National Reading Panel: phonemic awareness, phonics, fluency, vocabulary, and comprehension (National Reading Panel, 2000). Many have called for the inclusion of writing as a core skill as well.

Throughout this book, we use the term "L1" to represent the concepts "language one," "native language," "heritage language," or "first language," and the term "L2" to mean "second language" and sometimes "subsequent language," or "additional language."

All of these same literacy features need to develop in order to acquire literacy in a new language as well. Some aspects of these features can be learned once, in the first language, and positively applied to acquiring the same skill in a new language. Other features, however, require obtaining *language-specific* skills in the new language, that is, features that are unique to the structures of that particular language.

The skills needed may be acquired unconsciously in some cases and in others must be consciously learned. Language-specific skills are not necessarily facilitated by knowing the same skill in the first language; they may sometimes even be hindered by it, depending on such factors as the structure of the two languages (Birch, 2007), the L1 and L2 proficiency levels of the learner, and the nature of the task.

English as a New Language: Four Domains and the Fifth Domain

Learning a new language is usually divided by those in the language teaching field into four large domains: listening, speaking, reading, and writing (Canale & Swain, 1980). These domains, stated in this order, also represent a *general* pattern of *second-language acquisition (SLA)*. Sometimes listening and reading are characterized as "receptive," and speaking and writing as "productive," but we caution against using those labels because they fail to capture the active meaning making that takes place during both listening and reading. The four domains need to be included in instructional planning and assessment of L2 proficiency, in the same way that the framework for foundations of literacy needs to be used to build a *balanced literacy* program.

Each one of the large domains has many skills nested within it. Furthermore, many language activities spill into more than one of the language domains—language is like that. There are times when one domain or skill should be the object of focus, and other times when the focus should be on constructing and communicating meaning through integrated activities that span the language domains. A sound instructional model has room to develop both small skills that belong mainly to one domain, and large integrated operations.

In a literacy curriculum, there are numerous small skill areas across the four language domains, such as learning where to place a comma in a list or being able to anticipate the next word of the sentence when someone says "Neither my family _____." However, the goal is ultimately to absorb each of them into the reading and writing process until they become automatic and unconscious. The approach that favors mixing smaller skills within a framework of large meaning-based activities is usually called "balanced literacy."

In addition to the skills, operations, and domains mentioned here, a fifth domain can be considered both a result of the other four and at the same time a contributor to them: communicative competence (Hymes, 1971). *Communicative competence* can be described as "the ability to know when, where, and how to use language in a variety of contexts or situations" (Rothenberg & Fisher, 2007, p. 38). Communicative competence is composed of many features. Those who developed the concept divide them into grammatical, sociolinguistic, discourse, and strategic competence (Canale, 1983), which in turn guide language users in making appropriate language choices for different social and academic purposes.

Communicative competence can be demonstrated in many different ways. It can be expressed through word choices, syntax, vocal intonations, body language and gestures, and through socially constructed rules for verbal communication that guide different social settings. Communicative competence cannot be taken for granted; it may take a long time to acquire, and its ingredients vary for differing purposes. Good L2 instruction infuses all the language domains with authentic activities that build up communicative competence in a natural, ongoing way. For example, when students learn the *idiom* "You're pulling my leg!" they need to learn not only its idiomatic meaning, but the kinds of settings in which it would be appropriate to use the idiom.

Appendix 1.1 is a grid that can be used as a point of departure for thinking about ways to account for the five domains and the three functions of language learning in lesson planning on a regular basis. Understanding these domains and functions builds teacher expertise in teaching reading to ELLs. Developing key literacy skills affects the development of L2 reading, and the development of L2 reading in turn affects literacy skills.

Language-Centered Factors Influencing SLA

What kinds of forces and factors contribute to creating proficiency in a new language? Research converges on several factors, which we briefly discuss here.

The Input Hypothesis and Comprehensible Input

The first factor is that learning a language requires having sufficient exposure to the language, and at a manageable level, for learners to be able to comprehend it. Stephen Krashen (1985) grasped this understanding in his revolutionary *input hypothesis*, which states that people acquire a new language similarly to the way they acquire their native language as long as they are exposed to enormous amounts of spoken or written language, which he calls "input." Furthermore, the input needs not only to be very large; it must also be delivered at a level close to that at which learners can comprehend it. Krashen uses the term *comprehensible input* to describe language delivered to the learner at a level at which he or she can understand most of it.

We all deploy comprehensible input intuitively when we modify our speech for a specific listener. For example, we speak "baby talk" with an infant, using gestures and exaggerated intonation to get across our meanings (linguists call that simplified kind of talk *motherese* or *caretaker speech*). If we are mindful, we might use our intuitive understanding of comprehensible input by modifying our language to assist limited English speakers. (If we are not mindful, it may sound like we're producing baby talk!) Input may also be modified for us when we travel in places where we don't know the language and native speakers modify it for us by adding gestures or throwing in a few words of English. A person might make input comprehensible by simplifying words, repeating words or phrases, speaking more slowly, breaking speech into smaller units, using exaggerated intonation or stress, or adding facial features or gestures. As learners gain proficiency, the level of comprehensible input becomes progressively more advanced as well. When learners are immersed in both oral and written language that is not too hard or overwhelming, they are able to internalize it.

The input hypothesis and the concept of comprehensible input have been enormously influential in the ESL field. They have affected the development of all major ESL programs and instructional materials.

Finally, the comprehensible input needs to be meaningful on some level. Like the old joke, "What is the difference between ignorance and apathy? I don't know and I don't care!" people do not learn language for its own sake, but to fulfill real purposes. Even if it's comprehensible and there's enough of it, language acquisition requires some kind of authentic communicative purpose.

The Output Hypothesis

For successful language learning, learners need opportunities not just to be exposed to spoken or written language, but also to interact with it. Meryl Swain's (2005) *output hypothesis* attempts to address this. Swain noticed that Canadian L1 English speakers in bilingual education programs immersed all day in French language content instruction over many years did not speak and write at the same level as their L1 French-speaking counterparts. The "input" was the same in quantity and quality; the missing piece was the "output." L1 English speakers were not being pushed to use grammar accurately or meaningfully. There was no urgency to develop communicative competence.

Having lots of comprehensible input alone isn't enough to learn a new language, Swain reasoned; the learner needs abundant opportunities to create comprehensible output in situations that matter to the individual. *Comprehensible output* takes place through contact with a more competent other, such as a teacher or conversation partner, or in interactive situations such as collaborative dialogue (Swain, 2005, p. 478) or simple problem solving.

Comprehensible input helps explain the conditions for learning that are most likely to influence listening and reading, whereas comprehensible output helps explain the development of speaking and writing. Input and output are constantly interacting, however, and communicative competence is a constant overriding goal, no matter which processes are in play.

Nonlinguistic Influences on SLA

Many nonlinguistic factors have been shown to influence success in learning a new language, but we have chosen to highlight three we consider to be very important.

The Affective Filter

Affect, or emotional state, is closely associated with language learning outcomes. The emotional aspects that influence language learning are referred to as the *affective filter* (Dulay & Burt, 1977), that is, the emotional response to the language learning situation. Put briefly, many believe "the lower the level of anxiety, the better the language acquisition" (Krashen, 1987, p. 39). Learners' attitudes about their cultural or family background, the target language, the classsroom climate, their feelings about their age or prior educational experiences, and many other factors influence the affective filter.

Motivation

The purposes for which a person learns a new language are also at the forefront of language success. Motivation for learning a new language can be separated into the following four categories: integrative motivation, instrumental motivation (Gardner & Lambert, 1972), assimilative motivation (Graham, 1984, cited in Richard-Amato, 1988, 2003), and intrinsic motivation. *Integrative motivation* is the motivation a person feels when he or she wants to join a community. Voluntary immigrants have historically been those most interested in integrating into their new culture, and it has an effect on the way they pursue language learning. *Instrumental motivation,* occurs when a person needs to learn a language for a specific reason, such as school, a job, or a spouse. Students in foreign universities, people in international business, and those in English-dominant professions such as airplane pilots, ship navigators, and air traffic controllers have instrumental motivation to learn English in the realms needed for their purposes. When someone wishes to fully merge their identity with a target group (Richard-Amato, 2003), they are exhibiting *assimilative motivation*. Learners with assimilative motivation want to construct a new personal identify along with the new language. They are less likely to want to maintain their heritage language and culture. This group fits more with the "melting pot" idea that everyone "melts" into a single national or language identity. With integrative motivation, on the other hand, members want to mix but not melt.

The fourth kind of motivation, which is less specific to language learning per se, is *intrinsic motivation*. Those who have this kind of curiosity want to learn a new language or anything else for its own sake. Many of us who choose the language learning or language teaching profession have strong intrinsic motivation and find the study of languages captivating.

In addition, classroom motivational practices adopted by teachers should never be discounted. The way teachers structure and present content has a measurable effect on the motivation level and the success of ELLs (Guilloteaux & Dornei, 2008).

Resiliency

Resiliency describes a person's ability to persevere to overcome possible obstacles. A U.S. Department of Education–funded study of 1,000 fourth- and fifth-grade ELLs looked at the differences between resilient students, who were defined as high achievers who excelled on standardized tests and in daily schoolwork despite challenges; and nonresilient students, who were low achievers, were not motivated, and had low attendance (Padrón, Waxman, Brown, & Powers, 2000). They found that resilient learners stayed on task more of the time in class, had higher satisfaction with their classes and a better self-image, got in trouble less, and had better relationships with their teachers. Significantly, they also used more metacognitive strategies while reading, and they did not consider reading to be their hardest subject.

Resilient children were also found to speak more of their L1 with their parents and friends. These findings suggest that reading proficiency and use of the L1 as a resource may be factors in building resiliency and overall success for ELLs—or that resiliency contributes to building them.

Padrón et al. (2000) suggest the following ways that teachers can build resiliency in the classroom:

- Offering students opportunities to develop close relationships in the classroom.
- Increasing students' sense of mastery in their lives.
- Building social competencies in addition to academic skills.
- Reducing stress.
- Finding and generating school and community resources to serve the children's needs.

Language Teaching Approaches and Methods and the Role of Reading

Throughout history, there have been many approaches to teaching new languages. We briefly highlight four important approaches used in a wide variety of ESL programs over the years, with particular reference to how they approach the teaching of reading in a new language: (1) grammar translation, (2) audiolingualism (Fries, 1945; Lado, 1977), (3) the communicative approach (Canale & Swain, 1980; Savignon, 1983), and (4) content-based instruction (Anderson, 1999; Chamot & O'Malley, 1994; Freeman & Freeman, 1992; Peregoy & Boyle, 1997; Snow, 1994; Stoller & Grabe, 1997). We use the terms *approach* and *method* interchangeably in this section.

The Grammar Translation Method

The focus of the *grammar translation* method is on reading and translating a text back into one's first language. Once learners understand the specific grammar rules embedded in various reading passages, they begin writing in the target language. Little or no attempt is made to build communicative competence. A grammar translation lesson usually consists of the teacher introducing a text in the new language and explaining the grammar rules that the text illustrates. Students often receive a list of vocabulary words and phrases to facilitate their reading. The grammar translation approach is most widely used in language learning methods designed for instrumental purposes. Its users include those training for the clergy or for advanced degrees in certain academic disciplines. Latin, Greek, Hebrew, and Sanskrit are often taught by this method. Grammar translation is also a component of language teaching in countries where there are not many native speakers of the target language, so that the book and its related exercises serve in many ways as the "teacher." Elements of grammar translation may even be used for teaching very young children.

Incidentally, when students learn English in a non-English-speaking country, it is called *English as a foreign language*, or *EFL*. Within an English-speaking country, English language learners are said to be studying *ESL*, or

English as a second language. The learners of English as a new language are commonly referred to as English language learners, or ELLs. These terms are widely used in the language teaching field. Also, some professional standards for teachers of ELLs such as those in Illinois, for example, are called ENL standards (English as a new language standards). The terms L1 and L2, on the other hand, are used mainly in applied linguistics as a shorthand for the language being referred to at the moment.

Audiolingualism

Audiolingualism, or the audiolingual method (ALM), is a language learning method in which *oral proficiency* in the target language takes precedence over reading and writing. This is reflected in its title—"audio" representing listening, and "lingual" representing speaking. It developed as a countermovement to the heavily text-centered nature of the grammar translation approach. The initial impetus for ALM in the United States was to develop fluent speakers of the world's languages for national defense purposes. A modified form of audiolingualism is still used in the United States to prepare people for the Peace Corps and for diplomatic and other international assignments, and it is the method used by many independent language academies.

An audiolingual lesson consists of students learning and repeating dialogues with the teacher and other students and practicing sentences based on the dialogues through oral drills. The dialogues are often rehearsed in a language lab, making it an essential element of the method. Students may memorize and perform a dialogue at the end of a unit. Rules are presented sequentially through the dialogues, but not formally explained. Pronunciation gets a lot of attention in ALM. Reading is not a focus of audiolingualism and is not generally introduced until the third year of study.

The Communicative Approach

The *communicative approach* changed the focus of ESL instruction by putting communicative competence at center stage. Canale and Swain (1980), Savignon (1983), and others recognized that the social functions of language and meaning-making in language were too often missing from language teaching methods, in particular ALM.

Brown (2001) describes the goals of communicative competence this way:

> Communicative goals are best achieved by giving due attention to language use and not just usage, to fluency and not just accuracy, to authen-

tic language and contexts, and to students' eventual need to apply classroom learning to previously unrehearsed contexts. (p. 69)

The approach is learner centered and consistent with constructivist notions of education. Although reading and writing occur, they are seen as a means to greater communicative competence; academic language is not a focus. Students use authentic texts for speaking and reading activities, and these may come from a wide variety of genres, such as menus, newspaper articles, or even medicine bottle labels. Grammar, when taught, is contextualized and is considered a means to enhance communication. The communicative approach is widely used in EFL settings outside of English-speaking countries and with adult learners. Until the advent of content-based instruction, it was also the most widely used approach used in K–12 schools within the United States.

These three approaches have been successful in helping many people learn new languages. They have all been widely used with adult learners. However, all of them presuppose a certain "grace period" before the language must be used for literacy purposes, which does not address the reality of ELLs in K–12 academic settings. These young people must learn English at the same time they are learning content matter in English, in the areas of social studies, math, science, and language arts. In addition, they need to learn the language used to perform overall academic tasks, such as listening to directions and taking standardized tests.

Content-Based Instruction

Addressing this pressing need of ELLs to learn English and at the same time learn content through English is the goal of *content-based instruction* (*CBI*; Chamot & O'Malley, 1994). This approach represents a major paradigm shift in English language teaching.

For too long, it had been assumed that ELLs would naturally pick up the academic language that native speakers in schools are already likely to possess, but all too often, this was not at all the case. Using the CBI approach, all teachers, whether ESL, bilingual, or content teachers, and regardless of their instructional setting, need to know the language, strategies, and techniques for teaching academic language to ELLs. By the way, these same techniques also help in teaching native speakers of English!

CBI consists of two equally important components: building language proficiency and building content knowledge. The model for the approach encompasses setting clearly defined language and content goals and using a modified curriculum, supplementary materials, and authentic assessments.

On the language side, key competencies include learning the forms of English (grammar), learning its uses (functions), and becoming automatic in their spoken and written use. The language includes not only "survival" English, social English, and academic English, but has also incorporated the language of various content area and language proficiency standards. Naturally, survival English and social English have roles in the communicative approach, too; the unique contribution of CBI is its inclusion of teaching academic English as an explicit goal.

On the content side, key competencies of CBI include learning the specific language of the *content areas* (the various subjects students are studying in the classroom) as well as the content knowledge itself. Students must master a wide range of language demands, such as understanding oral and written directions and understanding and using content-specific vocabulary and concepts. The content vocabulary may be found not only in textbooks and lectures, but also in other print and online materials, including oral text sources. In addition, a goal of CBI is to help ELLs learn to produce language output at a level appropriate to the academic benchmarks for their grade levels. They must be able to demonstrate this ability in both oral and written forms, in the course of both instruction and assessment (Teachers of English to Speakers of Other Languages, 2006, p. 18).

In the past, teachers believed that introducing individual content words about a topic would take care of the language needs of learners, whether native speakers or ELLs. However, the missing ingredient for ELLs was accounting for the language activities students required to perform the cognitive tasks of the classroom. For example, third-grade ELLs learning about dinosaurs need two kinds of vocabulary. They need to learn the words to understand dinosaur species, their habitats, and the geological time periods in which they lived. They also need academic language to process and demonstrate their understanding of the content, such as "Speculate about why the dinosaurs became extinct," or "Include supporting details with your thesis statement," or "Summarize what you have learned." These are more complex procedures than meet the eye! CBI recognizes that the academic activities that accompany learning about content are just as important as the study of content itself. CBI is performance based, and the performances measures mirror the activities native-speaking children are expected to master to achieve academic success at each grade level.

CBI-Based Instructional Models

Three CBI-based instructional models have gained widespread acceptance in the United States. The *cognitive academic language learning approach* (*CALLA*; Chamot & O'Malley, 1986) was the first to recognize that it was necessary to put greater focus on English features and strategies in order to help ELLs academically. The *specially designed academic instruction in English (SDAIE)* model, developed in the 1990s and used in California, has three main components: making content comprehensible and engaging, developing academic language, and providing strategies students can use for independent learning. The *sheltered instruction observation protocol (SIOP)* model (Echevarria, Vogt, & Short, 2004) was designed for teachers with ELLs in their grade-level classrooms but is now used in several classroom configurations, such as ESL, bilingual, and sheltered models. The SIOP model has eight major parts and includes more than 30 sheltering strategies in order to build students' language skills while they are learning grade-level content. Teachers using the SIOP model are encouraged to be trained in its implementation, and a number of books are available to guide teachers in its use.

All of these models—CALLA, SDAIE, and SIOP—are *sheltered instruction* models. They activate the prior knowledge of the learner, provide supports for developing academic skills and language, provide manipulatives for hands-on learning, give generous time to generate output, and include authentic assessment. Sheltered instruction pedagogy is based on the CBI model.

These instructional models and others that subscribe to CBI use subject-matter content as the basis of instruction, while helping learners develop many cognitive and metacognitive strategies. However, it's also important that CBI programs provide enough time for ELLs to engage in daily oral language that is not on academic topics but develops social skills.

The Influence of Vygotsky's Theories on Second-Language Learning

Both Krashen and Swain's hypotheses include the assumption that students' L2 proficiency increases when they engage in activities that allow them to understand or produce language at the next level to which they aspire. Therefore, they benefit from opportunities to connect with a language user at a level just above their own current one. Their theories mesh nicely with those of Lev Vygotsky, a Russian psychologist whose works were largely unknown during his own lifetime but are becoming increasingly influential with language researchers, child psychologists, and educators.

Vygotsky's theories have contributed two important ideas to the field of L2 acquisition. One is his characterization of learning as being *socially constructed.* Our social interactions and the language we use to perform them provide us with the mental tools that allow us to learn. School settings are a place where "socially organized events" are likely to occur, so they are important to our language growth, which is in turn the basis of our cognitive growth. One application of that idea is that we learn through interactions that take place during schooling, family time, work, and play.

The other idea is Vygotsky's concept of the *zone of proximal development (ZPD)* (Vygotsky, 1978). He describes this as "the discrepancy between a child's actual mental age and the level he reaches in solving problems with assistance" (Vygotsky, 1986, p. 187). Vygotsky described an effective learning setting as one in which the learner has multiple opportunities to grow within that zone. The teacher's role can be described as something like collaborative coaching "in the zone." Research on effective second-language instruction supports Vygotsky's idea that ELLs thrive when the teacher models and collaborates in *instructional conversation* (Tharp et al., 2003; Waxman & Tellez, 2002). Many educators have begun to embrace the powerful idea that a student can attain a higher level of proficiency with assistance from a near peer or "expert other" than with a teacher lecturing from the front of a room.

The concept of ZPD acknowledges not only the dynamic process of learning, but also the importance of differentiating instruction among learners within a classroom. When we factor in the developmental continua of human learning along with L2 acquisition, we are not surprised at all the varieties of achievement that result! After all, no two people are alike, and no two language learners are ever at exactly the same stage.

The way I visualize learning a new language "in the zone" is by thinking of an island in the South Pacific. Formed by strong forces, the island forms as more and more material is pushed up from below and becomes rich island soil. Following the metaphor, as we learn more language, more material is added to the rich soil, and that in turn increases the base. After a while, there is enough to stand on, and things begin to grow. In time, you might have enough space to live upon.—KRISTIN

Research into Effective Teaching Strategies for ELLs

Only a decade or two ago, research about best practices for teaching ELLs was spotty. Most of the research had been conducted on adults in academic settings, but far less was known about how children who speak a language other than English at home could achieve biliteracy and academic success. Now, there is increased national awareness, and resources are being harnessed to conduct research about what teaching practices work best for ELLs.

Several major metastudies have examined best practices for teaching ELLs (August & Shanahan, 2006; Echevarria et al., 2004; Gersten & Baker, 2000; Gersten et al., 2007; Tharp et al., 2003; Waxman & Tellez, 2002; Williams, Hakuta, Haertel, et al., 2007). From them, it is possible to identify a number of recurring characteristics, as follow:

• *Collaborative learning communities.* ELLs thrive in cooperative learning and small-group settings due to having lowered affective filters, more opportunity to practice language, and reasons to use language for authentic communicative purposes.

• *Multiple representations of content.* ELLs benefit when they have several points of entry into content, especially when content is combined with visual images. Computers and the Internet provide even resource-poor schools with many potential visual and auditory enhancements to boost learning. Auditory sources, including music, and real life objects, called *realia*, can also be brought in. Realia might include pictures from mailers and magazines, common objects found in the home, and the environmental print found on the labeling and packaging of common products. The same visual support that can enhance comprehensible input for ELLs can also be used to help them demonstrate their comprehension through drawing, labeling, collages, photo essays, or posters.

• *Building on prior knowledge.* When time and care are taken to activate prior knowledge before engaging in reading, writing, or any kind of academic activity, it's easier for ELLs to hook into many topic areas and respond positively. Setting a purpose for reading, preteaching key vocabulary, giving students choice in their writing topics, and reviewing previously covered lessons before beginning new material are some of the ways to support ELL students.

• *Instructional conversation.* When ELLs have extended instructional conversation with both peers and with the teacher, their understanding of academic concepts increases and spills into all their literacy activity. Academic conversations that build higher-order thinking include not only reading and writing topics, but also common classroom topics, such as planning activities for the day and discussing classroom dynamics. In this area, the teacher serves as both a model and a full participant.

• *Culturally responsive instruction.* Like any students, ELLs need to see themselves and their home cultures reflected in some of the readings and topics offered in the curriculum. Although this is widely understood, many classrooms and schools have still not taken up the challenge to make resources that respect and affirm ELL children's home cultures and languages available and visible. Teachers can easily set the tone by establishing a welcoming classroom and showing openness by encouraging use of the students' first language as a support when needed. Inviting families and cultural representatives into the classroom as resources and leaders is another way.

- *Technology-enriched instruction.* Technology has opened new vistas for teaching ELLs. Computer-assisted programs allow students to work at their own pace and on their own lessons, allowing differentiation in mixed-level or mixed-language classrooms. Technology makes colorful and amusing resources available for supplementing background knowledge. Additional audio, visual, and interactive cueing systems make many learning tasks easy and enjoyable. Technology also gives a chance to students who "speak technology as a first language" to share what they know with classmates and the teacher.
- *Challenging curriculum.* When adapting language for different English proficiency levels, it's easy for teachers to become inadvertent "enablers." Students should be challenged to not only meet standards, but to exceed them. We must maintain a delicate balance to prevent the "comfort zone" from becoming a "work-free" zone. When challenging material and standards are presented and students are asked to meet them, ELL students rise to the occasion. Some ELLs should be invited to take part in gifted education, just like their L1 peers, in districts that have such offerings.
- *Strong and explicit vocabulary development.* Vocabulary development in both oral and written forms is at the core of all academic learning for ELLs. Students need to learn the language of the content areas and to experience new words as they are modeled, heard, spoken, written, and used in context.

We discuss all of these areas in more detail in the ensuing chapters.

HOW DOES THIS LOOK IN THE CLASSROOM?

Planning Work in the Five Domains

ELLs need daily experience using all five domains, both in isolation and integration. Is each student in the class taking part in some listening, speaking, reading, writing, and communicative activity every day?

Provide Comprehensible Input

The key word here is *comprehensible.* A person can have a TV on all day and call it language "input," but that doesn't make it comprehensible. Input can be made comprehensible by breaking it up into smaller chunks, using visuals, simplifying language, adding captions, and providing repetitions or other supports, while checking comprehension regularly.

Pushing Output

Pushing output is a way to describe a classroom that has less teacher talk and more pair and small-group talk. When teachers push output, students have many opportunities to construct, practice, and perform pieces of language created for some real communicative purpose, with developmental feedback that will allow them to raise their output to ever-higher levels.

Lowering the Affective Filter

There are many ways to create a learning environment that is at once comforting, nurturing, and challenging. One teacher reports, "The atmosphere in my high school ESL class improved a lot when I dropped the closed-book tests and quizzes." Other ways are to give students choices about ways of responding, allow sufficient wait time for students to formulate answers, and provide opportunities for students to present in small groups instead of presenting to the entire class. Laughter, games, songs, skits, and brain teasers also help. Celebrations and parties show caring, build community, and contribute to the general ambience as well.

QUESTIONS FOR FURTHER STUDY

1. If you had to choose three important ideas from this chapter, which would you choose? How can you apply these ideas to your larger knowledge of teaching English as a new language?

2. What are some ways that input has been made comprehensible in a teaching or learning setting with which you are familiar—not necessarily a language-learning situation?

3. Make a chart comparing and contrasting comprehensible input and comprehensible output. What do they have in common? How do they differ?

4. Analyze your own foreign language learning in terms of the four different kinds of motivation listed in the chapter. How did the presence or absence of that motivation affect the success of the language-learning task? What other tasks in your life have been guided by integrative motivation? Instrumental motivation? Intrinsic motivation?

5. Do you think resiliency and intrinsic motivation are determined entirely by environment and upbringing, or are they something some people are born with or without? Discuss.

6. Try to think of a time you have modified your speech or writing to create comprehensible input for someone. What techniques did you use to ensure it was comprehensible?

7. If you have access to a classroom setting with ELLs, take an inventory of daily activities to see how much time, if any, is devoted to the five domains of listening, speaking, reading, writing, and communicative competence. How do you think the proportion should change for different age levels? Proficiency levels? Instructional settings?

8. What are some ways one might keep track of the development of communicative competence in English language learners? If you were to create a rubric or checklist for this, what kinds of skills would it include?

9. Look at the circle in Figure 1.1. Think about a classroom you know and try to classify the daily activities to see which of them teach language, teach content through language, or teach about language. How do you think the proportion among them might change for different age levels? Proficiency levels? Instructional settings? From your own experience, which of the functions do you think is most often overlooked in instructional settings?

10. Of the overview of best practices in the list at the end of the chapter, which do you feel are most similar to best practices for native speakers? Least similar?

11. If you are in a teaching setting, see how the chart in Appendix 1.1 corresponds to your current practices. In which of the five domains or three functions of language learning do you want to fortify your practice?

Planning Guide to Include the Five Domains and the Three Functions of Language Learning in Instruction

	Learning language	Learning content through language	Learning about language
Listening	Beginning/emergent: Intermediate/ advanced:	Beginning/emergent: Intermediate/ advanced:	Beginning/emergent: Intermediate/ advanced:
Speaking	Beginning/emergent: Intermediate/ advanced:	Beginning/emergent: Intermediate/ advanced:	Beginning/emergent: Intermediate/ advanced:
Reading	Beginning/emergent: Intermediate/ advanced:	Beginning/emergent: Intermediate/ advanced:	Beginning/emergent: Intermediate/ advanced:
Writing	Beginning/emergent: Intermediate/ advanced:	Beginning/emergent: Intermediate/ advanced:	Beginning/emergent: Intermediate/ advanced:
Communicative competence	Beginning/emergent: Intermediate/ advanced:	Beginning/emergent: Intermediate/ advanced:	Beginning/emergent: Intermediate/ advanced:

CHAPTER TWO

First-Language Influence in Second-Language Acquisition

New Vocabulary in This Chapter: *contrastive analysis, interdependence hypothesis, compensatory model of second-language reading, hypothetical model of the reading process, language distance/linguistic proximity, orthographic distance, cross-linguistic influence, transfer, decoding, positive cross-linguistic influence (PCI), interference, lingua franca, metalinguistic awareness, interactive process, bottom-up skills, top-down skills, threshold hypothesis, threshold theory, short-circuit hypothesis, basic interpersonal communication skills (BICS), cognitive academic language proficiency (CALP), academic writing, English language proficiency, explicit instruction, TESOL (Teachers of English to Speakers of Other Languages)*

Although many mysteries remain, a good amount is known about how new languages are learned. It doesn't take a book like ours to convince you that learning a new language is not a matter of starting from scratch. Our first language serves as "an already established system of meanings" (Vygotsky, 1986, p. 197). Some parts of that system of meanings are embedded within the structure of the specific first language, however, while others can be applied directly and indirectly to learning a new language.

To understand the complex topic of first-language influence on second-language acquisition, we think it helps to introduce some of the thinking that predated current understandings and beliefs. We review several key hypotheses here.

The Contrastive Analysis Hypothesis

The *contrastive analysis* hypothesis emerged in the 1950s and 1960s, when linguists extensively analyzed features shared and not shared by languages. They predicted that learners would have an easier time learning the features of a new language that were similar to features of their first language, and a harder time learning features of a new language that differed from their first language. Contrastive analysis (CA) was the linguistic basis of the audiolingual method (see Chapter 1), and the result was that materials and lessons were designed around predictions about what patterns of difficulty could be expected in learning L2.

Over time, it was found that the CA hypothesis did not explain many phenomena teachers observed in their students, and that the exercises and drills based on predictions from contrastive analysis were not useful in developing language proficiency. Also, important research such as that of Dulay and Burt (1974) revealed that English morphemes were acquired in a certain predictable order regardless of the first language of the learner. However, the CA hypothesis still helps us understand that certain challenges learners face in learning English are directly related to their L1 system. We discuss this further in the chapter on orthography (Chapter 4).

Language as an Innate Human Endowment

At the same time, the Chomskyian revolution blew away the concept that a first language is learned. Linguist Noam Chomsky's theories state that language acquisition is innate, universal, and automatic, a uniquely human endowment (Chomsky, 1965, 1972). As people in the second-language learning field became exposed to Chomsky's theories, they in turn wondered what aspects of second-language learning might also be reframed as acquisition. Over time, a paradigm shift occurred, and many new ideas about language learning and acquisition began to emerge (Krashen, 1982). This has deeply affected second-language pedagogy, as described here by Freeman and Freeman (2004, p. 84) in an example pertaining to how ELLs attain English phonemes:

> Earlier methods of language teaching, based on a learning model, have been replaced by current methods that are based on an acquisition model. . . . the premise is that English phonology is simply too complex to be learned through either direct, explicit teaching or implicit teaching in the context of carefully sequenced drills. Instead, students acquire phonology in the process of developing the ability to communicate in a new language.

The Interdependence Hypothesis

The *interdependence hypothesis* (Cummins, 1979, 1981) emerged during this period. In examining research about bilingual children, Cummins attempted to address how a common underlying proficiency between two languages could help these students achieve high levels of literacy in a pre-K–12 setting. Cummins made the case that L1 literacy level closely correlated with L2 literacy level, all other things being equal. The implications of this hypothesis were that native language literacy would inherently assist L2 literacy. This hypothesis provided strong support for the bilingual education movement.

Like the CA hypothesis, the interdependence hypothesis explained many things, but it also had some limits. Many came to believe that transfer of L1 academic skills to L2 academic skills was both universal and automatic, but research has shown that this is not always the case. In particular, the linguistic proximity between languages is influential. However, Cummins's hypothesis has provided important affirmation for the value of L1 literacy.

The question of L1 influence on L2 development is more nuanced today, and we hope readers of this book will develop an appreciation of those nuances. Now, there is a recognition that some aspects of L1 literacy may "work" in developing the second language, and others may not, depending on a wide variety of factors (Birch, 2007; Koda, 2005; Van-Gelderen et al., 2007). For example, learning which words use capital letters in English is specific to the conventions of English, but learning how to draw inferences from text is universal across languages, even though specific strategies may differ. We explore the complexities of this interaction in the remainder of this chapter and throughout the book.

L2 Reading Models

The myriad factors that need to be accounted for in a model of L2 reading have made it confoundingly difficult to construct a model. A good L2 reading model must encompass not only all languages on both the L1 and L2 sides of the equation, but also learners of all ages and L1 literacy levels. We have found two models that we consider to be powerful and useful.

Bernhardt's (2005) *compensatory model of second-language reading* (Figure 2.1) accounts for several factors and complexities. She examined research about L2 reading over a number of years to construct a model that could accommodate a large number of combinations of L1 and L2 language groups. In this model, L1 literacy accounts for about 20% of second-language reading proficiency, and L2 proficiency (which she defines as

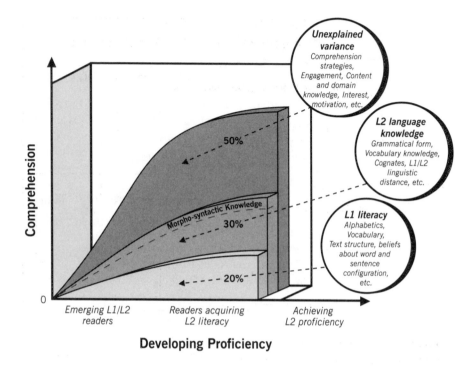

FIGURE 2.1. A compensatory model of English language reading. From Bernhardt (2005). Copyright 2005 by Cambridge University Press. Reprinted by permission.

word knowledge and syntax) accounts for another 30%. Beyond those two identifiable areas, there is another 50% of proficiency whose features have yet to be fully explained. We cite some of these in Chapter 1 as contributing to the "syndrome of success."

Birch's (2007) *hypothetical model of the reading process* (Figure 2.2) is not specific to second-language reading per se but seamlessly applies to it. The two large domains, which work in parallel, are the processing strategy domain and the knowledge domain, each of which comprises two parts. On the right side of the model are the two parts of the knowledge base domain, world knowledge, which can be obtained in any language, and language knowledge, which is language-specific, acquired both unconsciously and consciously, and includes literacy. The processing strategies domain on the left side of the model encompasses cognitive processing strategies, which are universal in nature, and language processing strategies, which are language-specific. The language processing strategies are needed in order for a person to read or write, and they need to be learned for each language in which someone wants to read or write.

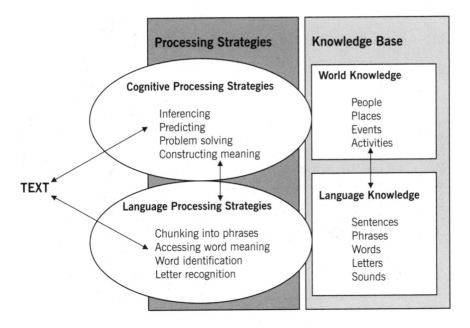

FIGURE 2.2. A hypothetical model of the reading process with some sample processing strategies and types of knowledge. From Birch (2007). Copyright 2007 by Lawrence Erlbaum Associates, Inc. Reprinted by permission of Routledge, member of the Taylor & Francis Group.

Now let's look at the model horizontally instead of vertically. If we look across the top of the model, we see world knowledge and cognitive processing strategies. These are not language-specific, and they can be deployed in many settings, not just in reading. We can use them in a group meeting, for example, to establish a procedure or to solve a problem. They are necessary but not sufficient for reading.

The language processing strategies and language knowledge at the bottom half of the model, on the other hand, are the pieces that must be in place to allow the rest of the model to work. These are specific to a particular language, and without them reading cannot occur. The two domains are porous, and activity in each informs the other. However, language knowledge and language processing strategies are indispensable to crack the code of reading, and they have to be learned separately in each language.

I call the language processing strategies the "dirty little lie about reading." They look so insignificant but they are so decisive. Without those lan-

guage processing strategies, like chunking text into phrases or accessing word meaning, it doesn't do any good to have the higher-order strategies or world knowledge because reading won't work.—LEAH

By separating out these four aspects of the reading process, Birch helps us understand that language-specific skills need to be learned in a new language or else the other universal aspects of language cannot be accessed for reading. In brief, without the nitty-gritty skills of language knowledge and language processing, the higher-order skills just can't be used. Paolo Freire's phrase "Read the word so that you can read the world" might be used as a slogan to represent the way language knowledge unlocks reading (Freire, 1970).

To discuss how first languages influence reading in a new language, it helps to have some precise terms. One of the terms we consider helpful is that of language distance.

Language Distance or Proximity

Language distance (Odlin, 2003, p. 443) can be thought of as an inventory of how many characteristics two languages share. (This same concept can also be called *linguistic proximity* when focussing on the similarity between languages.) Language distance or linguistic proximity can be seen in the similarities in the phonology, morphology, syntax, and semantics that are built into different languages, as well as the number of cognates, or words with shared roots. Languages that come from the same family are more likely to have greater linguistic proximity.

As a general rule, the greater the linguistic proximity, the easier it should be for people to learn each others' languages. Of course, many considerations affect the undertaking, including age, motivation, L1 literacy, socioeconomic class, and instructional setting. Still, those languages with historically close provenance will show greater linguistic proximity. French, Spanish, and Italian, for example, are "sister languages" that share syntax patterns, sounds, an alphabet, and many words.

When my friend and I went camping in Europe, our campsite was next to an Italian family's. They spoke only Italian, and we had both studied French and Spanish. Using words we knew and listening hard to similar-sounding words in the languages we didn't know, we all managed to converse for an entire weekend, with the help of added gestures and many laughs. Because of the similarity of the three languages and our determination to make it work, we somehow got ourselves across, and parted great friends.—KRISTIN

At the same time, languages can also be so close that they cause confusion because a person is not expecting to find a difference. For example, the letter *j* exists in English and German, but it is pronounced differently. German ELL children learning to read in English are likely to pronounce an English word such as *joke* with a /y/ at first, like *yoke*, because the letter *j* is pronounced with a *y* sound (/y/) in German, rather than with the English sound /j/. Teachers can help learners notice those differences through mini-lessons and extra opportunities to practice. Still, it can be said that the common linguistic features of sister languages make them easier to learn.

Orthographic distance is a subset of language distance. It describes the degree of similarity between the writing systems of two languages. Sometimes, two languages use different writing systems, such as Chinese and English, and a learner must learn the new writing system from scratch. Other times a common writing system is in use for languages from the same language family, such as the roman alphabet used in Spanish, Italian, Portuguese, and French. It should take less time for native speakers of one of those languages to read words in the other. However, still other times a writing system may be in use for languages from very different families, such as English, Swahili, Vietnamese, and Icelandic, all of which use the roman alphabet, but in dramatically different ways. Although they share an orthography, or writing system, they are orthographically distant because the same letters are used in different combinations and used to represent different sounds. The relationship between the writing systems of two languages influences how quickly and how well people learn to read in the new writing system.

For example, Spanish and English share 26 letters of the roman alphabet, and Spanish has an additional four letters. Because of the high amount of overlap, it is fairly easy for Spanish ELLs who can read Spanish to recognize the letters of the English alphabet. The Thai alphabet, however, does not share any letters with the English alphabet, so we can expect Thai ELLs to struggle longer with learning the English alphabet, due to the greater orthographic distance between Thai and English. In this book we embed the idea of language distance in the context of literacy development; as a result, we pay most attention to features of orthography, morphology, and cognates; however, all the other structural systems of a language also affect the ease of learning a new language.

Cross-Linguistic Influence and the Problem with "Transfer"

Cross-linguistic influence can be defined as the action, conscious or unconscious, of applying features of a first language to the learning of a new language, in this case, English (Koda, 2006; Odlin, 2003).

In this book we use the term cross-linguistic influence for what is often referred to as "transfer." *Transfer* can be defined as "influence resulting from similarities and differences between the target language and any other language that has been previously acquired" (Myles, 2002, p. 7; Odlin, 1989). However, we prefer not to use the word "transfer" for four reasons.

First, as described earlier, it is too often assumed that any language skill attained in the first language will be automatically available in the second language as well, but that is not so. Grabe (2001) summarizes the fallacy this way: "Few researchers would deny that transfer of literacy skills from the L1 to the L2 occurs, but many researchers believe that positive transfer occurs consistently only after students have had much practice in the L2, have automatized basic L2 language skills, and have been trained to use these potential transfer effects" (p. 32). Cross-linguistic influence cannot be considered to be either automatic or inevitable, and even when it occurs, it may not always be the most efficient route to a new understanding.

Another problem with the word *transfer* is that it implies a facilitating process, but first-language reading knowledge doesn't necessarily make learning to read in English easier, at least until ELLs master English *decoding*. Birch (2007) summarizes it thus: "It is true that transfer may facilitate reading the L2, but it is equally true that it might interfere" (p. 12). In fact, the other written system might be a seriously complicating factor for learning to decode in English, at least in the short run, and attention may need to be paid to this fact. The L1 knowledge and skills that are available for use in English may be very dependent on some features specific to the first language.

The third problem we have with the word *transfer* is that it implies that the L1 knowledge is conveyed immediately. Sometimes, an area of potential cross-linguistic influence might lie waiting in the wings, perhaps for years, until it surfaces or can be rendered usable. This is discussed in more detail in the section on the threshold theory.

Finally, Ellis (1997) regrets the use of the word *transfer* for another reason, explaining, "When we transfer money we move it out of one account and into another, so one account gains and the other loses. However, when language transfer takes place there is usually no loss of L1 knowledge" (p. 54).

Positive Cross-Linguistic Influence and Interference

We prefer a more global concept of cross-linguistic influence, one that includes not only "corresponding or analogous skills, but also metalinguistic or meta-cognitive skills that emerge from competence in the first language" (Genesee, Geva, Dressler, & Kamil, 2006, p. 161). In this book, we refer to the facilitating effects of the first language on second language literacy as *positive cross-linguistic influence (PCI)* and obstacles to second-language literacy based on first-language features as *interference*.

Although there are many examples of cross-linguistic influence in action, ironically, it's often easier to spot interference than PCI. That's because the interfering feature stands out—it doesn't look or sound like the target item in the new language. Interference is noticeable, whereas PCI is likely to resemble the production of a native speaker. We can think of PCI and interference like traffic rules. We don't keep track of all the traffic rules we obey perfectly in a day, but when we break a rule, we are very aware of it, especially if it causes a ticket, accident, or other mishap. It's a challenge for a teacher of ELLs to take note of their learners' PCI and successful use of new forms even when they are imperfect, and not just notice errors caused by interference.

Examples of PCI

There is plenty of research to support the assertion that literacy experiences from the first language can benefit acquisition of a new language. The research covers many of the component areas of reading, including phonological awareness, syntactic awareness, vocabulary knowledge, sentence and discourse processing, text structures, and comprehension. For a very thorough review of research into the cross-linguistic relationships that inform learning to read in English as a new language, we recommend Koda's excellent review of the research (2005).

Those of us who have taught or learned another language are likely to be able to think of many examples in which our knowledge of one language helped facilitate learning the other. Most of us can think of English words we know that we can also recognize in spoken or written form in another language. If we learn to write in a language that is written from left to right, we can apply our knowledge of the directionality of English without ever giving it a conscious thought. We may be able to apply the adjective + noun word order of English to languages that also place an adjective before a noun, such as Dutch. In addition, the influence of English as a world *lingua franca* has introduced English words into many languages around the world, and this makes PCI more likely. Teachers who already know or take the time to find out which characteristics are common to English and the L1 of their learners will help to raise the occurrence of PCI and the English proficiency of their students.

In general, good readers in a native language are more likely to be good readers in another language, and that's encouraging to bear in mind.

However, many small steps must be taken in order to become a good reader, and many of these require explicit, language-specific instruction on a wide range of skills and strategies.

Examples of Interference

Interference occurs when structural features of the first language impede acquiring or using a similar feature in the target language. Not all learner errors constitute interference; they may be due to developmental stages of understanding or individual interpretations of an item that have nothing to do with the first language. Interference can occur at many levels, including phonological, sound–symbol correspondence, vocabulary, and syntax. Following is an example of each of these.

Phonology

A foreign accent occurs when phonemes and phoneme patterns of a person's L1 are overlaid onto the phonemes and phoneme patterns of a new language. For example, English has two "th" sounds, and these sounds are not found in many other languages. Therefore, ELLs whose first language does not have the two "th" sounds of English are likely to pronounce English words with the voiced /th/, such as *this*, as /dis/ instead, since the sound /d/ is a voiced consonant formed very close to the sound /th/ in the mouth. Similarly, an English word with the voiceless /TH/, such as in *thing*, is often pronounced as /ting/, since /t/ is a voiceless consonant formed very close to /TH/ in the mouth.

Sound–Symbol Correspondence

Another area of interference that can affect reading is when there are conflicting sound–symbol patterns in the two languages, even when they share an alphabet, such as the example of the German and English pronunciations of *j* mentioned previously. ELLs who have learned to read and write in their first language show spelling errors due to interference from the way sounds and sound patterns are represented in their L1 writing system (Dressler & Kamil, 2006, p. 203). For example, when a Spanish ELL spells the word *beat* as *bit*, he or she is trying to transfer knowledge that Spanish represents the sound /iy/ with the letter *i*. This is a very common spelling error of L1 Spanish ELLs, by the way, and differs from the developmental spelling of native speakers of English (Bear, Templeton, Helman, & Baren, 2003).

Vocabulary

Vocabulary can also be an area of potential interference. Some words sound or look the same in both languages, but have different meanings. In other cases, two or more words combine differently in one language from another, and a word-by-word translation results in a strange utterance. For example, "Tengo veinte años" which translates from Spanish to the English "I'm twenty years old," is often rendered by Spanish-speaking ELLs as "I have 20 years," its word-by-word translation.

There are also cases in which the words are comprehensible, but the cultural meanings differ in the new language, as can be seen in this story from Tenena's early days in the United States:

> *I remember asking for the toilet in the museum, and when the man pointed me to a sign for the rest room, I thought the guy didn't understand what I meant because I wasn't tired. I imagined there was a couch there where you would go and relax after you had walked around. Even though I knew the words, I didn't know the cultural connotation of "rest room."*—TENENA

Syntax

Word order differs among languages, and trying to construct the same sentence in a new language can create errors. The sentence "The woman who I called her is at home" is a rendering of Arabic word order in English. Since Arabic doesn't delete the direct object inside a relative clause like English does, there is an extra word that sounds non-native to an English speaker.

Professionals involved in the education of ELLs will benefit by being aware that there are both PCI and interference effects that will affect their students' learning, and, to the extent possible, they should be alert to what those effects are likely to be and plan instruction accordingly.

Metalinguistic Awareness Facilitates the Study of New Languages

Metalinguistic awareness can be defined as the ability to think about, reflect upon, and manipulate the forms and functions of language apart from its meaning (Chaney, 1992; Koda, 2005; Pratt & Grieve, 1984). It develops the third language function in Halliday's classification, learning about language. Examples of metalinguistic awareness might include being able to do the following:

- Distinguish real words from nonwords.
- Hear the phonological error of a mispronounced word and correct it.
- Hear an error in a syntax pattern and correct it.
- Segment a spoken phrase into its individual words.
- Play with words to make jokes.
- Create new words or labels for unknown objects or people.
- Make a mental translation.
- Recognize cognates or false cognates.
- Recognize a foreign accent.
- Detect structural ambiguities in sentences.

Some aspects of metalinguistic awareness are a natural byproduct of acquiring one's native language, but many others, especially those connected with the written word, emerge through schooling. Metalinguistic awareness goes hand in hand with literacy achievement. In several studies, when children were given training or practice in developing metalinguistic awareness, it resulted in increased reading comprehension (Zipke, 2008). The metalinguistic awareness learners develop in their first language is also a helpful tool available for use when they are introduced to a new language. Moreover, the very process of learning a new language builds metalinguistic awareness as new sounds, spellings, and words unfold, each with its own peculiarities.

How do children develop a sense of metalinguistic awareness in English? Before becoming literate, they may hear rhymes and make jokes about language, such as the puns in "knock-knock" jokes (e.g., A: "Knock knock!" B: "Who's there?" A: "Boo!" B: "Boo who?" A: "Why are you crying?"). Jump-rope rhymes, camp songs, clapping games, circle games, and word games played on road trips can enhance the skill even before literacy is introduced. When children enter school, metalinguistic awareness can increase as they learn to sort out sounds and letters, engage in wordplay and word games through activities such as word sorts, listen for rhymes, write poems and songs, look for common roots across words, tell jokes based on words or syntax, write skits, listen to books or songs that include word play, and so forth. Favorite English language children's books such as the Amelia Bedelia (Parish, 1986–2008) and Junie B. Jones (Park, 1990–2009) series or poems by Shel Silverstein (1974, 1981) are full of wordplay and quizzical questions about why language is a certain way. They include funny misinterpretations of idioms and figures of speech. Metalinguistic awareness can be cultivated in any language. The common feature is having a word-conscious or word-rich environment.

ELLs benefit from practicing metalinguistic skills in the ESL classroom, and these activities can be introduced from an early age (Bouffard

& Sarkar, 2008). Metalinguistic activities can also help learners understand the concepts of language distance, PCI, and interference as they build awareness of the way words work in their native language and in English.

Incidentally, metalinguistic awareness also works in favor of learning a third language (Clyne, Hunt, & Isaakidis, 2004). Wilga M. Rivers, a famous author in the field of teaching ESL, learned five languages over the course of time. She decided to keep a daily diary of her study of Spanish, her sixth language, and her diary is full of fascinating evidence of her highly developed metalinguistic awareness (Rivers, 1981, pp. 500–515).

Vygotsky (1986) pointed out that studying a foreign language also helps our understanding of our own. "A foreign language facilitates mastering the higher forms of the native language," he says. "The child learns to see his language as one particular system among many, to view its phenomena under more general categories, and this leads to awareness of linguistic operations" (p. 196). Clearly, metalinguistic awareness helps with language learning in general because it helps us "learn about language"— the third function in the language-based theory of learning (Halliday, 1993).

How LI Reading Differs from Reading in a New Language

Reading is an *interactive process* (Birch, 2007; Rumelhart, 1980) that takes place between the text and the reader's processing strategies and background knowledge. To read, we need to master a set of word-level skills, which we will call *bottom-up skills*. These skills combine to allow us to be able to decode connected text. These are represented in the Birch reading model as language processing strategies and language knowledge (see Figure 2.2).

As we learn to decode, we also learn a large set of strategic reading skills, which we will call *top-down skills* and strategies, that readers use in concert with background knowledge to construct meaning from text. These are represented in Birch's model as world knowledge and cognitive processing strategies. To summarize, bottom-up skills refer to the word-level skills that are required for decoding, and top-down skills refer to the analytical and cognitive skills that are needed for comprehension. They interact and overlap throughout the life of a reader. Both skill sets require making many rapid judgments about words and keeping the words in working memory as we form reasonable interpretations about possible meanings.

Surprisingly, the bottom-up skills are the ones that may cause the greatest hurdles for ELLs who read in another language, both because of the effects of interference and the particular features of English. This is counterintuitive for teachers of L1 children because the bottom-up skills are something teachers expect children to have firmly in place by the end of second grade. Teachers who don't teach in the K–2 grades may take for granted that ELLs in their classrooms already have the bottom-up decoding skills in place. Indeed, they may have these skills in place in their native language, or they may not. However, even if they do, the bottom-up skills are language-specific, and as a result, they need to be learned at whatever age ELL students begin to study English. Furthermore, the details of English word decoding are exceptionally difficult to learn. In effect, even literate ELLs need to learn to read twice, because they have to crack two different codes.

The top-down comprehension skills that learners hone over many years of schooling include multipart strategies readers use to engage in summarizing, inferencing, evaluating, and so on. These strategic aspects of reading are more likely to benefit from PCI because they are less language-specific. For example, if Talia knows how to put historical events in chronological order in her first language, Hebrew, it will be much easier for her to learn to do the same in English.

The problem is that the strategies cannot be fully activated until the lower-level, language-specific processes are in place. Put another way, ELLs will not be able to make use of higher-level reading skills that cross languages until they master the lower-level skills that are specific to English. Furthermore, the lower-level, bottom-up skills of English are more difficult for students whose L1 has more linguistic distance from English, even if they are literate in their first language. This, then, is the critical way in which ELL reading differs from learning to read in English as a first language.

Literacy-Related Hypotheses about SLA

In addition to the concepts of positive cross-linguistic influence and interference, there are three other important theories about SLA that bear on any discussion of learning to read in a new language: the threshold hypothesis, the threshold theory, and basic interpersonal communication skills (BICS) and cognitive academic language proficiency (CALP). We describe each briefly.

The Threshold Hypothesis

The commonly known *threshold hypothesis* of Jim Cummins focuses on the cognitive benefits that accrue to becoming a "balanced bilingual" (Cummins, 1976, 1979). He describes three levels of language proficiency. At the first level, L2 instruction is introduced before L1 academic language is developed; at the second level, there is some L1 and L2 academic language development, but not at a level high enough to give real cognitive benefits. Only the third and highest level, when learners attain both L1 and L2 academic language proficiency, affords learners the real benefits of bilingualism, Cummins hypothesizes. This hypothesis, like Cummins's interdependence hypothesis described earlier, lays out guiding principles that bilingual program models can use to foster biliteracy for academic success. The hypothesis has been widely applied in the design of Canadian and American bilingual programs. In order to appreciate the efficacy of this model, it is important to note the difference between bilingualism and biliteracy. Learners can become orally bilingual without achieving the cognitive benefits of biliteracy. Biliteracy, on the other hand, facilitates positive cross-linguistic transfer because both bottom-up and top-down skills are developed in two languages.

The Threshold Theory

The *threshold theory* (Alderson, 1984, 2000), not to be confused with the threshold hypothesis, holds that it is not first-language literacy, but second-language proficiency that determines whether a second-language learner will become a proficient reader and writer. The theory incorporates an understanding of the importance of L2 language-specific skills that are needed for L2 learners to be successful readers. The needed "threshold" may vary according to the purpose for reading and the text being read, and it will vary among learners. Clarke's *short-circuit hypothesis* (Clarke, 1980), less well-known but very influential, complements this theory; he notes that even successful L1 readers cannot read for comprehension in a new language until they have adequate proficiency in it. Until that level is reached, then, their reading process will "short-circuit." Alderson summarizes the threshold theory by saying, "Second language knowledge is more important than first-language reading abilities" (2000, p. 39).

There is some support for this theory in reading and L2 research. Fitzgerald (1995) found that in academic tasks, the ways ELL readers use reading comprehension strategies become more and more like those of good L1 readers as they become more proficient. There are complex variables in the way students read in two languages, according to the learners' reading level in the two languages, the reading task, and the nature of the texts (Fender, 2001; Garcia, 2000; Pritchard & O'Hara, 2008; Royer & Carlo, 1991). Following are a few examples of how the threshold theory can help explain observed phenomena in the areas of reading strategies, spelling, and writing.

Reading Strategies

A study of high school–age Spanish-speaking ELLs who were also proficient in English found that the strategies they used to read in Spanish were not the same strategies that they used to read in English. The authors conclude, "We cannot assume that proficient readers (much less struggling readers) will automatically transfer the ability to use those strategies from Spanish to English" (Pritchard & O'Hara, 2008, p. 637).

As bilingual children advance in their literacy development, their dominant language will differ at different points in time. Moll, Estrada, Díaz, and Lopez (1997) found that Spanish–English bilingual students demonstrated use of comprehension strategies during Spanish reading but used graphophonemic strategies during their English reading. Looking at it through the lens of the threshold theory, it could be that the students weren't yet able to apply the comprehension strategies they had achieved in Spanish reading to English reading because they still needed to master the sound–symbol relationships of English, their new language.

Spelling

Spelling development is another area where the nature of PCI and interference changes over time. Zutell and Allen (1988) found that L1 Spanish ELLs made more spelling errors showing Spanish influence when they were at a lower proficiency level; their higher-proficiency peers tended to make errors that were more like those of their L1 English counterparts.

Writing

Sasaki and Hirose (1996) found that well-developed L1 writing ability may not be able to be positively applied to L2 writing until the learner reaches a certain threshold in the new language.

Language Loss

Conversely, when children cease to study their first language in a school setting, their L1 literacy skills may reach a plateau or even decline over time. This, in turn, may result in less PCI and lowered metalinguistic awareness. In addition, a sense of alienation and loneliness can occur as one moves further away from one's heritage language, and this can have negative consequences (Rodriguez, 1982). Although L2 proficiency may influence what L1 literacy skills can be activated, achieving and maintaining a high level of literacy in one's native language is very important and valuable.

So in this complicated set of theories, hypotheses, and research from all kinds of settings, we can say that what "kicks in" from L1 for use in L2 varies across the spectrum. Alderson's threshold theory gives us a valuable analytical tool to talk about why some elements of L1 literacy may not be deployed in the L2 at some points in time. Sometimes ELLs' L2 proficiency may have to reach a certain level of maturity in order for the value of their L1 literacy skills to be realized.

Basic Interpersonal Communicative Skills and Cognitive Academic Language Proficiency

Cummins is best known for the twin notions that he described as *basic interpersonal communicative skills (BICS)*, which he also calls "conversational language" (Cummins, 1981), and *cognitive academic language proficiency (CALP)*, which he also calls "academic language proficiency" (Cummins, 1979, 1991, 2008). BICS and CALP are key constructs in the field of teaching English as a new language. In his research and literature reviews of young second language learners, Cummins noticed that they often did well in their language classes but had trouble with academic tasks, including reading comprehension, once they entered grade-level classrooms. Similar findings were reported by Skutnabb-Kangas and Toukomaa (1976) with bilingual Finnish children in Sweden and in research with Spanish-speaking ELLs in the United States (Pritchard & O'Hara, 2008).

Cummins hypothesized that there were two distinct forms of language, whose characteristics we have summarized in Table 2.1. The first, BICS, is a body of simple English that can be acquired in everyday, natural settings, without formal instruction, which Cummins calls "context-rich" language. Verb forms are simple, the context makes it easy to understand, and it takes place in the "here and now." This conversational language is often referred to as "playground language" or "survival language."

The other, CALP, includes the much larger and more complex academic vocabulary of school. This language, sometimes called academic language, instructional language, or expository language, is needed for reading and writing in the content areas of not just the language arts, but also science, mathematics, and the social sciences (Fang, 2008). This language becomes more specialized as students are exposed to higher levels of knowledge in different fields; without this language, they will be unable to reach those advanced levels (Zwiers, 2008). CALP language has limited contextual information to aid readers' comprehension. It uses more tenses, assumes an unseen audience, and requires more formal instruction. Until CALP develops, it is also difficult to do *academic writing* because it requires addressing an unseen reader.

TABLE 2.1. Some Characteristics of BICS and CALP

BICS (context-rich, social, survival) language has some or all of these characteristics	CALP (academic, expository) language has some or all of these characteristics
Utterances are in fragments or memorized chunks.	Utterances and sentences are long and often contain embedded clauses; word order is varied.
Vocabulary consists of high-frequency words with general meanings.	Vocabulary consists of abstract, subject-related content words, often with specialized meanings.
Verb forms are in present tense or progressive aspect.	Verb forms include modal auxiliaries, perfect tenses, and passive voice.
Negative is indicated by the word *no*.	Correct syntax is developed or developing.
Conversation topics are related to the here and now and are context embedded.	Topics focus on subject content and may be context reduced.
Understanding relies on background knowledge.	Understanding depends on language in addition to background knowledge.
Language tends to be conversational, personal, and egalitarian.	Language tends to be distanced, impersonal, and authoritative.

The reason that the BICS and CALP concepts are so critical in teaching ELLs is because ELLs are often misjudged to have high language proficiency just because they have developed BICS skills. However, we know that students acquire BICS language years before they have mastered CALP language (Thomas & Collier, 2002). Teachers of ELLs must take care to make sure that CALP language—academic language—is developing in their ELLs to a level comparable with that of L1 students at the same grade level.

To understand what kinds of language CALP language encompasses, we must consider the vast range of mental and verbal activities that take place in classrooms over the course of a school year and over the course of the years of school. CALP language crosses all the domains of language acquisition. In some classrooms, the CALP language will be the language of science experiments; in others, it may be expository language needed to provide the definition of a word. Defining a word is a CALP language skill because the definition is abstracted from the word and is produced out of the context of the communication. The ability to define words has been shown to be correlated with reading comprehension in ELLs (Carlisle,

Beeman, & Shah, 1996). CALP language is the language of written texts, standardized tests, English language proficiency standards, and content areas of the curriculum.

The concept of BICS and CALP has been very influential in improving the way ELLs are assessed, placed, and exited from programs. Before these ideas became well known, ELLs were often considered "fluent" and put into mainstream classrooms on the basis of their BICS alone. Now there is widespread understanding that reading and writing skills take much longer to develop in a new language, and that it can be misleading to judge proficiency on the basis of listening and speaking skills. By recognizing the differences between social and academic language and incorporating them in our planning, we can ensure that ELLs transition into full academic achievement.

Standardized tests for ELLs such as the ACCESS-ELL test (WIDA Consortium, 2004) contain separate and distinct yearly assessments of language proficiency for ELLs in all four domains of listening, speaking, reading, and writing. These tests are in place to ensure that ELLs are not allowed to exit ESL programs until they reach a satisfactory level of academic language.

The field of ESL teaching has changed dramatically since the No Child Left Behind Act of 2002 required schools to demonstrate that ELLs were making adequate progress toward achieving *English language proficiency*. Combined with greater knowledge of how languages are best learned, the teaching of ELLs has come of age. Now academic language, not just social and survival language, is valued, and all three functions of language learning are included in the curriculum: learning the language, learning content through the language, and learning about the language.

As we look at our own experiences in second language learning, we can analyze our respective knowledge of BICS or CALP in other languages and clearly see how it influences what we are able to do. Here is a reflection of that sort by Beth Dominguez, a bilingual Spanish special education teacher who works with hearing-impaired Spanish ELLs:

> *I can carry on basic conversations using sign language or Spanish. I've been asked to interpret IEP [individualized education plan] meetings, sporting lessons, and conferences using sign language or Spanish, but have found that extremely difficult because I don't always have a more advanced knowledge of the respective vocabulary/terminology required. Interpreting for IEPs or conferences requires CALP in the L2, which I haven't acquired. When I student taught, I was required to interpret a high school chemistry class for a hearing-impaired student in sign language. I only had two sign language courses previously, which taught a*

BICS vocabulary! I had to study a sign language dictionary of chemistry terms to pick up the CALP vocabulary.—BETH DOMINGUEZ

It is also important that BICS and CALP terms be carefully applied. We have observed some common misunderstandings about the notions of BICS and CALP as we have come to understand them, and we describe them briefly in Table 2.2. BICS and CALP are controversial among linguists because Cummins's use of the terms is descriptive and not completely definitive; however, they are unquestionably a powerful "shorthand" for helping teachers describe the needs and progress of their ELLs.

TABLE 2.2. Fallacies and Realities about BICS and CALP

Fallacy	Reality
BICS is oral and CALP is written.	BICS is usually oral, but could be written, too: it consists of high-frequency words and phrases that are highly contextualized through visual and contextual clues. For example, an illustrated menu could be considered a BICS text even though the items are written down because the words can be easily accessed on the spot. CALP can also be oral, such as a college lecture that requires a listener to carefully follow a topic.
BICS will take care of itself; all attention must be paid to CALP.	If children have learned English as a foreign language in a non-English-speaking country and then immigrate to the United States, they may have acquired some academic English because of the method in which they studied English, but lack conversational English or communicative competence. Older children with strong formal education in their native language will also have more CALP skills to transfer from their L1, but may need help acquiring BICS, especially if they are very self-conscious. It should never be assumed communicative language will take care of itself. If ELLs don't have conversational abilities in English, they will be isolated from their peers, and school will be an unpleasant experience for them.
Teachers should wait until BICS is in place before beginning CALP.	Exactly the opposite is true. It is never too early to introduce CALP language and skills, even when students are not totally proficient in BICS, and even if they are not fluent decoders. CALP skills can involve oral analysis and listening vocabulary as well as written words.
BICS and CALP transfer automatically between languages.	This book is devoted to laying out some of the complexities of the landscape for developing English reading proficiency. Although some skills can be used automatically or easily in a new language, others are language-specific and require care and conscious attention.

BICS and CALP are dynamic ideas that have evolved over the years. Cummins has recently revised his ideas related to BICS and CALP (Cummins, 2003, 2008) and has included a third domain of discrete language skills that includes phonology, literacy, and grammatical knowledge. These skills can be developed in conjunction with BICS and CALP, but they require teachers to use *explicit instruction*, in which teachers demonstrate or explain to students exactly how certain language features work. Zwiers (2008) has also laid out some of the ways to address the specific demands for English in different content classrooms. Explicit instruction, in addition to the best practices described in Chapter 1, helps students to develop both BICS and CALP while learning content in authentic communicative contexts (Cummins, 1981; Rothenberg & Fisher 2007).

Performance Definitions for ELLs

How do we describe what an English language learner is able to do? This used to be a daunting task because there were no standards against which to judge performance. As a result, it was impossible to apply the criteria used in one ESL program to another. What might be called "advanced" in an ESL or bilingual program might still be below grade level in a classroom of native speakers. Now, *TESOL (Teachers of English to Speakers of Other Languages)*, the field's premier professional organization, in conjunction with the World Class Instructional Design and Assessment (WIDA) Consortium, a multistate working group, has created standards that describe performance goals for ELLs (TESOL, 2006). We adopt the language used to describe the six proficiency levels in the TESOL/WIDA standards as we move through the book: (1) Entering, (2) Beginning, (3) Developing, (4) Expanding, (5) Bridging, and (6) Reaching. What makes the standards unique and valuable is that they address the actions students need to be able to take in order to perform academic tasks at grade level, whatever their age. For a description of the English language proficiency levels across the different domains, please see the Performance Definitions in Appendix 2.1.

HOW DOES THIS LOOK IN THE CLASSROOM?

Using Academic Language

Using academic language in daily dialogue will help students get accustomed to hearing CALP language and make it easier for them when they encounter the words during reading and testing. When teachers feel comfortable talking in an academic English register, it helps give ELLs repeated exposure to the words they need to know. One of the ways to build CALP language is to adopt the language used in the TESOL/WIDA standards. For example, a teacher might say to young ELLs, "You sang that so well—can we replicate that performance in the assembly later on today?" *Replicate* is one of the verbs in the formative assessments of the WIDA standards. To build written CALP use, it is also important to put CALP vocabulary words up on word walls and to give positive reinforcement when the words are used.

Considering Every Learner's L1 a Language Resource and a Metalinguistic Resource

The first language can be a wellspring of understanding for the second language because talking about languages requires CALP vocabulary. Students can be asked to figure out what things the two languages they are learning have in common, and charts can be made. Metalinguistic awareness can be fostered with many activities, including children's books such as *Who Says a Dog Goes Bow wow?* (De Zutter, 1993), *CDB!* and *CDC?* (Steig, 1987, 2003) and others that build metalinguistic awareness.

Lowering the Affective Filter

Lowering the affective filter is something that good teachers do naturally, but it is worth thinking about even more when teaching ELLs. It has been our experience that when ELLs are validated in class and teachers express an interest in what they have to say, these learners will meet the teacher halfway. One small but significant item that helps establish a trusting classroom is learning to pronounce the names of all of the students correctly, and using their names often. This also helps other children in the class learn their classmates' names. Learning about the educational and family background of ELLs in the class and asking friendly questions about their siblings, elders, and celebrations is another way to "roll out the welcome mat."

QUESTIONS FOR FURTHER STUDY

1. If you had to choose three important ideas from this chapter, what would you choose? How can you apply these ideas to your larger knowledge of teaching English as a new language?

2. How would you appraise your own metalinguistic awareness? What are some examples of it? Do you think there is an optimal age to develop this awareness? If possible, discuss with a partner.

3. Try to find three examples of positive cross-linguistic influence (PCI) and three examples of interference from your own language teaching or foreign language study. Which examples were easier for you to find?

4. How could you help ELLs understand the concept of language distance more easily? What visual or kinesthetic means could make it more accessible? Do you think it would be easier to explain the concept in a class in which all the ELLs came from the same language background, or from different ones?

5. Look at the examples of metalinguistic awareness listed in the chapter. Which of them can be introduced at Entering or Beginning levels of English proficiency? Which might require a higher level of proficiency, or a possibly a higher grade level? Can you think of ways to build metalinguistic awareness that can be done at any level?

6. Sometimes ELLS who come to the US in mid- or late adolescence have strong CALP skills in their L1, but lack any English BICS. Think of some ways to build BICS skills for these students.

7. Lesson plans often account for CALP skills in the domains of reading and writing. What ways can CALP skills be supported in practicing listening and speaking?

8. Looking at the language(s) you have studied or acquired, evaluate your own BICS and CALP skills in them. What kinds of teaching methods do you think encourage the development of BICS? CALP?

9. Consider the example of the children in the Moll et al. (1997) example on p. 36. What kinds of observation or assessment might the teacher use to determine these students' English proficiency level in order to know how to address their English literacy instruction needs?

10. How can ESL instructors incorporate some of the understandings of the threshold theory when creating assessments for ELLs?

Performance Definitions for the Levels of English Language Proficiency

At the given level of English language proficiency, English language learners will process, understand, produce, or use:

6—Reaching	• specialized or technical language reflective of the content areas at grade level • a variety of sentence lengths of varying linguistic complexity in extended oral or written discourse as required by the specified grade level • oral or written communication in English comparable to proficient English peers
5—Bridging	• specialized or technical language of the content areas • a variety of sentence lengths of varying linguistic complexity in extended oral or written discourse, including stories, essays, or reports • oral or written language approaching comparability to that of proficient English peers when presented with grade-level material
4—Expanding	• specific and some technical language of the content areas • a variety of sentence lengths of varying linguistic complexity in oral discourse or multiple related sentences or paragraphs • oral or written language with minimal phonological, syntactic, or semantic errors that do not impede the overall meaning of the communication when presented with oral or written connected discourse with sensory, graphic, or interactive support
3—Developing	• general and some specific language of the content areas • expanded sentences in oral interaction or written paragraphs • oral or written language with phonological, syntactic, or semantic errors that may impede the communication, but retain much of its meaning, when presented with oral or written, narrative, or expository descriptions with sensory, graphic, or interactive support
2—Beginning	• general language related to the content areas • phrases or short sentences • oral or written language with phonological, syntactic, or semantic errors that often impede the meaning of the communication when presented with one- to multiple-step commands, directions, questions, or a series of statements with sensory, graphic, or interactive support
1—Entering	• pictorial or graphic representation of the language of the content areas • words, phrases, or chunks of language when presented with one-step commands, directions, WH-, choice or yes/no questions, or statements with sensory, graphic, or interactive support

From Teachers of English to Speakers of Other Languages (2006). Reprinted by permission.

CHAPTER THREE

ELL Oracy

*Listening Comprehension
and Oral Language Development*

New Vocabulary in This Chapter: *oracy, literacy, listening
comprehension, comprehension of oral language, auditory comprehension,
phonological awareness, phoneme segmentation, concept of word, stress
patterns, content word, function word, contrastive stress, intonation
patterns, paralinguistic features or cues, oral text, auding, gist, listening
vocabulary, simple view of reading, ellipsis, discourse markers, context-
reduced oral language, level of difficulty, purpose for listening, interactive
dialogue (collaborative dialogue), silent period, intensive listening activities,
extensive listening activities, dictation, cloze, total physical response (TPR),
interactive read-alouds, story grammar, prompts*

In this chapter we talk about comprehending and using spoken English,
which is composed of listening comprehension and oral language production. These two skills together lay the groundwork for the emergence of
reading and writing. Sticht and James (1984) refer to the listening and
speaking level reached by native speakers before they learn to read as their
"reading potential," and refer to the combined skills as *oracy*. They chose
the term oracy to serve as a parallel to *literacy*, which had been considered
at that time to consist of only reading and writing. To some extent, cur-

rent views of literacy encompass oracy, but we use the term to refer to the listening and speaking skills taken together. Students with strong oracy levels in English are more likely to develop strong literacy levels in English as well.

Oracy develops in different ways for ELLs than it does for children acquiring their native language. To explore those ways, we begin with a discussion of the nature of listening comprehension, how it develops in English language learners, and its role in reading. Then we look at how speaking skills develop in ELLs and how they interact with reading development. Finally, we look at how teachers can support developing strong ELL oracy in the classroom setting as a path to literacy and competence in English as a new language.

Listening Comprehension in English as a New Language

Listening is one of the primary modes through which we learn about our world; if listening is weak, overall comprehension suffers. *Listening comprehension*, which is sometimes referred to as *comprehension of oral language* or *auditory comprehension*, is the ability to understand spoken language, and, in this case, the spoken language of English. That might seem self-evident, but the listening comprehension we acquire more or less unconsciously in our native language, just by being around and interacting with people who speak it, encompasses many different complex skills we don't even realize we have mastered. These include:

• The ability to figure out which spoken sounds are meaningful parts of language and which aren't. Children learn very early on which speech sounds to ignore and which to attend to as they interact with caregivers.

• *Phonological awareness*, or the ability to recognize the sounds of speech, is present in all hearing human beings and begins at birth. Over time, it becomes honed to the specific sounds, or phonemes, of one's native language. Phonological awareness develops in the young child through nursery rhymes, wordplay, rhyming games, and songs. When children begin school, they further refine their phonological awareness. Children learn to recognize the order of sounds within an individual word by practicing rhyming and phoneme substitution games, such as seeing pictures of a ship and a sheep, and talking about the difference in the sounds. We will refer to this key reading skill of breaking down the phonemes of a word and putting them back together as *phoneme segmentation*.

Phonological awareness is one of the strongest predictors of reading comprehension in L1 children (Geva, 2007). Phonological awareness helps ELLs in three distinct ways:

1. They imitate the sounds and thereby learn to say the word.
2. They obtain a tool that helps them recognize the word when they hear it because the sequence of sounds gets stored in their long-term memory.
3. Once they begin to read and write, their phonological awareness, in particular their ability to do phoneme segmentation, will greatly assist them with decoding, writing, and spelling new words in English.

• As we acquire a language, we learn to perceive the boundaries between words even though they blend together in spoken form. The ability to distinguish word boundaries within the flowing stream of speech is called *concept of word* (Morris, 1993). When we hear people animatedly speaking a language we do not know, we hear it as a torrent of connected sound without form or meaning. However, once we know a language, we can tell where one word ends and the next begins, and how the words taken together have meaning.

• The ability to recognize the *stress patterns* of English words. Stress patterns are audible differences in how long and how loudly a speaker pronounces a word or groups of words. Stress patterns are not random; they follow a complex set of rules that are among the structures of each language. Each word of more than one syllable carries a stress pattern, and we learn to predict the stress patterns of unknown words by generalizing from patterns we already know. For example, we can predict that the low frequency word *concatenation* will be pronounced with its strong stress on the "na" syllable because there are so many other words that do so: *elation, station, graduation*. We can view spoken stress patterns through voice-imaging software.

• Stress patterns are also distributed in phrases, clauses, and sentences. They help signal to listeners which parts of a sentence carry more meaning than others. In English, *content words*, such as nouns, verbs, adjectives, and adverbs, are usually the strong-stressed words; they are normally pronounced longer and more loudly than the smaller, shorter *function words*, such as conjunctions, prepositions, pronouns, and articles. Strong-stressed words help listeners catch key points even if the message is degraded somehow by background noise or other interference. In addition to learning to recognize the stress patterns of English, we also develop an ear for when speakers alter the regular stress pattern for emphasis, such as when a parent says to a child, "I said to be home in *ten* minutes, didn't I? It's been 25 minutes." Changing the stress patterns of phrases or clauses for added emphasis is called *contrastive stress*.

• The ability to interpret the *intonation patterns* of speakers of English. Intonation patterns are vocal changes of pitch that occur in the normal course of speaking. They differ according to factors such as the region, dialect, gender, and age of the speakers, and even the speaker's attitude. Americans may have difficulty understanding an English speaker from a different English-speaking country because of their differing intonation patterns, such as an English speaker from New Zealand. Even among members of the same dialect group, changing intonation alone can completely alter the meaning of a sentence. Part of listening comprehension is being able to tell that two sentences with the same words can have different meanings, based solely upon their intonation.

Another related ability is knowing the meanings of gestures, body language, and facial expressions that accompany speech. Gestures and body language are not universal—they are language- and culture-specific. Linguists call the non-word-based cues *paralinguistic features or cues*. Although these are not part of listening comprehension per se, they do contribute to meaning. Paralinguistic features work in concert with the *oral text*, the words that are being spoken, and help us understand the meaning of the words.

The Active Nature of Listening Comprehension

Once we understand the components of listening comprehension, we realize why listening must be considered an active process. Like reading, however, it is sometimes wrongly labeled as a "receptive" skill, as if acquiring it were a passive process. If listening didn't require active engagement, we could understand speech when we weren't paying any attention to it, by osmosis, like a plant receives and processes sunlight! Native speakers can still keep track of some of the drift of oral language even when they are not concentrating on it, but only the most proficient L2 learners have that luxury. That's because comprehending oral speech in a new language requires constant attention. In fact, it is such hard work that it can be downright exhausting (Igoa, 1995). Active listening is an intense mental workout—it's no wonder many children listening to a new language all day feel fatigued. It's even possible that the focus problems and restlessness some ELLs experience is related to listening fatigue. Here is how author Francisco Jimenez (1997) describes his first attempts to understand spoken English in his first-grade classroom in the book *The Circuit*:

> Miss Scalapino started speaking to the class and I did not understand a word she was saying. The more she spoke, the more anxious I became. By the end of the day, I was very tired of hearing Miss Scalapino talk because the sounds made no sense to me. I thought that perhaps by paying close attention I would begin to understand, but I did not. I only got a headache, and that night, when I went to bed, I heard her voice in my head.

For days I got headaches from trying to listen, until I learned a way out. When my head began to hurt, I let my mind wander . . . but when I daydreamed, I continued to look at the teacher and pretend I was paying attention because Papa told me it was disrespectful not to pay attention, especially to grownups. (pp. 17–18)

"Auding": A Way to Describe Listening Comprehension

Auding is a word used to describe active listening. It is a term coined by Brown (1950) and subsequently adopted by Carver (1981) as a way to describe not just hearing, but active listening. During auding, a person actively constructs meaning from an oral text similarly to the way a reader actively constructs meaning from a written text. Auding does not require literacy, but the two skills develop hand in hand. We like this term because it reminds us of the interactive nature of listening comprehension. Auding is an interaction between active listeners and oral texts as listeners rapidly process oral texts through their mental systems. These systems include all the previously presented listening skills, in addition to the listener's background knowledge, interpretation of the setting, and cultural and emotional filters.

As we perform these complex maneuvers, we also hold the message in short-term memory and later store it in long-term memory so that it can be retrieved for later use. In auding, we do not remember the exact form in which a text was conveyed to us unless there was something very striking about the words themselves, or about their delivery. Instead, we remember the main idea, or *gist* (Pinker, 2000). Richards described this in the following way: "The basic unit of meaning in oral communication is the proposition or idea" (quoted in O'Malley & Valdez-Pierce, 1996, 58). Propositions are the way the brain processes input and stores it in memory, focusing on the predicate, or verb, of the message and the information attached to it. When we are trying to get the gist of an oral message in a second language, however, we may not capture the key idea, due to missing or misunderstanding part of the message, as demonstrated in this anecdote from an ESL teacher:

As a newly arrived student in Taipei, I had studied Chinese for only 2 years and had very limited experience listening to normal-speed speech. In addition, the local accent was different from the accent of the teacher I had primarily studied under. During my first week, I got lost trying to find my college and asked directions of someone on the street. He understood my carefully rehearsed question, and the rehearsal clearly made me sound more capable than I actually was. He gave me rapid directions, which I in turn thought I understood. Unfortunately, the speed of his speech caused me to fail to remember a few essential steps. I got the "gist," but for follow-ing directions around a city that just isn't enough. I ended up far from home, even more lost, and having to sacrifice my very limited funds to take a cab back. I finally found the college the next day, when I made sure to have written directions.—JANIS MARA MICHAEL

Research into the listening processes of ELLs has shown that they are more likely to home in on content words and miss some of the shorter function words (Field, 2008). Those little words, so common and so short, can be the pivots for comprehension, and it takes a long time to learn to hear them in context. Often, a wrong preposition can literally set a person off "in the wrong direction."

Now that we have unpacked the complex skills of listening comprehension and further realized that these intricate processes occur in real time, without the benefit of any kind of "instant replay," we gain a new appreciation of how remarkable it is that we can process messages and texts as fast and as well as we do, especially in a new language!

Similarities between Comprehension in Listening and Reading

There are striking similarities between the comprehension processes involved in listening and reading, as summarized in Table 3.1. Listening involves learning how to make "reasonable interpretations" of an oral text (Brown & Yule, 1983, p. 57), whereas reading involves the same process for a written text. There are other similarities as well. Listening comprehension is the knowledge of language that includes all of the content of a language—its vocabulary, syntax, meanings—that can be borne by the oral text alone, whereas literacy situates all of that language content within a written system. Oracy acts as the bridge between a natural language process, which is listening, and an unnatural process, which is reading.

All of us learn to listen in our native language, and the habit of listening comprehension becomes automatic and unconscious by the time we begin school. Once we become literate, we only reference our *listening vocabulary* when we are trying to retrieve something specific, such as a new or tricky word we are trying to spell, understand, or decode.

I always have to say "Wednesday" to myself in order to spell it correctly.—TENENA

I have to whisper "curmudgeon" to myself to access its meaning.—LEAH

I have to read "miniseries" aloud to myself or else I think it's "ministeries." Also true for "outage" and "outrage." The missing letters really confuse me.—KRISTIN

TABLE 3.1. Similarities between the Listening and Reading Processes

1. Both require active construction of meaning, with interaction between the text (oral or written) and the person.

2. For both reading and listening, text is remembered as the "gist," not the exact words.

3. Both listening and reading require phonological awareness.

4. Both the reading and listening processes benefit from larger vocabularies.

5. Reading and listening comprehension require having the concept of word (as a unit of meaning which can be manipulated).

6. English has many similar-looking and similar-sounding words, and these can be confusing.

7. Longer words are harder to store, retain, and retrieve from memory.

8. When context is stripped away, comprehension becomes much more difficult.

9. Automaticity facilitates the ability to construct meaning for both listening and reading, and this can be developed.

10. Learners need to become familiar with different genres and what can be expected from the structure of the genres.

11. Listening or reading tasks vary according to different purposes, different texts, and different contexts.

12. Both intensive and extensive practice are needed to improve listening and reading levels.

13. Both listening and reading require knowledge of English syntax patterns in order to make good guesses about what is coming next.

Listening Comprehension Is Language-Specific

Even though different languages share many words and parts of words, it doesn't mean ELLs will recognize those words when they are spoken in English. We have to learn a whole set of sounds and stress combinations in a new language, very much like an infant, and the set of sounds from our first language may provide PCI or interference, or both. Therefore, listening in many ways requires "starting from scratch."

ELLs and Listening Vocabulary

Native speakers come to school with a large storehouse of listening vocabulary—an estimated 5,000–7,000 words by the time they start school (Grabe & Stoller, 2002). ELLs, however, do not have this storehouse of remembered English words, which we will call their listening vocabulary. Although they have undergone the same universal processes of acquiring listening comprehension in their L1 that native English speakers have in theirs, the set of words and sounds is not the same. Therefore, the similar features that would allow a smooth transition from oracy to literacy such as those in Table 3.1 do not apply because listening is language-specific. Until the English listening vocabulary of an ELL is well established, the skills that can be imported from listening to reading cannot come into play.

The Simple View of Reading

The *simple view of reading* (Gough & Tunmer, 1986) considers reading comprehension to be the product of listening comprehension and decoding. In fact, there is considerable research to support the idea that listening comprehension is a decisive factor in reading comprehension (Biemiller, 1999; Dymock, 1993; Gough & Tunmer, 1986; Stanovich, 1996).

For example, Dymock (1993) studied L1 English middle school students with good decoding but poor comprehension skills to see whether they also had poor listening comprehension skills. She reasoned that if the students were so preoccupied with decoding that it detracted from their ability to construct meaning from text, their listening comprehension scores should be higher than their reading comprehension scores. If, on the other hand, their listening comprehension scores were at a level similar to their reading comprehension scores, it would prove that their reading comprehension level equaled their listening comprehension level, once decoding was removed as a factor. She found that poor comprehenders also had poor scores on listening comprehension, leading her to conclude that "once a child has become a good decoder, differences in reading ability will reflect differences in listening ability" (p. 90).

Biemiller (1999) points out that building a strong listening vocabulary base through listening is a decisive competency needed for later reading tasks. A strong listening vocabulary allows students to recognize many words once their decoding catches up with their listening vocabulary. Royer and Carlo (1991) found that Spanish ELLs' English listening comprehension assessed in fifth grade was one of the strongest predictors of English reading comprehension in sixth grade. Others found that English listening comprehension and quality of vocabulary definitions could account for 50% of the variance in reading comprehension scores of teenage Mexican ELLs (Carlisle et al., 1996). This kind of evidence makes the simple view of reading intriguing to those interested in second-language acquisition.

The simple view of reading implicitly accepts the idea that oracy is the foundation for literacy. It also helps explain why ELLs need to have listening vocabulary in place before they can comprehend text.

The Grammar of Oral Language

The grammar used in spoken English differs from that of written grammar. Native speakers of a language do not, typically, use full sentences when speaking. Spoken language usually uses less specific vocabulary, looser syntax, pronouns instead of nouns, and a lot of *ellipsis* (missing words that can be understood from context) because the setting and the interaction provide many clues to meaning. Spoken language uses more *discourse markers*, such as conversational fillers and other sounds, as well as the paralinguistic cues mentioned earlier, in order to help listeners keep track of where in the course of an utterance the speaker is at a particular moment (Brown & Yule, 1983). These fillers serve as an informal kind of "oral punctuation." Brazil calls this real-time process a "step-by-step assembly of a spoken utterance" (Brazil, 1995, p. 17).

Slang and idioms particular to a time and place abound in spoken language. In addition, pronunciation may be less precise. Because oral language happens in real time, it can afford to be somewhat fragmentary because there are other cueing systems available to the listener in the context. However, *context-reduced oral language* (Cummins, 1996), such as language exchanged during telephone conversations, lacks the extra cueing systems that we use to compensate when our auditory comprehension breaks down. Context-reduced listening tasks can be very stressful for ELLs, even when their proficiency in other areas is high.

Oral language comes in many forms. It may be informal or come in more formal contexts, such as lectures, in-depth news reports, speeches, or sermons. Like in reading, the *level of difficulty* and the *purpose for listening* change from task to task, and these changes require flexibility and strategic listening. If the percentage of unknown words is too high, comprehension breaks down. Also, if the sheer quantity of spoken words is too great, or the duration of the listening task is too long, concentration will also break down. When the spoken language is beyond the learner's zone of proximal development (ZPD; Vygotsky, 1986), the input is no longer comprehensible. This can result in full-scale frustration, mental shut-down, and a resulting lack of academic progress.

Oral language varies according to the listening task, and those tasks can range from informal communicative (BICS) language, to more academic (CALP) language, which is used in classrooms. When students are put in listening situations in which the contextual cues are reduced, the listening task gets harder because the words alone must convey the meaning. Here is one account by a second-grade ESL teacher that captures the nature of the challenge not only for the students but also for their instructors:

> *I speak Spanish, but would by no means call myself bilingual. However, I often have to speak Spanish in my school with both students and parents. If I am called upon to make a phone call in Spanish, I tend to panic because I cannot see the person talking to me and therefore do not have*

any body language to interpret, or anything visual, for that matter. I also translate for conferences, and by the time the night is over, I am mentally exhausted. And when analyzing why, I think that listening to the parents and making sure I am understanding what exactly they are saying is pretty stressful. And then to translate that to the teachers, then translate back to the parents is really tiring. People can "zone out" while someone is speaking their native language and still get the gist of what they are saying, but to do that in a person's second language is just not possible.—
VICKI MUSIAL

All of these factors—the fleeting nature of spoken words, the fragmentary nature of oral grammar, the casual pronunciation of words, idiomatic vocabulary, different purposes and difficulty levels for listening tasks, and cultural factors—combine to make it challenging for ELLs to achieve a high level of listening comprehension. Because listening remains effortful for ELLs for a long time, it is important to practice it with them in manageable amounts and at the appropriate level.

Assessment of Listening Skills

Appropriate assessment of listening skills is a key component for placing ELLs in the programs and at the levels that best suit their needs and in assessing their comprehension of academic work. Notwithstanding its importance, the listening comprehension level of ELLs is often hard to assess. Because listening comprehension cannot be easily seen, teachers may have a false sense of how much an ELL understands. On the one hand, if students' oral language has not reached a threshold that allows them to produce connected sentences, they may comprehend but not be able to demonstrate their comprehension verbally. On the other hand, teachers may find that when they stop to check their ELL students' comprehension, students may signal that they understand even when they don't because they simply don't want to call attention to their confusion.

Oral Proficiency in English as a New Language

The second component of oracy is oral proficiency, sometimes called the speaking skill. Although being able to speak a language well does confer many benefits that come with having greater opportunities for self-expression, oral proficiency in itself doesn't predict reading proficiency (August, Calderon, & Carlo, 2002; Geva, 2007). For ELLs, reading proficiency is more affected by the core decoding skills, which include phonological awareness, letter identification, word recognition, and knowledge of English grammar (Bernhardt & Kamil, 1995), in addition to the listening comprehension described previously. The National Literacy Panel called for greater attention to English oral proficiency as a core goal for ELLs (August & Shanahan, 2006), basing its conclusions on studies that focused on a mixture of speaking and listening skills.

Effective oral language is an important part of academic development in classrooms in the United States, and it is important that ELLs learn to engage in instructional conversation (Saunders & Goldenberg, 1999; Tharp et al., 2003; Waxman & Tellez, 2002), which can be defined as "planned, goal-directed conversations on an academic topic between a teacher and a small group of students" (Tharp et al., 2003, parag 6).

Whether or not ELLs have rich instructional conversation in their native language, they need opportunities to engage in instructional conversation in English. Therefore, English instructional conversation is best supported when it takes place in the classroom, and it is very important for teachers to provide ample opportunities to develop this kind of language.

Instructional conversation uses CALP language. As we explained in Chapter 2, CALP language can be both written and oral. ELLs need to engage in probing conversations about instructional topics with peers and expert others, including the teacher. These kinds of conversations help them learn such skills as conveying information, discussing, analyzing, inferring, debating, summarizing, evaluating, and synthesizing and the vocabulary that accompanies each of them.

As children advance in the grade levels, more and more CALP language is found in the instructional conversation of the classroom. The pedagogical implication of this is that teachers need to provide early opportunities to engage in challenging oral conversation in class. It is all too tempting for teachers of ELLs to simplify speech, becoming inadvertent "enablers" of lowered expectations and not giving ELLs that CALP "workout" they need (Zwiers, 2007, p. 107). When teachers finish a sentence for the student, steer answers, affirm too quickly, or oversimplify, students pay the price. On the other side, students learn to engage in instructional conversation when teachers ask more focused questions, provide sufficient wait time, and pay attention to the thinking process of the students rather than supplying answers or steering them toward a "correct" answer.

Oral language is tremendously important for other, more universal reasons. Oral language is the main way we interact with the world, through the all-important medium of dialogue. *Interactive dialogue* (sometimes called *collaborative dialogue*), which includes instructional and social conversation, develops language, thought, and content knowledge, as well as our personalities and beliefs, and our ability to form relationships (Swain,

2000). If we think of oral language not as a product but a process that evolves over a long period of time, it's easier to understand why interactive dialogue is so important in L2 acquisition.

Stages of Oral Language Development in ELLs

Children learning their first language produce speech in roughly the same order no matter what their native language is: they start with nouns, followed by verbs, then adjectives (National Institute of Child Health and Human Development, 2004). Young ELLs go through similar stages of oral language development, moving from single-word production all the way to complex sentences, which, including literacy skills, take place in the space of about 5 to 7 years (Thomas & Collier, 2002). Development is influenced by such factors as the age at which the learner begins to learn English, L1 oracy and literacy, the amount of prior schooling, the presence of English-speaking siblings, motivation, learning style, and related factors. Of course, progress is also affected by the instructional setting.

One of the phenomena in the stages of oral language development of which every teacher of ELLs must be aware is the preproduction or *silent period*. During the silent period, which may last as long as a year, the learner focuses on bearing the listening load of spoken English and may not produce any oral language. The silent period is similar to the pre-speech period of native-speaking children, but it can occur at any age. Although it may appear on the surface as if no learning is occurring, the silent period is very dynamic. During this period, ELLs are actively gaining knowledge of the sounds and patterns of English, and teachers can have full confidence that learning is taking place. At the same time, while respecting that children may not be ready to speak, teachers need to continue to actively include and engage such students by asking them to point or gesture, perform motor activities, manipulate objects, act, pantomine, or create some kind of visual art to show what they have understood. Clear speaking and expressive oral reading by the teacher are important sources of modeling for students during this period.

> *I have witnessed an extreme example of the silent period in a seventh-grade student whose first language was Chinese. She was in an ESL class, and although her father, a bilingual Chinese–English speaker, went over the English lessons with her every night, she wouldn't say a word in class. For 9 months she was mute, and the district was getting ready to test her for a learning disability, but then summer came. Although she spoke only Chinese during the summer, she came back the following fall and, after a week in school, was speaking full sentences and carrying on conversations in English, like a native speaker, with no accent or anything.*—LEAH

Of course, teachers need to be careful not to mistake a silent period for a student just "tuning out" or detaching. It's important that teachers of ELLs not put the children "out to pasture" by failing to include them in activities. Mohr and Mohr (2007) point out that teachers in one study claimed they were allowing an extended silent period for new ELLs, but to observers, "the students seemed neglected" (p. 443).

Importance of Oral Language Development for School Success

Research shows that children who come to school with strong oracy are at an advantage, and those with limited oracy are more likely to have difficulty learning to read (Scarborough, 2001; Tracey & Morrow 2002). Conversely, early delays in the development of oracy are reflected in low levels of reading comprehension, which in turn lead to lack of academic success (Biemiller, 1970). Thanks to the inborn proclivity of children to learn language, children who are learning English can easily develop oral vocabulary. In fact, at least one study has indicated that kindergarten-age ELLs learned more English vocabulary in a classroom than their English-only counterparts did (University of Chicago Press Journals, 2007).

It should also be noted that children whose home language is not English will also benefit from developing strong oracy in their first language. When their oracy is strong in their heritage language, they will bring more vocabulary, background knowledge, listening skills, and self-confidence to the English-learning endeavor.

For all of these considerations, then, bringing ELLs' oracy to a high level is an important ingredient of their long-term reading success.

HOW DOES THIS LOOK IN THE CLASSROOM?

To boost listening skills, we suggest alternating *intensive* and *extensive* practice activities.

Intensive listening gives students a chance to focus on discrete features of the sounds of English in a controlled setting in which they can hear the oral text more than once and analyze its features and sound combinations. The insights gained from intensive listening can be applied to other listening experiences. Intensive activities can be embedded within extensive activities.

Intensive Activities

Here are some intensive listening activities which will help build listening comprehension.

Using Clips from Movies, TV, or the Internet

Using media excerpts is a great way to demonstrate pronunciation features because they can be played again and again, unlike a real speaker. While listening to them, features of American English pronunciation can be highlighted. For example, in American English, when one word ends with /t/ and the following pronoun begins with a /y/, we normally produce a "ch" sound, such as /downchuw/ for *don't you*. Once that is explained and demonstrated, students discover many other examples of [-t] + [y-], and many formerly impenetrable sounds suddenly make sense to them.

Transcribing a Song

Split the class into small groups, ask each group to write down the words of one verse or chorus of a chosen song, and then play it. Members of each group then huddle to put together their verse and write it on the board. Then the whole class looks at the lyrics while listening to the song a second time. Finally, the teacher passes out the complete lyrics and students check their work against the lyrics. Sometimes the words the students think they hear can be very funny! What's more, transcribing opens a great discussion about how words are spelled in comparison to how they sound.

Dictation

Dictation practices phonological awareness and concept of word—two of the key components of listening comprehension. To prepare a dictation, a teacher reads a connected text aloud, preferably one students have already seen, and asks students to write down all the words they hear. A teacher can take a phrase or sentence from the lesson, read it with pauses at the phrase and clause breaks, and gradually increase the length of the sentences. Over time, students become proficient at holding more words in working memory as they transcribe them. It is a great way to spot-check development of ELLs' syntax, and it provides spelling awareness at the same time. A prerecorded text can also be used for dictations.

A modified version of the dictation is a *cloze* dictation, in which some of the words are provided and others are left blank. The words that are left blank can be selected according to a teaching focus, such as past-tense irregular verbs in a ballad, or left out at fixed intervals as students listen to a speech or dialogue. When preparing a cloze for song lyrics, make sure the blanks are far enough apart for students to have enough time to write in the missing word.

Using Closed Captioning

Many video and audio tracks contain closed captioning or subtitling options. On YouTube, for example, many songs can be played with a lyric crawler underneath the image, allowing ELLs to read along as they listen to the sounds of the words. Karaoke programs offer written lyrics sung softly under a musical track. Cable stations and DVD formatting also allow for subtitles in several languages. This is a great way to jump-start the sound-to-letter correspondences of English, and they can be great aids to building listening comprehension inside and outside the classroom.

Extensive Activities

Extensive listening activities, on the other hand, give students practice in getting the gist of an utterance as they develop strategic listening skills in authentic but low-stress contexts. Here are some of the ways ELLs can practice extensive listening.

Total Physical Response, Pantomime, and in the Manner of the Word

Total physical response (TPR) is a popular ESL teaching technique in which students act out a word, sentence, or scenario (Asher, 1988), demonstrating their listening comprehension. It works well for the earliest learners who cannot write or speak English yet but can indicate comprehension through movement. Anne Grossmann of Gary School, in the Chicago Public Schools, says that her school's bilingual and ESL classes use this technique extensively in the early grades. For example, she might give an ELL the word "cry" and ask the learner to act it out in pantomime for his or her classmates. The class guesses the word together. As students become more advanced, the nature of the TPR task can get more sophisticated. For example, a student can be given a piece of paper with an adverb not known to the rest of the class and read a fairy tale "in the manner of the word," as students try to guess the adverb from their classmate's tone of voice and body language.

Watching and Listening to Classmates, a Guest Speaker, or a Video

This is a great way to practice listening comprehension. If learners are more proficient, they can combine the listening with note taking or by filling in a graphic organizer that has been prepared in advance by the teacher. Although less immediately exciting than a "live" visitor, a video or webcast can also be used.

Interactive Read-Alouds

Teachers read books or stories to students, stopping at key points in the story to model thinking aloud. Teachers ask students to speculate about what is coming next in the story and to apply what they have just heard to their own experiences. In addition to building oracy, *interactive read-alouds* build crucial background knowledge of people, places, and events needed by ELLs (Chen & Mora-Flores, 2007). As ELLs hear more stories, they develop a sense of *story grammar*, the events that a listener or reader can expect to occur in the normal course of an English language story. Learning story grammar helps children begin to make predictions that will later be used in their reading and writing. Reading informational text aloud also builds knowledge of text structures for reading and writing. Studies have shown that native-speaking students can benefit from read-alouds even through eighth grade (Biemiller, 1999; Chall, 1996); high school students probably benefit as well, but research is lacking. We find no upper age limit on its benefit for ELLs.

Using Music and Recorded Books

These help both listening and reading comprehension. Songs are great motivators; they give cultural information; their vocabulary is informal and often contains colorful idioms; and they can be played again and again. Also, the multiple cueing systems available through recorded books help ELLs fill in the gaps in their listening vocabulary and their reading vocabulary as they draw upon both sources. Internet downloads make it easy and affordable to find enjoyable songs to practice listening comprehension while building classroom community (Lems, 2002).

> *I ask my high school ELLs to give a formal presentation on their favorite piece of music, musician, or musical genre. As each student presents, the others take notes. Some students show examples of the singer in live performance as they give the presentation, and it gets others in the class really excited about the music. Later, some students found YouTube sites of the same artists with subtitled lyrics, so the whole class was able to sing along.—*KRISTIN

Breaking Text into Smaller Units

Because the sheer volume of listening is exhausting for ELLs, oral text should be broken into more manageable pieces. Lectures should be avoided in instructional settings with ELLs—including lengthy teacher explanations of what is planned for the day! It is particularly important for content teachers to find interactive ways to get across course content without lecturing and reading from the textbook. PowerPoint and other tools make it easier to put key points in a visual format, and this can guide ELLs as they listen.

Making an Inventory of Listening Tasks

Teachers should figure out in advance of a curricular unit what listening tasks will be needed in their classrooms and provide aids to comprehension whenever possible. This might involve visuals, graphic organizers, and walk-throughs of procedures.

Infusing the Class with Interactive Dialogue

Younger learners develop their oral skills partly through the natural interactions that occur when speaking English socially. However, interactive dialogue, as described earlier, ensures that students develop oral language at a cognitively challenging level. When students are involved in problem solving together, they create integrated projects through interaction and talk about their own processes as they do so. Through dialogue, students explore the topic at hand and their own linguistic processes and their actual language use. Swain summarizes the process in this way: "A student's talk about language crystallizes ideas" (Swain, 2005, p. 479). Dialogue gives ELLs opportunities to simultaneously learn language, learn content through language, and learn about language (Halliday, 1993; Swain, 2000). Teachers can examine their own language to ensure that it scaffolds and supports ELLs, not only in developing answers in response to fact-based questions with right or wrong answers, but also for higher-order thinking. Like all students, ELLs need to be challenged with targeted but open-ended questions and held to high academic expectations (Zwiers, 2008).

Assessment of Oracy

When assessing activities using oral text, it's important for teachers to allow students adequate processing time. Timed tests that require speedy responses to oral *prompts* do not give a fair assessment of what an ELL may know. Whenever possible, listening assessments should include an opportunity for ELLs to hear the texts and the prompts more than once. When rubrics are used to assess ELLs' oracy on a continuing basis, they should account for the developmental nature of learning a new language and give credit for finding resourceful ways to communicate, even with limited vocabulary and the presence of errors.

QUESTIONS FOR FURTHER DISCUSSION

1. If you had to choose three important ideas from this chapter, what would you choose? How can you apply these ideas to your larger knowledge of teaching English as a new language?

2. Can you think of something someone said to you that you remember exactly, with a great deal of detail? What do you think was so striking about the words? Why do you think we remember some words we hear exactly, but most only for their gist?

3. Have you had any experience, either as a teacher or a language learner, in which it seemed somebody understood an oral text until it was shown that they didn't? Describe it.

4. Think of a recent example in which you engaged in instructional conversation. Whom did you share it with? What were some of its characteristics?

5. With a partner or alone, think of some "meaning-bearing" gestures and body language commonly used by teachers in schools. Talk about ways those gestures could be taught to ELLs. If you have the opportunity to ask ELLs about this, you may find that they have perceived gestures that adults have missed!

6. Choose a favorite short rhyming poem and have a proficient English speaker read it to you. As you listen, mark its stress patterns. Now make a table to see what parts of speech the stressed words are. Are they nouns/pronouns, verbs, adjectives, adverbs, or prepositions? Does your list reflect the general statement about English stress patterns made in this chapter?

7. Talk about ways that a person's body language might reveal as much or more about them than their words. Do body language and words ever give contrary messages? How could you help ELLs discover this difference?

8. Make a list of at least six word combinations that create the /t/ + /y/ = / ch/ pronunciation mentioned in the chapter. Can you think of ways to make this into a classroom activity?

9. We often hear the lyrics of a song but interpret them completely differently, changing the meaning of the song to our own skewed interpretation. Do you have any examples of this phenomenon? Share them with others.

10. Can you think of any words that you need to subvocalize to yourself in order to access their meaning or spelling? If you can, try to analyze what it is that makes that word tricky.

11. When you look at a TV show or movie without sound, what do you catch and what do you wonder about? How does it compare with hearing a TV from another room when you cannot see the picture? Have you ever looked at a TV show or movie in a language you didn't know, with no subtitles? What could you figure out from the body language?

12. Looking at Table 3.1, talk about which similarities between listening and reading you had realized prior to reading this chapter, and which were new to you. Can you think of any others?

CHAPTER FOUR

Learning to Read, Write, and Spell Words in English as a New Language

New Vocabulary in This Chapter: phoneme, grapheme, word recognition, decodable word, sight word, recoding, phonics, probabilistic reasoning, alphabetic orthography, alphabet, logographic writing system, syllabic writing system, syllabary, generative, transparency, shallow/ transparent orthography, deep/opaque orthography, opacity, orthographic depth, word calling, onset, rime, morpheme, morphophonemic, digraph

In this chapter we discuss how learning to read is influenced by the orthography of the target language, in this case, English. Each written language in the world has an orthography, or writing system, and English uses the roman alphabet. The way words are represented in the English writing system affects the way everyone, including ELLs, learns to read in English. The experiences ELLs have with the English alphabet can be influenced by the writing system of their first language and its orthographic distance from the English writing system. Adjusting to the English writing system is important and too often overlooked in designing instruction for ELLs.

We begin by taking a look at how native speakers of English learn to recognize words and decode connected text.

How Word Recognition Occurs in English

To read English words, we learn to match sounds, or *phonemes*, with letters, or *graphemes*. When we learn to read English words, we learn to perform several steps very rapidly. First, we identify the first letter(s) of the word and try to find a matching phoneme. Then, working left to right, we match the rest of the graphemes and phonemes of the word. Holding the sounds in our working memory, we recombine them to form a mental representation that we attempt to match with a word from our listening vocabulary. Once that lightning-fast process has occurred, we can access its meaning. Of course, if we are reading out loud, there are additional steps needed in order to pronounce the words.

Accessing and recognizing individual words is called *word recognition*, and recognizing the sound and meaning of words across connected text is what we call decoding. There are two broad categories of words in English: those with easy-to-match phonemes and graphemes, called *decodable words*, and those that have to be memorized as a whole, called *sight words*. Decoding and sight-word recognition are the primary word-attack skills used for English word recognition. There are good reasons that English words are taught through both decoding and memorization, which will become clear as we proceed through this chapter.

On the other hand, when we write to represent words in written form, which is sometimes called *recoding*, we retrieve the word from our listening vocabulary and try to write the letters that represent the sounds of the word, proceeding in order from left to right. We also learn to write some English words not by matching them with the sounds, but from sheer rote memorization. Like decoding, recoding words in English can proceed in two possible ways, by putting letters in order, or by learning how to write some words "by heart," without breaking them apart. Although some of the shortest and most common words are sight words, overall the great majority of English words are decodable, and learning to decode is unavoidable in order to read and write in English.

Put another way, when learners decode English words, they start with the letter symbols and match them with the sounds, and when they write English words, they start with the sounds and match them with the letter symbols. No matter which end we start from, both processes involve matching the English sound and letter symbol combinations. The skill of matching sounds and letter symbols is called *phonics*. Phonics knowledge requires a good understanding of how the English sound and writing systems map onto each other. In order to help learners develop the phonics skill, teachers need to understand how the phonemes and graphemes of English work together in the English writing system. The teacher also needs to appreciate how the orthographies of ELLs' first languages resemble and differ from English and how that affects learning to read. Exploring those similarities and differences is the principal purpose of this chapter.

For a native speaker of English, the process of learning to read and write words usually begins before or in kindergarten and continues until it is in place by third grade. This is a lengthy and often laborious process, and must be cemented into place before the focus of reading changes from "learning to read" to "reading to learn." Learners of English as a new language need to go through this process just like native speakers, but it might take place at any age or grade level, depending on when ELLs begin to learn English as a new language. Phonics skills are critical to cracking the code for reading English and must be accounted for in any comprehensive instructional program. As Calderon (2006) nicely summarizes, "Whatever the grade level, teachers with ELLs will eventually have students who need instruction in these basic skills, before they can comprehend a text" (p. 131).

Probabilistic Reasoning

Even though the relationship between phonemes and graphemes is not regular in the English writing system, L1 English readers "know" that when a consonant or vowel occurs in a certain context, it is likely to be pronounced in a specific way. They rely on a mental processing strategy known as *probabilistic reasoning*. The term, used in the computer science and cognitive science fields, explains that the way readers process text is partially based on their sense of the likelihood that a letter or combination of letters will stand for a certain sound or combination of sounds (Birch, 2007; Edwards & von Winterfeldt, 1986; Rachlin, 1989).

This reasoning skill is honed through the stages of reading development. As we get to know print better, we get better and better at predicting what the next letter of a word is likely to be and how it is likely to sound. When we become really proficient at it, we can even fill in missing letters, or missing words, when the message is compromised somehow. The game show *Wheel of Fortune* is a contest pitting the probabilistic reasoning skills of contestants who try to guess a hidden phrase with the fewest letters revealed.

We can also recognize probabilistic reasoning in the editing settings on word processing programs. If we activate it, it will "guess" the most probable word as we type in the first couple of letters. If a person types in "st," for example, the program brings up the most high-frequency word starting with *st*, such as *stay*. The concept of probabilistic reasoning boils down to being able to predict what is most likely to come next, based on what we already know. It's something ELLs must strive to develop to a native speaker level in their reading. English learners need to learn the sounds and letters of the new language as well as the actual vocabulary words and sentence patterns that they are endeavoring to read or write.

Once we realize that we are talking about the brain's ability to assess probabilities, we realize that "rules" are really just highly probable events, and "exceptions" are less probable events. Seen that way, we can approach the teaching of the ways words are written and spelled with a different perspective.

Now let's look at how different writing systems are organized in order to better understand how sound and letter combinations work in English.

Major Kinds of Writing Systems

Over time, human beings have developed many kinds of orthographies. All of them are attempts to capture and preserve the information contained in speech; however, the level of detail of the phonemic information contained in them varies considerably. The way an orthographic system represents spoken language influences how people learn to read. There are many kinds of orthographies, but they can be classified into three large systems: alphabetic, logographic, and syllabic (Birch, 2007; Omniglot, 2009). Each of these large orthographic systems is represented in the languages of immigrant groups in the United States.

When we learn to read in a new language, we need to learn its orthographic system. If we are literate in our first language, we also carry the knowledge of its orthographic system. When the two orthographic systems are similar, they have greater language proximity, as described in Chapter 2, and the reverse is also true. Learning how to use the English writing system may be facilitated or impeded by prior experience with a different orthography. When an ELL is literate in an orthography that is similar to English, there may be a positive cross-linguistic influence (PCI), but it can also be a source of potential interference because of the different associations between some sounds and letters. On the other hand, when an ELL is already literate in an orthography that is not similar to English, it can also be a source of potential interference or PCI. For example, punctuation marks such as commas and periods are used very similarly in both English and Chinese. The facilitating or complicating aspects of native language orthographies are too often overlooked in planning instruction for ELLs from different language backgrounds.

Alphabetic Writing Systems

An *alphabetic orthography* represents each sound with a symbol or symbols and includes both consonants and vowels. The set of all the units that can make up words is called an *alphabet*. Many languages use alphabetic orthographies. These include English, Russian, Spanish, Arabic, and many more. Within alphabetic orthographies there are many different alphabets. English uses the roman alphabet, as do many other languages; however, the relationship between the roman alphabet letters and the sounds they represent differs from language to language. For example, the letters *ch* represent the /ch/ sound in English, such as the word *church*, but the /sh/ sound in French, such as the word *chateau*.

The Cyrillic alphabet is another widely used alphabet for languages such as Russian, Ukrainian, and Bulgarian. ELLs who read and write in a Cyrillic alphabet need time and practice to learn to decode in English because they don't know the English letters yet.

Another common alphabet is the Arabic alphabet, whose letters represent all of the consonant sounds but only some of the vowel sounds, and which is written from right to left. Arabic is the alphabet used for not only Arabic, but Urdu, Persian, Malay, and other languages spoken by many ELLs. When ELLs read and write in a language using Arabic letters, they need not only extra practice learning the ways to say and write vowel sounds in English, but also practice in reading and writing from left to right.

ELLs whose first language is represented by an alphabetic script will have an advantage in learning to decode English words because they already know that the letters of the alphabet represent sounds. In addition, ELLs from languages with roman alphabet letters have an added advantage because the letters of their first language share more characteristics with English.

Logographic Writing Systems

No writing system in the world is devoid of a phonological element. However, those that use a *logographic writing system* contain some characters that have no phonological information and others that do. Chinese has the best known logographic writing system. A Chinese word is composed of a radical that contains semantic information to which a phonetic component may or may not be added. Put together, this radical plus phonetic component is called a sinogram. Chinese has about 2,500 logograms that can be combined to create 60,000 sinograms (Yule, 2006), but additional words are being created all the time. It is a common fallacy that reading Chinese does not involve phonological processing; it does. For example, it has been demonstrated that phonological awareness, an important building block of reading, affects reading ability equally in Chinese and English (Pang & Kamil, 2003).

Logographic writing systems require more visual and less phonetic processing. It takes a long time to acquire a complete set of logograms (McGuinness, 2004). Logographic orthographies provide a direct pathway to meaning, allowing people to read and write "what they mean," not just "what they say" (Ellis et al., 2004, p. 438). An additional advantage of logographic systems is that, because they carry less phonological information, they can be used by a wide range of regional dialect speakers who otherwise wouldn't be able to understand each others' speech.

Syllabaries and Other Writing Systems

There are a number of other writing systems, and one of the most widely used is the *syllabic* writing system, in which each symbol represents a consonant–vowel combination that cannot be broken down further (Comrie, Matthews, & Polinsky, 1996). Languages that use syllabic orthographies include Japanese Hiragana and Katakana, Hmong, Bengali, Gujarati, and Cherokee. Words consist of combinations of syllables, and the complete set of syllables is called a *syllabary*. There are also a number of instructional writing systems, such as the International Phonetic Alphabet (IPA), a variation of which is used as a guide to pronunciation in this book.

Alphabets carry the added advantage of being *generative*. With a limited number of letters and sounds, they can be combined to generate an astronomical number of new words. The elegance and economy of an alphabetic system convinced the Chinese to use a transitional alphabetic system called pinyin to teach new readers Chinese. Once the sounds of the alphabetic system have given children the extra phonological information they need to decode a Chinese word, the phonological information is withdrawn and children read the logograms without support.

The differences children experience in learning literacy through these writing systems are profound, but proficient readers emerge through the medium of all of these writing systems. For a detailed inventory of the world's writing systems, we recommend the website called *Omniglot: Writing Systems and Languages of the World* (Omniglot, 2009).

Some of the orthographies used by members of immigrant and ethnic communities in Chicago are featured in the photo essay Chicago Orthographies (Figure 4.1).

Orthographic Transparency or Depth

An important concept of how predictably writing systems represent the sounds of words is called orthographic *transparency* or depth. Orthographic transparency describes how closely the sounds and symbols of a language correspond to each other. Various languages fall in different places along the continuum. *Shallow (or transparent) orthographies* are writing systems with a close match between sounds (phonemes) and symbols (graphemes).

Amharic sign on Ethiopian restaurant.

Chinese soybean seller in new Chinatown neighborhood.

Bilingual sign in Vietnamese and Chinese.

FIGURE 4.1. Orthographies found on signage in the Chicago area.

Georgian store with Georgian and Russian orthographies.

Skokie Public Library welcomes its residents in many orthographies.

FIGURE 4.1. *(cont.)*

Korean signs adorn stores in many Chicago and suburban neighborhoods.

Russian sign for hearing aid company.

Hindi sign on a restaurant.

FIGURE 4.1. *(cont.)*

Neon sign in "Greektown."

Arabic adorns all the panels of the door at this center.

English/Hebrew sign.

FIGURE 4.1. *(cont.)*

Sometimes referred to as "phonetic" orthographies, transparent orthographies include Italian, Spanish, Turkish, Korean, and Dutch.

Deep (or opaque) orthographies, on the other hand, have symbols that do not match closely with their phonemes. Examples include Chinese, French, Japanese Kanji, and most important, English. Languages that have kept the same written form for a long time are naturally more opaque, because written language changes more slowly than spoken language. Over time, the gap between the two forms widens. Such languages generally take longer to learn to read and write.

Because English has a deep orthography, many English words cannot be identified by sounding out the letters across the word. There are 40-plus phonemes in English (Ellis et al., 2004; Venezky, 1970), and only 26 letters to represent them; therefore, the alphabet must be combined in a large variety of ways in order to represent the sounds of English (McGuinness, 2004). "Read," for example, has two different pronunciations, depending on its context. It can only be understood through the words around it.

Historical Features Contributing to the Opacity of English

English has an opaque writing system because of at least three historical factors that have had a significant impact. The first of these is the effect of the Christianization of England, in which new writing systems were adopted by the indigenous peoples there. The second factor is the effect of the various foreign invasions that occurred, most notably the Norman Conquest in 1066, which infused the spoken and written language with thousands of new French words. The Norman Conquest introduced a second word for many words that already existed in English, but they took on different nuances. Examples of parallel Old English and French words found in English include *pig* and *pork, cattle* and *beef, sheep* and *mutton,* and *deer* and *venison*. The third factor is the effect of the wide diffusion of written materials that resulted from the invention of the printing press. Printed materials codified the spellings of some words and distributed them widely. All of these factors have contributed to the *opacity* of the English spelling system.

The opacity of English explains why not only ELLs but also native speakers of English have so much trouble with spelling. For example, they will have to figure out if the letter *c* is pronounced with a hard sound /k/, as in *coat*, or with a softer sound /s/, as in *city*. Some words even have silent letters, as in *comb* or *sign*, and these must be learned one by one.

A writing system need not be alphabetic to be opaque. Chinese is also deep, or opaque, because although Chinese contains some phonemic information in its characters (Li, 2002), the characters cannot be broken into a linear sequence of sounds. Also, Chinese has an old writing system that has traveled to many places, so its symbols are pronounced many different ways. As a result, the reader of Chinese employs a different kind of word identification strategy, as described earlier, which involves looking at the semantic element of a word as well as its pronunciation clues. Because reading in Chinese requires a different set of strategies and does not require the decoding skill needed for alphabetic orthographies, Chinese ELLs need extra guidance and time to develop English decoding skills. However, Chinese ELLs may have the compensating skill of looking carefully at the semantic elements of a word, which can serve as a valuable tool, especially at higher levels of English reading.

The Effect of Orthography on Learning to Read

Katz and Frost (1992) proposed the *orthographic depth* hypothesis to address the question of how different writing systems influence the ways children learn to read. They hypothesized that it would be easier for children from transparent orthographies to learn to read aloud and spell than for children from opaque orthographies, and that children from transparent orthography languages would use more phonologically based strategies to identify words. The hypothesis has been confirmed by a number of studies, including one that examined children learning to read in alphabetic, syllabic, and logographic orthographies. The children from transparent orthographies learned to read more quickly, read longer words more slowly, and were more likely to say "nonwords" or nonsense words when they made reading mistakes. Children from more opaque orthographies, on the other hand, took a longer time to learn to read, did not read longer words more slowly, and were more likely to substitute other real words when they made reading errors. In addition, they were more likely to skip words (Ellis et al., 2004).

These and comparable results have confirmed that readers from different orthographies undergo different processes in learning to read. Readers from transparent orthographies read across the syllables of a word, and as a result it takes longer to read a longer word. The fact that transparent orthography readers have a high occurrence of nonwords when reading aloud suggests that some may not be reading for meaning, at least initially. Clearly, the transparency advantage has a downside. *Word calling*, or decoding without comprehension, is a concern because the ease of decoding makes it possible to focus on the sounds alone, without analyzing the meaning of the words being decoded (Paulesu et al., 2000). Decoding is not really reading if it doesn't include comprehension.

When I read out loud in Korean in my school days, I often found myself decoding words without thinking about any meanings of the sentences, and now I understand what the reason might be. Also, I noticed that when I started learning to decode words in English, I couldn't comprehend much while reading aloud either because I mostly focused on decoding the words correctly.—SEUNG HEE MA

Readers from opaque orthographies, on the other hand, go through several different strategies as they learn to decode, including phonemic segmentation, whole-word recognition, probabilistic reasoning, and generalizing from rhyming syllable patterns found in short words, using *onset* and *rime*. An onset is the first consonant or consonant sound of a syllable, and the rime is the vowel, vowel + consonant, or vowel + consonants pattern at the end of a syllable. The fact that the Ellis et al. (2004) study shows a high number of real substitute words by opaque readers hints that they are probably learning a different set of compensating strategies to read for meaning as they struggle to learn to decode.

As we have discovered, the level of transparency in a writing system is a factor in determining how easily people learn to read in their first language. For an extended example, we highlight two languages, Turkish and Cherokee, whose writing system reforms created a marked effect on literacy.

Writing System Reform in Turkish and Cherokee

When nations and groups adopt reforms in their writing systems, the result can be an explosion of literacy.

Mustapha Kamil Ataturk (1881–1938), the founder of modern Turkey, brought a roman-based alphabet to Turkish, which had been written in the Arabic script for centuries during the Ottoman Empire. Arabic's symbols were not a close match with Turkish sounds, creating an opaque alphabet and difficulties in learning to read and write. Modern Turkish script, on the other hand, written in a modified version of the roman alphabet, matches the sounds of Turkish very closely, and is an easy alphabet to learn to read. Emel Gokcen describes the change in her family that occurred when Mustapha Kamil Ataturk introduced alphabet reform to Turkey:

[When Ataturk changed the alphabet] my father immediately had a teacher come to teach my mother the new Turkish, the new alphabet. My mother could write in the old ways. She had been schooled enough to write her own letters. But she told me that the old Turkish writing, the Arabic alphabet, was so difficult that it took years to learn, whereas the new one was not only easy to read and write but very easy to pronounce.

It is much easier to read than French or English because it is like Italian. You don't have to know the language. It was phonetically clear, very easy to learn. So all the grandmothers started reading books and learning . . . [the grandmothers hadn't been able to read before] . . . Reading spread like wildfire all over Anatolia and it reduced the tremendous ignorance of the population—the workers out in the fields and so forth; they could take part in a better government. (in Cherry, 2008, p. 25).

Another writing system reform was the creation, in 1821, of a phonetic writing system for the Iroquoian language spoken by the Cherokee. Sequoya, a Cherokee from North Carolina, created this syllable-based system, and "within a few years after its invention, a high level of literacy had been achieved within the Cherokee community" (Comrie et al., 1996, p. 207). Social studies teachers might highlight this remarkable man and his achievement.

Morphemes Help Us Learn Opaque Writing Systems

Languages with deep orthography make up for their phonetic inconsistencies by conveying semantic information in their morphemes. *Morphemes* are the smallest units of meaning of a word; we can often figure out a word's meaning by examining its morphemes. English is considered to be a *morphophonemic* language because English words contain both phonemic and morphemic information. Benczik (2001) points out that in deep orthography languages like English, spelling is included in the teaching of grammar because the spelling patterns are clues to meaning. (The morphophonemic nature of English is explained in Chapter 5.)

Despite the compensating information from morphemes in opaque languages, it is much easier to learn to read in a transparent language. Some call transparent orthographies "learner-friendly orthographies." They are also easier to read aloud because there are no unpleasant surprises. Another implication of *orthographic depth* is that children learning to read in a deep orthography need more training in phonological awareness (de Jong & van der Leij, 2002) because there are so many spelling patterns that need to be matched with phonemes.

Research published in *Nature Neuroscience* revealed that Italians were considerably faster in reading words and nonwords aloud in Italian than their English counterparts were in reading English. Positive emission tomography (PET) scans, which indicate which portions of the brain are in use while a person performs certain tasks, showed that the portion of the brain using phonological information was in greater use for the Italians than for the English speakers. Conversely, the portion of the brain used for naming objects and processing the meaning of words was used more with

English speakers (Paulesu et al., 2000). Greek children acquire decoding skills earlier than their English counterparts, due to the transparent symbol-to-sound orthography of Greek (Tafa & Manolitsis, 2008). The benefits of children learning to decode early on, however, do not necessarily translate into long-term superiority in reading comprehension (Ellis et al., 2004), because reading is so much more than decoding.

> *To me, learning to read in an opaque writing system is like learning to drive a car with standard transmission: it takes longer to learn, and there are more subskills involved, but once you've got it, it's just as smooth a ride. A driver learning to drive with automatic transmission is like a reader from a transparent orthography—they learn faster, but they may not have quite as good an understanding of how the car goes forward since it works just fine by pressing the pedal!*—KRISTIN

Two Aspects of Transparency/Opacity: Symbol-to-Sound and Sound-to-Symbol

Orthographies reflect transparency/opacity in two different directions: their symbol-to-sound similarity and their sound-to-symbol similarity. At first glance, these appear to be redundant, but they are not.

Symbol-to-Sound Matching

Symbol-to-sound matching is the extent to which a word "looks like it sounds." It determines how easily a reader can decode a word and pronounce it correctly. Symbol-to-sound matching is the aspect of transparency that is most widely referenced because it is so decisive in learning to read. When words have close symbol-to-sound matching, they are decodable and easy to learn to recognize. They can be "sounded out."

Spanish orthography, for example, has a transparent symbol-to-sound relationship. In Spanish, each letter or *digraph* (a two letter combination for one sound) matches with only one sound, with small variations caused by the influence of the letters around it and variations by dialect. As a result, once L1 Spanish children learn which sounds each letter or digraph makes, they have mastered decoding.

The letters of the opaque alphabet of English, on the other hand, can be pronounced with several sounds. The symbol-to-sound correspondence of English letters is messy, especially with respect to vowels. The letter *a*, for example, can be pronounced in at least six different ways: /ae/ as in *hat*, /a/ as in *father*, /aw/ as in *saw*, /ə/ as in *again*, /ey/ as in *say*, and /e/ as in *said*. As a result, children learning to decode in English take considerably longer to learn to decode words containing the letter *a*.

Sound-to-Symbol Matching

Sound-to-symbol matching, on the other hand, is important in learning to write and spell words. If a sound can only be spelled one particular way, it is easier to learn to write and spell in that language. If a sound can be represented by several different symbols, however, it takes a longer time to learn to represent words in writing or to spell words correctly.

Although Spanish "sounds like it looks" and is easy to learn to decode, it doesn't "look like it sounds" quite as consistently; as a result, Spanish writers do make spelling mistakes. The letter *h* in Spanish, for example, causes spelling problems because it is silent. Therefore, Spanish learners learn by trial and error where to place the "silent h" until they learn which words have one. There is nothing in the pronunciation of a word that tells us there's an *h* at the beginning of *hola*, or between the vowels in *ahora*. Overall, however, Spanish can still be classified as largely a transparent language, and both decoding and spelling will be easier to learn than the same skills in English.

Many children have trouble learning to spell in languages with opaque orthographies, such as English, even if they can read well. In school systems that place correct (often called "proper") spelling at a high premium, difficulty learning to spell may convince a lot of students that they can't write at all and set in motion a syndrome of failure.

> *A Mexican elementary school teacher in one of my classes said, "In Mexico there's no subject called 'spelling' like you have in America. That's because Spanish spelling, at least for most words, pretty much takes care of itself. When students start to write words in Spanish, they are easier to read than the invented spelling of kids in English."*—LEAH

In an opaque language like French, on the other hand, spelling is elevated to the level of an important subject. Classes in "Orthographe," or spelling, are part of a French learner's language study, just as spelling study is in schools in the United States.

Probabilistic reasoning is the strategy by which we learn to spell words, just as we use probabilistic reasoning to decode. The brain is wired to find patterns, and when patterns of spelling probability are included in the teaching of English spelling, learners learn to generalize to unknown words. Brains "actively resonate with regularities in the input, and automatically keep score of the probabilities of recurring patterns" (McGuinness, 2004, p. 47). That is why when spelling is taught as a "hit or miss," rote activity, learners, both L1 English and ELLs, will not develop the probabilistic reasoning they need to attack unknown words.

Table 4.1 is a list of selected languages and their transparency or opacity in symbol-to-sound and sound-to-symbol aspects.

Many languages are not represented here, and it may be possible to add them to the chart by asking a native speaker of the language, "Is it hard to learn to read in your language?" and "Is it hard to learn to spell in your language?" The first question addresses symbol-to-sound regularity, and the second question addresses sound-to-symbol regularity. McGuinness (2004) refers to languages which are transparent to decode (read) and encode (write) as "transparently reversible" (p. 39).

English: Opaque in Both Directions

English, alas, is opaque in both its symbol-to-sound and its sound-to-symbol relationships, making it a language that is both hard to read and spell! Because English sounds can be represented a number of different ways, spelling takes a long time to learn, and many never learn to spell very well. The trickiest part of English spelling is usually found in its vowels. The sound /ay/, for example, can be spelled in at least five different ways: *buy* (/bay/), *try* (/tray/), *sigh* (/say/), *height* (/hayt), and *lie* (/lay/). Also, the vowels of unstressed syllables in English are usually pronounced with the schwa sound /ə/, so it is impossible to "hear" the correct vowel even with good phonological awareness. The word "constant," for example, is pronounced with a schwa sound /ə/ for the *a*, and, based on sound alone, it would be just as logical to write *consent* or *constynt* as it is to write *constant.* There are thousands of words with reduced vowels.

Because English has a larger variety of vowel sounds than many other languages, and these vowel sounds have multiple spellings, an ELL must first develop the phonological awareness to perceive the (often subtle) differences in vowel sounds, and then, using probabilistic reasoning, try to match them with the grapheme or graphemes that seem most likely to go with the sound. Vowel sounds are the most malleable sounds of a language because they consist of air passing through the mouth, with the tongue and lips held in certain positions, and they are not tethered to the other organs of speech. Just think of the subtle differences between the sound of the vowels in "book" and "buck," for example. Think, too, of the different ways vowels of words are pronounced by people from different areas of the English-speaking world. Because it is hard to differentiate the sounds of English vowels to begin with, it is no wonder that it's hard to spell them.

When I first arrived in the United States, a friend was supposed to meet me at the airport. I waited in vain; he never showed up. After about three hours of waiting, I decided to take a cab. I told the driver that I was going to "Queen" Street. We drove around and around for another three hours

TABLE 4.1. Classification of Selected Orthographies by Two Aspects of Transparency/Opacity

Writing system	More transparent symbol-to-sound (symbols are mostly pronounced one way; easy to read)	More transparent sound-to-symbol (sounds are mostly written one way; easy to spell)	More opaque symbol-to-sound (symbols can be pronounced several ways; harder to read)	More opaque sound-to-symbol (sounds can be written several ways; harder to spell)
Spanish	X			X
English			X	X
Serbo-Croatian	X			
Greek	X			X
German	X			X
Albanian	X	X		
Hebrew	X			X
Finnish	X			
Dutch	X	X		
Japanese Hiragana	X	X		
Korean	X	X		
Italian	X			X
Welsh	X			
Turkish	X			
Japanese Katakana	X		X	
Arabic	X	X		
Persian			X	X
French	X			X
Chinese			X	X
Japanese Kanji			X	X
Portuguese			X	X
Danish			X	X
Russian	X			X
Ukrainian	X			X

Note. Data from Ellis et al. (2004).

looking for "Queen" Street. After a long drive around town, the cabdriver asked me if I had the address on a piece of paper. I said yes, and pulled it out from my folder and showed it to him. He went, "What are you talking about man?" It was Quinn Street; we had passed it again and again, and I didn't pay any attention to it. I was too busy looking for Queen Street.—TENENA

Spelling Changes Due to New Technologies

Text messaging is having a profound effect on the way words are spelled, not only in English but in many other languages. Although the "long" forms of words are still considered correct in the classroom setting, messages are increasingly using a combination of traditional spelling and alphabetic or numeric spelling of words. When students are just learning a new orthography, seeing a word with a number stuck in the middle can be very confusing. Alphabetic spelling occurs when an alphabet letter is written with the expectation it will be read aloud by its letter name. The most common example is *u* to represent *you*. Numeric spelling is the same thing for numbers; a number name is put in a word or sentence with the expectation that the number name will be read aloud. An example is *gr8* to mean *great*. These kinds of hybrid words are becoming more and more common in the literacy practices of young people and in advertising. Figure 4.2 shows some examples of alphabetic and numeric spelling and other simplifying techniques on license plates and signs.

When I was a kid, we had autograph books, and everyone wanted to write a message that used alphabetic and numeric spelling. In my book, my best friend wrote "U R A QT. G I N V U." As you can see, I still remember it to this day.—KRISTIN

Two wonderful books written several decades ago spoofed alphabetic spelling. They are called *CDB!* (1987) and *CDC?* (2003) by William Steig. The books consist of cartoons with captions created entirely of alphabet letters that contain a whole range of dialogue. However, they create a peculiar "accent" when read aloud! These are guaranteed to delight any class of any age or level.

Implications for Teaching

The "take-away" message is that ELLs come to English from languages with all kinds of different orthographies, with varying degrees of transparency. This means instruction in using the English alphabet should be differentiated according to the characteristics of the orthography from which ELLs

We don't miss the *e* in HLP because the consonants guide us.

A mix of standard and numeric spelling.

A mix of standard and alphabetic spelling.

A mix of numeric spelling and simplified spelling by vowel removal.

FIGURE 4.2. Use of alphabetic, numeric, and simplified spelling.

Simplified spelling on an awning.

Alphabetic spelling of "you" in a word play.

When *dough* changes to *do*, we lose the morpheme telling us it's made of dough.

Simplified spelling.

Simplified spelling by clipping first syllable.

FIGURE 4.2. *(cont.)*

come. If students have already learned to read and write in a transparent orthography, they may be used to phonologically based decoding, but may not stop to notice when they read nonsense words. It is important to teach them a number of strategies that L1 English readers use to construct meaning from print: developing probabilistic reasoning through practice in prediction techniques, recognizing onsets and rimes, breaking a word down into its individual sounds, and practicing getting the gist, among other strategies.

ELLs from languages with transparent orthographies that do not share the roman alphabet with English, such as Bulgarian, will need to learn not only ways to read for meaning, but also all of the details of the English alphabet and phonics system.

ELLs from other opaque orthographies, such as Chinese, will need extensive guidance and practice with phonological decoding because they have not used it extensively to read in their L1. They will need to learn all of the ways the English alphabet operates relative to the sounds of English. For these students, developing a high level of phonological awareness will really bear fruit because it will allow them to learn to decode unknown words.

Any learners who have not been exposed to basic principles of decoding in English will have to acquire them, no matter their age. In addition, any learner of English will have to learn that some English words are simply not decodable and must be memorized as whole words, sometimes called "sight words." There is no way around this, either for native speakers or ELLs, due to the opaque nature of English orthography. We have summarized the pedagogical direction that might be taken with readers and writers from different orthographies in Table 4.2. Of course, the amount of prior literacy in their L1 and other educational experiences will influence the direction taken, but these are some general guidelines.

Children who are beginning to read in English as a first language need to go through all of the skills in the list of items in Table 4.2 as well: learning the concept of an alphabet, phonological awareness, English phonics, reading for meaning, and learning sight words, among other literacy competencies.

Spelling: Taking a Reader's Temperature

We can think of spelling as a way to "take the temperature" of a student's reading, using the "thermometer" of spelling analysis. Student spelling errors show us the edge of their reading development and where to begin word study instruction. In that sense, spelling activities are a form of authentic curriculum-based assessment. Understanding spelling this way gives us an important tool in working with ELLs and makes it easier to help

TABLE 4.2. Ways to Differentiate Early Reading Instruction for ELLs Literate in Different Kinds of Orthographies

Orthographic system the ELL has been exposed to	Examples of languages	Focus should be on:	Less time needs to be spent on:
Transparent roman alphabet with some similarities to English	Spanish Polish Turkish Welsh	English phonics (focusing on differences from L1), reading for meaning, learning sight words	Phonological awareness, phonics for sounds/letters shared with L1
Opaque roman alphabet with few similarities to English	French Portuguese	Phonological awareness, English phonics, learning sight words	Reading for meaning
Non-roman orthography, either transparent or opaque	Ukrainian Arabic Mongolian Korean Gujarati	Reading for meaning (for transparent), phonological awareness (for opaque), English phonics, learning sight words	phonological awareness (for transparent), reading for meaning (for opaque)
Opaque orthographies that do not use an alphabet	Chinese Japanese Kanji	Learning the concept of an alphabet (representing sounds through symbols), phonological awareness, English phonics, learning sight words	Reading for meaning

them read and write words with confidence. Spelling helps assess reading because "what they can spell, we know they can read" (Bear et al., 2003, p. 76). Looked at this way, spelling (recoding) can be a source of information dynamically linked to reading (decoding).

Orthography Is Not Destiny . . . but It's Important

When we first discover how different orthographies influence the way students learn to read, write and spell in their L1, it's easy to conclude that it explains a lot about the way they learn English. However, we add a word of caution: L1 orthography is only one factor in the vast array of factors that determines how ELLs learn English as a new language. Wang and Koda (2007) summarize it well:

> L2 readers with different L1 orthographic backgrounds engage in both universal and language-specific processes. On the one hand, properties

of the L2 writing system affect L2 processing similarly across learners irrespective of L1 backgrounds. On the other hand, L1 reading experiences also come into play in L2 reading. . . . The properties of both L1 and L2 interact with one another, jointly contributing to L2 reading processes. (p. 201)

If students have tremendous difficulty learning to decode proficiently due to interference from their L1 orthography, their academic prospects will diminish. Teachers who find out about the orthographies of their ELLs' first languages are more likely to help contribute to their "syndrome of success."

HOW DOES THIS LOOK IN THE CLASSROOM?

Through lively implementation of engaging explicit instruction, guided practice, and communicative opportunities, we can help ELL students internalize the regular and consistent patterns of English graphemes and phonemes, regardless of their complexity.

Factoring in First-Language Writing Systems of Students Literate in L1

When students can already read or write in another language, the orthography of that language will have a huge influence on how they learn to read and write in English. Those who learned an opaque writing system have more practice in looking for word meanings and learning a set of patterns for sound and spelling. Those who can read in a transparent writing system have more practice in phonological decoding and less in looking for word meanings. Those who learned a writing system that is not alphabetic have not learned the concept of phonics at all. Table 4.2 gives some general guidelines for how to differentiate the skills and needs of ELLs who are literate in different writing systems.

Phonological Awareness and Phonics Skills

Phonological awareness and phonics skills can be developed through many enjoyable activities that build metalinguistic awareness. Word sorts that use words from the day's lessons are one way to do this. The students simply write the words to be sorted on index cards. Word walls can be organized by phonemes, not just first letters of words. For example, students can classify words according to their vowel sounds. You can also have a word wall focusing on the three possible pronunciations of the final -*ed* ending and the three possible pronunciations of the final -*s/-es* endings (see Appendix 5.3).

Combining the Study of Reading and Spelling

Combining the study of reading and spelling helps learners manipulate the written and oral code in both directions. "Make sure that encoding (spelling) and decoding (reading) are connected at every level of instruction via looking (visual memory), listening (auditory memory), and writing (kinesthetic memory)," suggests McGuinness (2004, p. 38). Since English is opaque in both directions, moving in both directions needs to be practiced in order for ELLs to develop probabilistic reasoning for both reading and spelling using modeling and thinkalouds. Teachers can help students reason through the most likely way a word might be spelled (recoded or "encoded") or read (decoded), beginning with high-frequency words and moving toward less common ones.

Practicing Word Patterns

Students can also engage in thinking of words that follow certain patterns. Here are a few possible sample prompts that give students a chance to practice generating words on specific sound and letter patterns.

1. Draw a picture that has five things that begin with the letters *sh.*
2. Write a story that contains five words that end with the sound /t/.
3. Make a list of items in the classroom that have a long *o* vowel sound.
4. Classify the animals in the picture according to how many syllables each animal name contains.
5. Write one sentence about your most recent birthday, and then find all of the silent letters in the sentence.

Reading Every Day in the Classroom

In order for ELLs to develop probabilistic reasoning for both reading and writing, they will have to read and write a great amount of English in and outside of the classroom. Good literacy programs ensure that reading and writing are cornerstones of every single day.

Celebrating Different Writing Systems

Celebrating different writing systems helps students gain an appreciation of the remarkable ways humans have devised to put words down in print. An innovative third-grade teacher, Theresa Kubasak, does this by organizing an annual Hangul-Nol Festival at her school. Hangul-Nol, which takes place on October 8, is a Korean holiday celebrating the invention of the Korean alphabet in 1444. It is touted as the most elegantly transparent alphabet in the world, both easy to read and easy to spell. At the all-school festival, parents from L1 languages with different orthographies are invited in to share their way of writing with children and other parents. Children and their parents circulate among the classrooms and learn how to write their own names in Arabic, Chinese, Devanagari, Cyrillic, and other scripts. Each language station uses different materials to write, such as black ink painted on rice paper for Japanese, silver pens on black construction paper for Arabic, and fine-tip pens for Cyrillic. Theresa adds, "Also we splashed the room with environmental print from the various alphabets, which is easy to obtain in Chicago through menus, posters, newspaper ads, wedding announcements. It is an amazing day in a classroom." Celebrating Hangul Nol helps all learners become more metalinguistic as they internalize the understanding that writing systems are widely varied, invented, and arbitrary, and that all of them are ways to represent speech.

QUESTIONS FOR FURTHER STUDY

1. If you had to choose three important ideas from this chapter, which would you choose? How can you apply these ideas to your larger knowledge of teaching English as a new language?

2. Besides the probabilistic reasoning used in e-mail programs and cell phones, what are some other examples of probabilistic reasoning in the tools you use every day?

3. Take one vowel sound of English, representing it with the phonetic symbol used in the Guide to Pronunciation (pp. xv–xvi). Try to discover all of its possible spellings in English words, giving an example of each. How many spellings were you able to find for the vowel sound? Can you find any words in which the sound is not represented by any letter?

4. Take one letter of the English alphabet and try to figure out all its possible sounds in English words. Include words that use the letter at the beginning, in the middle, and at the end, and use the Guide to Pronunciation (pp. xv–xvi) to represent the different sounds. How many distinct sounds for the letter were you able to find? Can you find any words in which the letter is silent?

5. Why were Polish and Spanish signs in Chicago not included in Figure 4.1?

6. A young adult immigrant from El Salvador never had the benefit of formal education. Now he wants to learn to read and write at a community college night school that offers a Spanish or English GED. His first language is Spanish, but he speaks some English. Would you advise him to learn to read and write first in Spanish, or in English? Why?

7. A Chinese ELL is typing names into a database and comes across a handwritten last name she cannot read. She types exactly what she sees: Sctubert. What do you think the name actually was? What is your guess

based on? Explain this anecdote in terms of probabilistic reasoning. How could you help a Chinese ELL develop the kind of reasoning you applied to solve the unreadable name problem?

8. What experiences have you had trying to read another writing system? What strategies did you use to try to decipher it? Which strategies helped, if any?

9. Reflect on ways a teacher with a classroom of mixed-language ELLs could differentiate instruction so that children from backgrounds with different orthographies from the roman alphabet could get the extra practice needed in decoding the roman alphabet and developing reading comprehension skills.

10. A quipu is a set of knotted strings that was used as a writing system during the Inca Empire to keep track of inventories and convey news about the Empire (see Figure 4.3). The knotting system was learned by select members of the court. The quipu was taken to the king by a runner, sometimes as far as 1,200 kilometers away, and "read" there. In what way can a quipu be considered an orthography? In what ways not?

FIGURE 4.3. Quipu from Peru.

CHAPTER FIVE

Using Morphemes
to Learn Vocabulary

New Vocabulary in This Chapter: root, bound roots, affix (prefix/ suffix), stem, free morpheme, lexical morpheme, lexicon, functional morpheme, modal auxiliary verbs, phrasal verbs, syllable, bound morpheme, derivational morpheme, grammatical category, inflectional morpheme

Think for a moment about all the varied ways a person can "know" a word. We can recognize it when it's spoken by others. We can pick it out when reading it in a word list. We can understand its meaning when it appears in a sentence of a text. We can recognize it as part of a phrase or idiom, or see it as part of a figure of speech. We can know how to pronounce it. We can use it in different social settings, we can make puns with it, we can spell it, and we can include it in our writing. Learning these many levels of word knowledge can be daunting in a first language—but it becomes truly frightening in a new language! Nevertheless, it is the ability to learn thousands of new words in a new language that, more than anything else, determines a learner's success, both academic and social.

In Chapter 3, we talked about the *phonemic* aspect of words—how words sound—and how ELLs can build an "oral word bank"—a listening and speaking vocabulary—that readies them for literacy in English. In Chapter 4, we discussed the *graphemic* aspects of words—how words look in different writing systems, how readers and writers process text in different languages, and how that affects learning to read in English. In this chapter, we focus on *morphemes*, the smallest linguistic units of meaning, look at the ways they combine within and across words, and see how they can help

ELLs learn English vocabulary. Understanding English morphemes is a practical and versatile tool for the literacy toolkit.

Morphemes: The Building Blocks of Words

Morphemes are powerful tools for building English vocabulary. ELLs who can break words down into smaller parts and make connections between words that have the same morphemes have increased success in vocabulary growth (Kieffer & Lesaux, 2009; Prince, 2008). Morphemes can be defined as the smallest unit of meaning in a word, or a "minimal unit of meaning or grammatical function" (Yule, 2006, p. 246). All words are made up of morphemes. When readers recognize the structure, meaning, and function of morphemes, they develop a lifelong strategy to figure out word meanings. Morphemes are especially important in helping English language learners develop that all-important academic vocabulary of the content areas.

English, a Morphophonemic Language

Due to the morphophonemic nature of English, in which words contain both phonemic and morphological information, a morpheme may be pronounced differently in different words because of the sounds of the letters around it. For example, the morpheme *please* has three different pronunciations in the words *please, pleasure,* and *pleasant*. Say the words aloud and you will hear that both the vowel sound and the pronunciation of the *s* differ according to the letters that come after it. Even though the neighboring sounds change each word's pronunciation, they all contain the same morpheme, carrying the same meaning. This is a key point for ELLs to understand as they try to master academic English. When students rely mainly on their BICS language, delivered mostly in oral form, they will not pick up on words with similar morphemes because they may sound different in different words.

> *After hearing the word* electricity, *my ELL students did not recognize its connection with the word* electric *because the* c *was pronounced differently. It was pronounced still another way in the word* electrician. *Once the three words were written on the board, their resemblance was very clear, and students began to grasp the morphophonemic nature of English—that neighboring sounds can influence the way a morpheme is pronounced, but its meaning is preserved.*—KRISTIN

Students need to understand these two key ideas:

1. Morphemes may be pronounced differently but still bear the same meaning.
2. Spelling patterns in English give us information about both morphemes and phonemes.

Once learners capture these abstract ideas, they will find they are able to recognize the meanings of many new words.

Another example of the morphophonemic nature of English can be found in the three distinct pronunciations of the -s/-es and -ed morphemes for plural and past tense. Consider these examples:

Pronunciation of *ed*	/t/	/d/	/əd/
	missed	tried	wanted
Pronunciation of *s/es*	/s/	/z/	/əz/
	gets	goes	misses

The ways the endings are pronounced depends on the sound that precedes them in a way that is completely regular and predictable. Once the regularities are learned, thousands of new words can be understood, both in listening and reading. An added benefit is that ELLs might be more likely to pay attention to adding those pesky word endings in their writing and speaking because they realize that morphemes aren't always going to be pronounced the same way in every word.

Along with changes in pronunciation, morphemes may also have variations in spelling. For example, the Latin prefix *in-*, meaning *into,* is spelled *im-* in such words as *imbibe* and *impress,* or even *en-* as in *engrave.* Spelling reflects modifications in pronunciation made by speech communities. Speakers of all languages generally pronounce words in the easiest possible way while still preserving the word's identity.

In the previous chapter we looked at the opaque nature of English orthography and the fact that its sounds and letters do not "map" neatly. Sometimes words don't "sound like they look" or "look like they sound." Now we can see that the same idea can be applied to morphemes: Morphemes do not necessarily "map" neatly onto their pronunciation or spelling. Nevertheless, the morpheme retains its meaning even when it has variations in pronunciation or spelling. This linguistic insight applies to English and, indeed, all languages. When teachers can clearly understand and explain to students that morphemes preserve their meanings even when their pronunciation or spelling changes, they can dramatically advance ELLs' reading, spelling, and writing. Any users of English, in fact, can benefit from this linguistic insight.

Roots, Affixes, and Stems

Words are composed of three kinds of morphemes: roots, affixes, and stems. *Roots* are morphemes "that cannot be cut up into any smaller parts" (Pinker, 2007, p. 128). They may form complete words, or they may need other morphemes added to them to form a word. There is even a small category of roots that carry meaning but cannot form words unless combined with other morphemes. These are called *bound roots* and are discussed later in the chapter. *Affixes* attach to roots and are called *prefixes* when they are at the beginning of a word and *suffixes* when they are at the end of a word. Affixes are morphemes but they are not words, and they cannot stand on their own. They can also be "coupled" like train cars: many words contain several affixes. *Stems* consist of a single root plus one or more affixes. Sometimes stems form complete words, and other times they must be combined with additional morphemes to form words. For example, *stars* is a word that is also a stem consisting of the root *star* and the affix *-s*. The stem *descript-*, on the other hand, is a stem but not a word. It consists of an affix, *de*, and a root, *script*, but in order to become a word, it still needs an additional affix. When the suffix *-ion* is added, the stem becomes the word de*scription*. Alternately, the affix *non-* could be added at the beginning of the stem to form the word *nondescript*. Stems are often used as a synonym for roots. Teachers, however, may find it useful to distinguish between roots and stems because it helps readers understand that some words can be broken into smaller units of meaning and others cannot.

English words can be taken apart and put together in different ways depending on their linguistic sources. Some words from Old English origins, such as *sparrow* or *father*, are two syllables but have always been a single root that cannot be separated into smaller units. Another example is *goodbye*, which consists of a single root that is contracted from what was once four words, *God be with ye;* or the word *awful*, which is a single root, but once contained the two morphemes, *awe* and *-ful*. The important point is that many of the high-frequency older English words are roots, but not stems—they cannot be broken down (Fry, 1980) even when they are composed of more than one syllable. That means that morpheme-combining activities will not work with those particular words.

Understanding morphemes helps students figure out the meanings of words, and it also gives clues about the grammatical categories, or parts of speech, that words occupy within a sentence. The previously introduced terms are commonly used in the classroom to explain how words can be put together and taken apart; however, we believe there is also value in understanding the terms linguists use to talk about morphemes in terms of the places they occupy within and among words in a sentence.

Four Categories of English Morphemes

Linguists have identified four major categories of English morphemes. We begin by describing free morphemes, which consist of two subcategories: lexical and functional morphemes. Then we describe bound morphemes, which also consist of two subcategories, derivational and inflectional morphemes. The category the morpheme belongs to determines where it can be used in the English grammar system. The inverted morphemes pyramid (Figure 5.1) helps us see the distribution of these four categories at a glance.

The top two levels of the inverted pyramid represent words. The vast majority of words are lexical morphemes. Although not as many, there are also more than 100 functional morphemes. The bottom two levels of the inverted pyramid are morphemes that are not words, called bound mor-

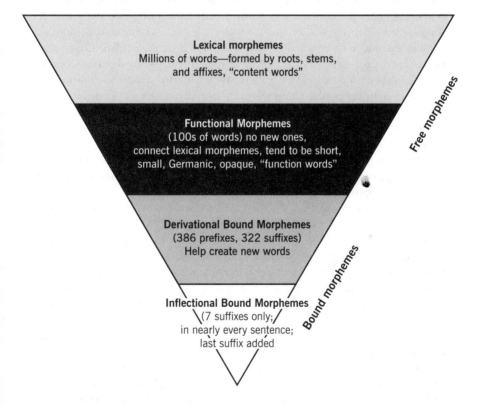

FIGURE 5.1. Inverted morphemes pyramid. From Lems (2008). Reprinted with permission from Kristin Lems.

phemes. They are divided into two groups, called derivational morphemes and inflectional morphemes. Let's take a look at each of these four categories.

Free Morphemes

Free morphemes are words and consist of roots or stems. Free morphemes can be subdivided into two categories: lexical and functional. We introduce lexical and functional morphemes below and immediately relate them to the study of English as a new language.

Lexical Morphemes: The "Vital Organs"

Lexical morphemes comprise the vast majority of the words of a language. Also referred to as content words, lexical morphemes include nouns, verbs, adjectives, some prepositions, and adverbs. Some examples of lexical morphemes are *spinach, meet, brown, get over,* or *quickly.* Content words can be considered the "vital organs" of the body of language. English can accommodate an unlimited number of new lexical morphemes. Also, existing meanings can be changed when lexical morphemes combine with other morphemes to form stems. No wonder there are so many English words! Not coincidentally, *lexicon* is the word usually used to mean "all the words in a language."

Lexical morphemes contain both BICS and CALP vocabulary, and they become more difficult to learn as curriculum content becomes more advanced and abstract. Therefore, they are rightfully the center of most ELL vocabulary study.

Functional Morphemes: The "Connective Tissue"

Functional morphemes, on the other hand, include most prepositions, articles, pronouns, conjunctions, modals, and auxiliary verbs, and are also referred to as function words. Examples of functional morphemes include *of, the, she, and, modal auxiliary verbs,* such as *can,* and auxiliary verbs such as *is.* These words define the relationships among the content words around them, stand in for a content word (in the case of pronouns), or provide nuances of meaning (in the case of modals). They could be considered the "connective tissue" in the body of language.

New function words cannot be added to English, and the function words that already exist cannot be changed by attaching other morphemes. For example, we can't put *-ed* on the word *of.* Functional morphemes are also bound by the rules of syntax for each language, and the order of English morphemes can be very complicated to learn. For instance, ELLs need to be considerably advanced to correctly produce the following sentence with all of its function words: "I would have eaten if I had known you weren't going to feed me." (A comprehensive explanation of function words can be found in Freeman and Freeman, 2004, pp. 177–179.)

Although the list of functional morphemes is short, they are very frequent. Function words abound in English and are found in nearly every sentence. Of the 100 most common English words, 79 of them are function words; for the most common 50 words, all but three of them are function words (Fry, Kress, & Fountoukidis, 1993) (See Appendix 5.1). In fact, few sentences of more than two or three words exist without them! Without function words, English doesn't make sense because the relationships among the words cannot be expressed.

The Trouble with Function Words

The focus of vocabulary learning in schools is usually on learning lexical morphemes (content words), but functional morphemes are equally important for ELLs. It should not be taken for granted that ELLs know these all-important functional morphemes. In fact, they are harder to learn than content words for the following three reasons:

1. *Function words are opaque.* First, because function words tend to have been in the language for a long time, their spelling is more likely to be opaque, that is, not decodable. This makes them harder to read and spell. Think about how hard it is to read or spell the function words *of, could,* and *though.* In addition to not looking the way they sound, some function words are homophones (*to, two, too; there* and *their*). Furthermore, some of the most common function words look bafflingly similar to beginning readers and writers, such as words with the letters and letter combinations of *h* and *th,* found in function words such as *the, then, them,* and *when* (Hiebert, Brown, Taitague, Fisher, & Adler, 2004). ELLs also have trouble with common function words with a silent *l,* such as *would, could,* and *should,* and those spelled with a *g* or *gh,* such as *through* or *although.* Because older, high-frequency words, including function words, have less decodable spelling and pronunciation, and they often cannot be broken down into smaller units of meaning, they need to be taught as "sight words" to be memorized as a whole unit rather than decoded.

2. *Function words are not cognates with Latinate languages.* The second reason, related to the first one, is that English function words tend to be words of Old English origin and are not cognates of words in the Latinate languages of many ELLs in the United States. That means that these words will not look or sound familiar to ELLs from Latinate languages such as Spanish.

> *When my kids and I were visiting my Dutch family last year, we could hardly recognize any Dutch content words, but a number of function words, en for the English word and, dis for this, and bij for by or near were very easy for us to pick out. Due to the Germanic roots Dutch shares with English, we had the strange sensation of not knowing the topic of a sentence, but being able to tell more or less where the sentence was going.*
> —KRISTIN

3. *Function words can cause interference* The third and most important difficulty with English function words for ELLs, however, is that the relationships they signal are language-specific. In English, native speakers use thousands of combinations of verbs and prepositions (called *phrasal verbs*) in their everyday speaking and writing. Those particular word combinations are not the same in other languages. For example, in French the preposition *de* is used in the verb *se souvenir de*, which means *to remember*. A French ELL might be likely to say "I remember from her" instead of "I remember her" because the word *de* in French is sometimes equivalent to the word *from* in English. Unfortunately, these small but important differences in the distribution of prepositions must be learned one by one in a new language, and very little PCI occurs to assist in the process. In fact, interference from function word distribution patterns in another language can cause considerable problems in learning to read, write, listen, and speak in English.

To further complicate the situation, some ELLs come from languages that signal functions without using function words to show relationships like English does. Languages such as Polish or Arabic use "case endings" attached to the end of words to indicate some of the relationships that English signals with prepositions. For students who come from languages using case endings, the "function of function words" may need to be taught explicitly, through mini-lessons. A list of some representative languages that use case endings can be found in Table 5.1.

Despite the challenges, function words deserve attention in the ESL classroom. Figuring out how function words work within phrases and sentences can be a revelation to ELLs who understand the content words around them but are tripped up by the "little words" in between.

Dangers of Analyzing Words by Syllables

The *syllables* of English are its allowable set of consonant–vowel patterns, and they are based on a word's sound. Sometimes they have a one-to-one correspondence with a word's morphemes, but often they don't. Although syllables are useful for learners learning to read in transparent alphabets

TABLE 5.1. List of Selected Languages Using Case Endings

Languages	Language Family
Sanskrit, Old English, Latin (historical languages)	Indo-European
Albanian, Bengali, Bulgarian, Czech, German, Gujarati, Hindi, Kurdish, Latvian, Lithuanian, Marathi, Nepali, Persian (Farsi), Pashto, Polish, Punjabi, Russian, Romanian, Serbo-Croatian, Sinhalese, etc.	Indo-European
Estonian, Finnish, Hungarian	Finno-Ugric
Amharic, Arabic, Hebrew	Semitic
Mongolian	Altaic
Chechen, Georgian (Caucasus)	Nakh-Daghestanian
Turkish	Altaic
Kannada, Malayalam, Tamil, Telugu	Dravidian
Tlingit	Na-Dene
Warlpiri	Pama-Nyungan
Quechua	Quechumaran

Note. The number or distribution of cases differs among the various languages. Data from Comrie, Matthews, and Polinsky (1996).

such as Spanish or Korean, they are more problematic in the English alphabet because of its opacity. For example, the word "played" is pronounced as only one syllable, but it contains two distinct morphemes, *play* and *-ed*. If we analyze it only by syllables, we will lose the information provided by the two morphemes, the root *play*, and the inflectional morpheme *-ed*, which indicates the past tense. Focusing on the syllable can negatively affect both reading and spelling the words.

Once ELLs are no longer at the Entering or Beginning levels of English and are beginning to read connected text, morphemes are a more useful tool than syllables. In fact, using a syllable-based decoding strategy may conceivably contribute to "word calling," a concern discussed in Chapter 7. When the phonemes and graphemes of a word, rather than its morphemes, get all of a reader's attention, it is possible that words may be pronounced correctly, but their meanings overlooked.

Some teachers ask students to look for words from letters in other words, such as finding the letters to make the word "bear" among the letters of the word "bread." We find this kind of activity much less valuable than one in which learners look for morphemes within a word because morphemes are more than letter combinations; they carry meanings.

When morpheme analysis is used as a tool for word attack, ELLs are more likely to pay attention to the meanings of words as they read. In the

Harry Potter books, for example, the young antagonist is named Malfoy. When ELLs learn the Latin root *mal*, meaning bad or evil, they will recognize it not only in that name, but as a root in words they encounter in the future, such as *malodorous, malefactor, malaria, maladjusted,* and *malfeasance.*

In oral reading, focusing on morphemes may create more pronunciation miscues in the short run, but it will pay off in the added attention students pay to comprehension. For example, if an ELL pronounces the word *musician* as /myuwzikiən/, it indicates that the reader recognizes the morpheme *music* in the word, and that kind of morpheme recognition is something we want to encourage. When ELLs make pronunciation miscues that signal recognition of a morpheme, teachers may need to provide guidance about the part of speech the word occupies, but should be reassured that the student does recognize the morpheme, and therefore is accessing part of the word's meaning.

There are other hazards of syllable-based analysis. If we break the word *antifreeze* into syllables, for example, we see three. One of them, *freeze,* is a free morpheme that carries a meaning all by itself. The other two syllables, *an* and *ti,* do not retain any meaning when they are split up; however, when we see them as a morpheme instead of two syllables, we find *anti,* a prefix that means "against" or "opposite." Looked at by syllables, we can't grasp the meaning of the word, but using morphemes, we can derive a meaning of "against freezing," the purpose for putting antifreeze in a car. Here is a similar example:

> *In my class last week, one of my ELLs broke up the word* altogether *into* "all to get her." *He said with excitement, "All the words are on the word wall!" And they were. But they have no relationship to the meaning of the word. I realized I needed to help them understand that some words can't be broken into smaller words—they are inseparable.*—MARGARITA (MARGIE) JAIME, 1–2 bilingual teacher, Berwyn, Illinois

The most striking example of the danger of dividing words across syllables instead of morphemes is the classic joke about the word *therapist.* It makes sense broken into its morphemes—*therap* from the Greek word "to treat medically," and *-ist,* a bound morpheme meaning "one who practices." However, if *therapist* is divided into syllables instead of morphemes, it can also look like *the rapist*!

Bound Morphemes

Bound morphemes are the other major category of morphemes. As noted earlier, here are two kinds of bound morphemes, *derivational* and *inflectional.* Unlike free morphemes, a bound morpheme alone cannot be a word. Bound morphemes need to be attached to other morphemes in order to make a word. Examples of bound morphemes are *pre-, -s, -ed, -un, -ment,* or *-ist.*

Derivational Morphemes

Derivational morphemes can be either prefixes or suffixes in English. Derivational morphemes are dynamic and rich. They are one of the devices that grant English its remarkable ability to generate so many new words, as we discuss in the following chapter on word formation processes. Derivational morphemes also change the *grammatical category,* or part of speech, of a word, such as adding *-ful* to *thought,* thus changing it from a noun to the adjective *thoughtful.*

DERIVATIONAL MORPHEMES FUNCTION IN THREE MAJOR WAYS

Derivational morphemes operate in three powerful ways within words:

1. The first way is that they can create words when added to a root (e.g., *pay + ment*), stem (e.g., *progress + ive*), or bound root (e.g., *ex + pel,* with *-pel* being a bound root).
2. The second way is that they change the meaning of an existing word. Examples include adding the derivational morpheme *non-* to the word *dairy,* creating *nondairy,* which means that a food does not contain dairy products, or adding *dis-* to *respect,* meaning not to respect.
3. The third way derivational morphemes function within words is to change a word's grammatical category and therefore its meaning. For example, the word *disrespect* can change from a noun to an adjective by adding the suffix *-ful* to make *disrespectful.* Knowing common adjective suffixes alone, such as *-ious, -able,* and *-ful,* we can unlock the meanings of thousands of unknown words. For this reason, they're well worth spending classroom time on. A chart of common derivational prefixes and suffixes appears in Appendix 5.2.

COMMON MORPHEMES USED IN CONTENT-AREA CLASSROOMS

Rob Schoonveld, an eighth-grade science teacher who has a class of mixed ELLs and native speakers, puts large cards with common science morphemes up around his classroom and refers to them regularly. He finds that the visual reminder of the morphemes helps students feel more confident with new science vocabulary. Table 5.2 shows morphemes used frequently in upper elementary and middle school science classrooms. These morphemes, a combination of roots and affixes, can also be found in many

TABLE 5.2. Some Key Science Morphemes

sol	aero	hydro	paleo	astro	physio
bio	ecto	endo	ortho	chemo	cyto
meta	geo	therm	eco	electr(o)	micro
macro	quant	qual	trans	techn	syn

TABLE 5.3. Some Key Mathematics Morphemes

grad	graph	deci	centi	milli	circ
meter	plex	numer	equa	tri	quad
angl	hemi	sphere	add	sub	tract
fract	penta	necto	octo	vert	hor

science words in a number of other languages, which provides substantial PCI for ELLs from those languages.

Putting common morphemes up around the classroom is also a good idea for mathematics, social studies, and language arts classrooms; Tables 5.3, 5.4, and 5.5 list common morphemes in those subject areas. In the case of language arts vocabulary, the words may be known to the students but not with their specialized language arts meanings. For example, *character* is a common word but has a specialized meaning when talking about a protagonist in literature.

TABLE 5.4. Some Key Social Studies Morphemes

multi	proto	poli	agri	metro	ethno
anthro	hist	demo	gyn	homo	andro
poly	mono	bi	mega	hetero	gen
morph	popu	arch	aqua	theo	psych
cult	edu	logy	soph	etic	emic

TABLE 5.5. Some Key Language Arts Morphemes

biblio	script	auto	comp	improv	infere
solos	meta	orat	studere	spect	littera
rhetoric	genus	narrare	krisis	dict	caput

Note. Some morphemes change spelling when adopted into English.

Inflectional Morphemes

There are seven *inflectional morphemes*, and they serve as grammar markers that show tense, number, possession, or comparison (Table 5.6). Unlike derivational morphemes, they do not create new words. They also do not change a word's grammatical category, or part of speech. In English, all inflectional morphemes are suffixes and the longest are only three letters (*-est* or *-ing*). Thus they are easy to overlook in both reading and writing, but they serve a key role in the meaning of sentences. Linguists disagree about how inflectional morphemes are counted, and the number may vary between seven and 11.

TABLE 5.6. The Seven Inflectional Morphemes of English

Inflectional morpheme	Grammatical function	Part of speech inflectional morpheme is added to	Example
-s or *-es*	noun plurals	noun	apples, buses
	third person singular in present tense	verb	makes, goes
's or *s'*	possessive for singular or uncountable nouns	noun	the book's, oil's
	possessive for plural nouns	noun	the students'
-ed	regular form of past tense	verb	talked, tried
	regular form of past participle	verb	(have) talked, (has) tried
-en (left over from Old English)	some plurals	noun	oxen, children
	some past participles	verb	written, given
	derivation from noun	verb	strengthen, threaten
	derivation from noun	adjective	golden, silken
-er	comparative form of adjectives and adverbs	adjective	friendlier
		adverb	faster
-est	superlative form of adjectives and adverbs	adjective	friendliest
		adverb	fastest
-ing	derivation from verb	noun (gerund)	swimming
	present continuous (present progressive)	verb	going, trying

Although insignificant in terms of letters, inflectional morphemes are both very common and very important in conveying grammatical information about English words. Furthermore, because English is a morphophonemic language, adding an inflectional morpheme to a word may affect the pronunciation of other parts of the word and confuse early readers and writers.

Since inflectional morphemes often don't "sound the way they look," they need to be explicitly taught. For example, when ELLs learn that the -ed morpheme has three distinct pronunciations that are determined by the immediately preceding sound, it is a revelation to them. That is especially true for ELLs from languages that do not have any silent vowels, such as Spanish. They are similarly surprised to learn the three distinct pronunciations of the -s/-es, marking plurals and third-person singular verbs. (The patterns for -ed and -s/-es pronunciations can be found in Appendix 5.3.) When teachers themselves know these patterns, they can help students learn and practice them in the classroom. ELLs will benefit dramatically and rapidly in their understanding of English. Once they understand that the morphemes may vary in their spelling and sound but retain their meaning, ELLs gain a powerful new idea that will improve their probabilistic reasoning for listening, speaking, reading, and writing in English. Suddenly, seemingly baffling items become very comprehensible.

A Special Category

Sometimes, we don't find understandable morphemes when we break a word apart. This is because, over time, the meanings of some morphemes become lost to the speakers of the language. These morphemes that seem to have no meaning of their own are called bound roots. A bound root has no identifiable meaning until it is combined with another root or affix to create a single morpheme. For example, the words *lukewarm, overwhelm,* and *cranberry* look like they have two morphemes in them because we recognize the free morphemes within them, in this case *warm, over,* and *berry*. However, the other half of the words, in this case *luke, whelm,* and *cran,* are bound roots—they do not have any meaning unless combined with another morpheme, and they cannot stand on their own.

Bound roots can also be found in some words that have an identifiable prefix, but when the word is pulled apart, the remaining morpheme has no meaning. Examples of this are the words *precept, receive,* and *inane*. When the prefixes *pre-, re-,* and *in-* are removed, the remaining morphemes, *-cept, -ceive,* and *-ane* do not have a recognizable meaning. Other examples of bound roots can be found in the words *reduce, conceive, impeach,* and *repeat*.

The "take-away" idea that teachers need to know is that some words appear to have more than one morpheme but actually only have one, and their meaning can only be found by looking at the word as a whole. There aren't many of them, but ELL teachers should be aware that when they use morphemes to teach vocabulary, some bound roots will crop up. The following ideas can be conveyed to students:

- Some multisyllable words may be composed of only one morpheme and can't be broken down any further.
- Although all morphemes carry meaning, not every meaning of every English morpheme can be figured out, due to the history of words.

How Morpheme Analysis Is Useful

Teaching Morphemes as Part of Any Vocabulary Development Program

ELLs benefit greatly from morpheme analysis at every grade level and proficiency level (Kieffer & Lesaux, 2009). Charts, word walls, word banks, and binders can contain not just words, but also morphemes. Examining the parts that make up words gives students a chance to learn word-attack skills at the same time they learn about the history of a word. For example, if we look at the two morphemes of *breakfast*, *break* and *fast*, we find added meaning in the idea that we are not only eating the first meal of the day, but "breaking our fast" from the night before.

Morphemes Help with Spelling

From time to time, writers call for "simplifying" English spelling to make it more phonetic. Freeman and Freeman (2004) see reform proposals as humorous and not to be taken seriously. In their opinion,

> What many reformers don't realize is that the current system is a good compromise. Writing systems are designed to serve two different groups of people: writers and readers. Changes that would make writing easier would make reading more difficult, and changes that make reading easier would make writing harder. Most reforms are aimed at simplifying the task of spelling words by making spellings more closely correspond to sounds. That is, the reforms favor writers. But most people read a great deal more than they write, so these changes would not be beneficial. (p. 106)

If spelling were simplified, we would lose morphemic information that helps us read in English. Homophones, such as *two*, *to*, and *too* would become indistinguishable. English spellings do not just represent the sounds of a word; they also point to its meanings and in some circumstances its origins.

Because English is a morphophonemic writing system, information may be contained in the visual display of a word that cannot be heard in its pronunciation. For example, the *p* in the word *cupboard* isn't pronounced, and the morpheme *board* is reduced to a syllable that sounds like the word *bird*, but if we look at the two morphemes in this compound noun, we get a clue about its historical meaning: it has something to do with a place where cups are stored.

The power of knowing morphemes is that changes in phonemes and graphemes may mislead students, but once they learn to identify morphemes, even with spelling or pronunciation changes, they will have a steadfast compass that points them toward the meaning of a word.

L1 Morpheme Study Can Help

All languages combine morphemes to create meaning, and learners can examine the morphemes of words not only in English but in their native language. Studying morphemes in their native language helps learners become more metalinguistic, and also helps students build their own L1 vocabulary. Looking at morphemes in a student's L1 can also highlight differences in the way a word's meaning is distributed across two languages. A good example is the Spanish word for birthday, *cumpleaños*, which comes from two Spanish morphemes meaning "complete" and "year." Thus, a birthday is the "completion of a year." In English, on the other hand, the word *birthday* comes from the Germanic roots "birth" and "day," a commemoration of the first day of a child's life. In a bilingual or dual language Spanish/English classroom, pointing out the morphemes for the Spanish word can help students recognize that when they "turn 10," 10 years of life have been completed on their birthday, and that is a useful mathematical concept. Learning other languages exposes learners not only to new words, but also to the new concepts found within those words. Identifying morphemes in one's L1 can potentially facilitate PCI with English.

HOW DOES THIS LOOK IN THE CLASSROOM?

Four Good Morpheme Games

Word List Contest

It's possible to learn a lot of new words by listing them by prefixes, suffixes, and roots. First, teachers put students in small groups and a secretary is chosen by the group. Next, the teacher writes or calls out a prefix, such as *pro-*, or a suffix, such as *-ment*. The groups have 5 minutes to generate as many words as they can that use the prefix or the suffix. After the time is up, the groups take turns reading them out loud. Any word shared by other groups is crossed out by all the groups. The group that has the largest number of words the other groups did not find wins the round.

This game can also be done using roots, but it is harder because the spelling of roots can change in different environments, due to the morphophonemic features of English described earlier. We would suggest differentiating this activity for more advanced ELLs. Teachers can use the roots charts we have included in this chapter, or others connected to their course content area. For example, the root *digitus*, the Latin word for *finger*, is found in many words connected to the word *number*, such as *digitize*, *digital*, *three-digit numbers*, or *prestidigitation*. Talking about the way people "count on their fingers" is a good way to help students see the relationship between these words. The list of words based on a root can be kept up and added to as they encounter new words in reading and speaking. Incidentally, this activity builds metacognitive awareness in L1 English learners, too.

The Compound Noun Game

Reena Patel, a second-grade ESL teacher in the Chicago public schools, created a game for ELLs based on the theme of recognizing and creating compound nouns. The game has two parts. She created cardboard tiles with pictures of lexical morphemes that can be used to create compound nouns. She gives one tile to each student in the class. They walk around the room and find the partner whose tile allows them to create a real compound noun. For example, one student had an image of a book, and another had an image of a bag. Together they formed the compound noun *bookbag*. Then, she re-collects the tiles, shuffles them, and lets each pair choose four tiles from the box. With the four tiles, all consisting of high-frequency nouns, she asks students to form at least two possible new words, create a definition for them, and share them with the class. For example, students in her class created the new compound noun *dream shelf*, a "place to put objects that will bring you happy dreams."

Animal Compound Game

Reena also compiled a list of compound nouns that are used in many animal names, such as *mole rat, butterfly, anteater*, and *muskrat*. She made separate cards for each of these words and asks students to combine them to create new imaginary animals, which they then illustrate and share with the class. It creates a wonderful menagerie of morphemes, and lots of laughs! For a set of game cards and full instructions for both of the games, see Appendix 5.4.

Compound Noun Chain Game

If you are in a classroom, split the class into small groups and give the whole class a free morpheme. Give them 3 to 5 minutes to come up with as many other compound nouns as they can by adding another noun in either direction. Then have each group read its words. If another group shares the word, cross it out. The group with the most words not thought of by the other groups wins. For example, *pot* can form part of compound nouns such as *flowerpot, teapot, crackpot, potholder* or *potbelly.* Some other nouns that combine with many other words include *moon, home, stop,* and *ground.* A variation of the game is to generate not only compound nouns but also phrasal verbs, listemes, and idioms from the word.

QUESTIONS FOR FURTHER STUDY

1. If you had to choose three important ideas from this chapter, which would you choose? How can you apply these ideas to your larger knowledge of teaching English as a new language?

2. Try to divide the following words into morphemes and classify them accordingly. If needed, look in a good dictionary that includes the etymology of words. Can you find any bound roots (words that look like they contain several morphemes but have only one) in the list?

If possible, split the word into its roots and affixes.	Root(s)	Derivational morpheme (prefix or suffix only)	Inflectional morpheme (suffix, 7 morphemes only)
1. trees			
2. preprinted			
3. city			
4. incorrectly			
5. insect			
6. backpack			
7. scratch			
8. apolitical			
9. inexcusable			
10. ours			

Now choose 10 words from a text and try the same procedure.

3. Make a simple chart summarizing the important characteristics of function words described in this chapter.

4. Choose a prefix or suffix and see how many words with it you can generate in 1 minute. Remember, the spelling of the affix may change in different surroundings.

5. Using Appendix 5.3, add -ed to the following words and classify their pronunciation (/t/, /d/, or /ed/):

   waste, live, save, raid, cook, start, play, interest, try, watch, toss, turn, sort

6. Using Appendix 5.3, add -s/-es to the following words and classify their pronunciation (for /s/, /z/, or /əz/):

   watch, mess, get, kick, sing, hold, help, wash, trust, hum, play, go, sign, stop, hang

7. Choose one of the sets of content-area morphemes in Tables 5.2 through 5.5 and look up the word origins of the roots in a dictionary or online etymology source. Were there any surprises?

8. Choose a root in a content area and see how many words you can find that contain it. Remember that spelling can change while still preserving the morpheme.

9. Choose another language you are familiar with and make a list of 6 to 10 affixes in it. Then compare them to similar affixes with the same functions or meanings in English. How could these similarities be displayed in a chart or table used in the classroom?

10. With others, have a contest to see who can find the word that contains the most affixes. Can you find one with four affixes? five? (For this game, let's omit antidisestablishmentarianism!)

11. In small groups, try to fill in the blanks of the chart in Appendix 5.1 and talk about what you have discovered.

12. Try to create a graphic organizer to show the morphophonemic effects of English on the spelling or pronunciation of words. Why do you think one teacher said, "It should be called the *morphophonemicgraphemic* principle"?

13. Look at the spellings *spilled* and *spilt*, or *burned* and *burnt.* Which spellings give more morphological information? Which give more phonemic information?

The First 100 Most Commonly Used English Words

The first 100 (including their variations) make up about 50% of all written material, and the top 1,000 make up about 90% of all written material.

100 most common words in English	Origin—Anglo Saxon, Germanic or Latin/Greek?	Content or function?	Root (R) or stem (S)?
1. the			
2. of			
3. and			
4. a			
5. to			
6. in			
7. is			
8. you			
9. that			
10. it			
11. he			
12. was			
13. for			
14. on			
15. are			
16. as			
17. with			
18. his			
19. they			
20. I			
21. at			
22. be			
23. this			
24. have			

(cont.)

100 most common words in English	Origin—Anglo Saxon, Germanic or Latin/Greek?	Content or function?	Root (R) or stem (S)?
25. from			
26. or			
27. one			
28. had			
29. by			
30. word			
31. but			
32. not			
33. what			
34. all			
35. were			
36. we			
37. when			
38. your			
39. can			
40. said			
41. there			
42. use			
43. an			
44. each			
45. which			
46. she			
47. do			
48. how			
49. their			
50. if			
51. will			
52. up			
53. other			
54. about			
55. out			

(cont.)

100 most common words in English	Origin—Anglo Saxon, Germanic or Latin/Greek?	Content or function?	Root (R) or stem (S)?
56. many			
57. then			
58. them			
59. these			
60. so			
61. some			
62. her			
63. would			
64. make			
65. like			
66. him			
67. into			
68. time			
69. has			
70. look			
71. two			
72. more			
73. write			
74. go			
75. see			
76. number			
77. no			
78. way			
79. could			
80. people			
81. my			
82. than			
83. first			
84. water			
85. been			
86. call			

(cont.)

100 most common words in English	Origin—Anglo Saxon, Germanic or Latin/Greek?	Content or function?	Root (R) or stem (S)?
87. who			
88. oil			
89. its			
90. now			
91. find			
92. long			
93. down			
94. day			
95. did			
96. get			
97. come			
98. made			
99. may			
100. part			

Words from Fry, Kress, and Fountoukidis (1993).

Common Prefixes and Derivational Suffixes

Prefixes

re- (back, again)	inter- (between, among)	un- (not)	pro-/pur- (forward, in favor of)
ad-/abs-/at-/aft-/ag-/al-/an-/ ap-/aq-/ar-/as-/at-/ (toward)	pre- (before)	post- (after)	ex-/e-/ef-/ (out, beyond)
sub-/suc-/suf-/sug-/sum-/sur-/sus- (under)	per- (though)	trans-/tra-/tran- (across, beyond)	di-/dis- (not, apart, away)
de- (down, away)	in-/ig-/il-/im-/ir-/ (not) in-/il-/im-/ir-/ (in/into)	ob-/o-/oc-/of-/op-/ (against, toward)	over- (above)
ab-/abs-/ (from, away)	non- (not)	com-/co-/col-/con-/cor- (with, together)	mis- (wrong/wrongly)

Data from Nation (1990).

Derivational Suffixes

Abstract noun makers	-ism idealism	-ery drudgery	-dom wisdom	-ocracy aristocracy	-age mileage	-hood neighborhood	-ing farming	-ship membership		
Concrete noun makers	-eer seer	-er teenager	-ess waitress	-ette etiquette	-let tablet	-ling changeling	-ster mobster			
Verb makers	-ate frustrate	-en quicken	-ify identify	-ize/-ise realize						
Adjective/ noun makers	-ese Pekingese	-[i]an Fijian	-ist royalist	-ite socialite						
Nouns from verbs	-age breakage	-al arrival	-ant deodorant	-ation indication	-ee trustee	-er wiper	-ing building	-ment amazement	-or sailor	
Adjectives from nouns	-ed hated	-esque Kafkaesque	-ful plentiful	-ic angelic	-[i]al genial	-ish hawkish	-less hopeless	-ly lovely	-ous porous	-y hairy
Adjectives from verbs	-able doable	-ive restive								
Adverb makers	-ly carefully	-ward onward	-wise lengthwise							
Noun from adjectives	-ity levity	-ness tenderness								

From Crystal (1996). Copyright 1996 by Cambridge University Press. Reprinted by permission.

Patterns of Pronunciation for -s /-es and -ed Inflectional Morphemes

Sound of base word	Pronunciation of -s or -es
Last sound is /p/, /t/, /k/, /f/, /TH/	/s/ taps, gets, takes, laughs, booths
Last sound is /b/, /d/, /g/, /m/, /n/, /ng/, /l/, /r/, /v/, /th/, or a vowel	/z/ sobs, bids, tugs, hums, gains, sings, pulls, stairs, loves, soothes, days, sees, tries, goes, who's
Last sound is /s/, /z/, /sh/, /ch/, /zh/, /j/	/ez/ places, phases, washes, touches, garages, judges
Sound of base word	**Pronunciation of -ed**
Last sound is /p/, /k/, /f/, /s/, /sh/, /ch/, /TH/	/t/ stopped, kicked, laughed, kissed, washed, watched, toothed
Last sound is /b/, /g/, /v/, /z/, /m/, /n/, /ng/, /j/, /r/, /th/, /zh/, or a vowel	/d/ grabbed, bagged, shoved, surprised, shamed, found, hanged, judged, stirred, bathed, stayed, agreed, tried, crowed, massaged, wooed
Last sound is /t/ or /d/	/əd/ waited, loaded

The Compound Noun Game

1. Print the game cards and cut into pieces. If possible, use card stock or laminate them. If class is larger, create more compound noun pairs. If students are at a very beginning level, pictures can be added to the words.
2. Each student picks out one card with half of the compound word written on it. They will walk around and find a person whose card completes the compound word (e.g., your word is *water*, you can make a compound noun with the person that has the word *fall—waterfall*).
3. Once the students find their partners, they discuss why it is a compound word and what it means. Explain to the students that sometimes compound words are made up of two random words (e.g., butterfly).
4. Now, collect all the words and mix them up. Have two sets of partners pick out four new game cards. Put them together in any order to make a new compound word! Be creative and have fun! Students can use the word in a sentence and draw a picture of the new word. They can also create an advertisement for their new word if it is an object.

ANIMAL COMPOUND NOUN GAME

Try doing this same activity with the set of animal compound words below. When the cards are shuffled, students can create their own animals!

catfish	dragonfly	bulldog	jellyfish	starfish
ladybug	anteater	bluebird	lionfish	grasshopper
sheepdog	seahorse	bullfrog		

When they create the animal, have them draw it and describe what it does.

ANOTHER COMPOUND WORD GAME (COMPOUND WORD LADDER)

1. Give the students a compound word. Take the word and think of another word that has part of the first word. Keep going to make a compound word ladder!

   Example: Snowman
   Snowball
   Basketball
   Football
   Footprint
   Fingerprint
   Fingernail

2. When you can't think of any more words, try a new compound word!

(cont.)

CARDS FOR THE COMPOUND NOUN GAME
(ENTERING OR BEGINNING LEVEL)

back	pack
day	dream
sail	boat
water	bed
book	case
flash	light
lunch	box

CHAPTER SIX

Word Formation Processes, Cognates, and Collocations

New Vocabulary in This Chapter: etymology, homonym, homophone, homograph, polysemeous words, coinage (neologisms), borrowing, compounding, clipping, acronyms, abbreviations, backformation, conversion (category shift), scale change, paired-word sound play, multiple processes, cognate, false cognate, cross-linguistic homograph, cross-linguistic homophone, collocation, listeme

The previous chapter showed ways that words can be learned through the tool of morphemes. In this chapter we show more vocabulary learning techniques at the word and phrase level, with a focus on English word-formation processes, cognates, and collocations. All of these ways of learning new words cross many languages, but we will look at them as they apply to English. Learning more about them will help ELLs build the toolkit they need for successful reading comprehension and good writing.

The Bottom Line for Reading in Any Language: Vocabulary

Educators have looked at the relationship between reading comprehension and vocabulary for many years and found it to be a strong one. Thorndike (1973) explored the relationship between L1 vocabulary and reading comprehension. He collected data from students in 15 countries who were learning to read in different first languages and found that students' vocabulary and reading comprehension correlated at a very high level across a wide range of grades. It stands to reason that the more word meanings one knows, the more easily one can construct meaning through reading. This strong relationship has been corroborated in numerous other research studies, some of which date back to as early as 1925 (Whipple, 1925).

For ELLs, vocabulary is just as decisive. A 2,000-word threshold is considered by many to be the minimum number of words learners need to function when they enter a school setting, but native speakers already have between 5,000 and 7,000 words in their listening vocabulary when they enter school (Grabe & Stoller, 2002). Although many ELLs are not even at the 2,000-word threshold, much less 7,000 words, they are expected make up the difference at the same time they are learning academic content. Meanwhile, the native speakers alongside them are busy adding to their vocabulary. For this reason, ELLs must acquire twice as much English vocabulary, twice as fast as native speakers, often without any exposure to hearing English outside of school. This is no small feat!

English, a Richly Generative Language

English has the largest vocabulary of any language in the world, with more than 100,000 words, and is growing even as we read this! It absorbs and allows for the creation of new words in ways that consume the careers of thousands of linguists and bedevil countless English learners. New English words are formed through many processes, some of which we will not be able to mention in this brief chapter. We refer you to Pinker (2007), Birch (2007), Crystal (1996), and Yule (2006) if you want to explore the rich word-making capabilities of English in detail.

The many sources of English words and the wide variety of English word-making options have a direct bearing on how easily ELLs acquire English vocabulary. Some aspects of English, such as its relatively straightforward word order and grammatical categories, are reasonably easy to learn; it's getting a handle on English vocabulary that can prove so challenging. When teachers of ELLs become motivated to learn more about words and how they are put together, it will naturally spill over into the word learning of their students.

Etymology

One of the reasons that English is so rich and widely used around the world is that there are many routes into the lexicon. Studying the history of how words are created and how they change is called *etymology*. It is a fascinating field for teachers and students alike. We can all become more metalinguistically aware when we learn about where words come from and how they change.

Good dictionaries, such as the *The American Heritage Dictionary of the English Language* or *The Oxford English Dictionary*, include the etymology of words. No classroom should be without a dictionary that includes etymology. (Please see Appendix 8.1 for some thoughts about the role of dictionaries in the ESL classroom.) There are also many captivating books that tell the amazing stories behind English words, such as *Mother Tongue* or *Made in America* by Bill Bryson (1990, 1994), or *The Story of English* by McCrum, Cran, and MacNeil (1986). In addition, excellent websites, such as *Online Etymology Dictionary*, trace the origins of thousands of English words. Since the Internet has made it easier to find out the origins of English words than it used to be, it is much more possible to include this study as part of the literacy curriculum.

Ambiguous Vocabulary in English

The opacity of English and the diverse sources from which words come into it combine to create many unusual overlaps, ambiguities, and multiple meanings of words. These can create challenges for learning to read in English! Words containing differing spellings, pronunciations, or meanings in English are often lumped into the catch-all term *homonyms*, but we prefer to divide them into three distinct categories: homophones, homographs, and polysemous words.

1. *Homophones* are words with the same sound but different spellings and meanings. Because English spelling is so opaque, these words abound. Homophones also account for a great number of spelling errors; students know the meaning and sound of a word, but they aren't sure which possible spelling pattern of the word represents the meaning they are trying to represent in writing. In addition to homophones with two spellings, such as slay/sleigh, bow/bough, weight/wait, and pair/pear, some common words are homophones with three spellings, such as there/they're/their, right/write/rite, and to/two/too.

2. *Homographs* are words with different pronunciations and meanings but the same spelling. They are unlikely to be misspelled, but they may be misread and their meaning confused with the other meaning of the word using that spelling pattern. Common homographs include the different words that are both spelled with the letters *bass, bow, wound, wind,* and *present*. In another example, the sentence "They read the book," is ambiguous because of the homograph "read."

3. *Polysemous words* are pronounced and spelled the same but have different meanings that may not appear to relate to each other. Sometimes they are different parts of speech. The root morpheme may give information about some of the meanings, but not others. Many very common English words are polysemous, and their additional meanings can be very misleading. For example, ELLs in a class we observed who were reading a basal story about native Americans were confident that they knew the meaning of the word *game*. Looking at its context, however, they realized that "they hunted *game* with bows and arrows" didn't make sense with the meaning of *something you play*.

Older, high-frequency English content words are likely to take on a wide variety of meanings in different content areas. The many distributions of the word *table* in math and science is such a case. Students need to learn both the common meanings and the specific content-area meanings of words for reading success. Therefore, any vocabulary learning system must be set up to include ways to account for polysemous words. Students should learn that it's not at all unusual or problematic to find multiple word meanings; in English, it's natural.

Both homophones and polysemous words are likely to be found in unintended puns, which are jokes based on wordplay. Many puns derive their humor from the second meaning of the word clashing with its first meaning, creating humorous dissonance.

Word Formation Processes in English

The technology of the Internet and cell phones have allowed new words to proliferate among speech communities much more rapidly. In the case of text messaging and instant messaging, the efficiencies created by rapid "thumb-spelling" of words may have long-term implications for English spelling. Dictionary editors and publishers are challenged to constantly introduce—and retire—English words for their latest editions, and in time this may give the edge to online dictionaries, which do not need to wait for a new printing. Although words seem to enter English randomly, they can be classified into certain linguistically distinct categories. Once students see how new words can be formed in English, they can find evidences of them every day, and can enlarge their own vocabularies.

Here are twelve ways new words can be formed in English. (Note: these are not the only ways words are formed in English. Also, these are only individual words. New meanings can also be formed by combining words.)

1. *Coinage* (*neologisms*). These words are made up from scratch to suit certain purposes. They often do not contain an identifiable morpheme. They are often invented by companies with new products and then extended to more generalized use. Examples: *Xerox; Kleenex; Vaseline, Band-aid, Tylenol, Viagra*

2. *Borrowing.* These words are taken from another language and incorporated into English. Sometimes the original meaning is altered, and the pronunciation may change. Since some words were borrowed long ago, it may be hard to recognize their foreign origins. Examples: *tortilla* (Spanish), *coup de grace* (French), *pajamas* (Hindi), *banana* (Bantu), *chipmunk* (Algonquin), *alfalfa* (Arabic)

3. *Compounding.* This common way to form English words consists of combining two free morphemes to create a new meaning. The new word may be hyphenated or combined without hyphenation. Sometimes compound nouns consist of two words with a space between them. In spoken form, the first of the two nouns receives the strong stress. Examples: *white board, sailboat, makeover, sandbag, bailout, nonprofit, giveaway*

4. *Blending.* This creative word-making tool of English consists of combining morphemes or even just phonemic fragments from two other words to create a new "hybrid" word with a new meaning. Examples: *brunch* (breakfast and lunch); *smog* (smoke and fog); *infomercial* (information and commercial); *guesstimate* (guess and estimate); *webinar* (Web and seminar)

5. *Clipping.* Words are made by shortening a longer word or phrase. The word may be clipped at the beginning, middle, or end of the longer word, and may even cross morpheme boundaries for ease of pronunciation. Examples: professional → *pro*, condominium → *condo*, laboratory → *lab*, zoological garden → *zoo*, telephone → *phone*, weblog → *blog*, handkerchief → *hankie*

6. *Acronyms.* The first letter of each word in a group of words is combined into a single word, which can be pronounced as a whole. The resulting word may be capitalized. When *acronyms* are well-established the words that make them up may be forgotten. Examples: *NATO* (North American Treaty Organization), *radar* (radio detection and ranging), *scuba* (self-contained underwater breathing apparatus), *pin* (personal identification number), *zip* (zone improvement plan), *UNICEF* (United Nations International Children's Emergency Fund), *AIDS* (acquired immune deficiency syndrome)

7. *Abbreviations.* The first letter of each word in a group of words is combined into a single word whose letter names are pronounced separately. Examples: *CNN* (Cable News Network), *NPR* (National Public Radio), *ASAP* (as soon as possible), *AKA* (also known as), *RIP* (rest in peace). A number of new words are also an alloy of acronyms and *abbreviations*, in the

interest of easier pronunciation, such as JPEG, a photo storage software, which is pronounced /jeypeg/, pronouncing the *j* as a letter name, like an acronym, and the *peg* in a syllable, as an abbreviation. "ASAP" is also moving in this direction with the pronunciation /eysap/. Abbreviations can be especially tricky for ELLs if they are spoken aloud without explanation. Maria Isabel Orescanin, a Panamian ESL teacher and herself an ELL, describes it thus:

> *I see a lot of abbreviations, and I am constantly asking people about them. I used to find these abbreviations as new words when going to the doctor, and it was very intimidating and uncomfortable. When I would hear them, I would not even know they were abbreviations, so my brain would be busy trying to figure them out. It was awful when it was medically related. It added unnecessary stress.*

8. *Backformation.* This is a process in which, most commonly, a noun is changed into a verb by lopping off the end of the noun and affixing a derivational suffix for a verb ending. Examples: television → *televise*, make priorities → *prioritize*, donation → *donate*, magnification → *magnify*, enthusiasm → *enthuse*

9. *Conversion* (also called *category shift*). Without changing any morphemes, the grammatical category of a word is changed. Examples: butter (N → V pass the *butter* or *butter* the bread), empty (adj → V, an *empty* bottle or *empty* the bottle), must see (modal V → N, you *must see* this movie or this movie is a *must-see*), chair (N → V, sit on a *chair*, *chair* the meeting)

10. *Scale change.* An existing free morpheme has a prefix or suffix added to it in order to change its dimension or scale. This would include an English affix that shows dimension in English, such as the /iy/ diminutive morpheme, added to the end of a word to make it smaller or more familiar (e.g., Bobbie, puppy), or the diminutive morphemes from other languages, such as Spanish (-*ito*, as in *burrito*) or French (-*ette*, as in *coquette*). Scale changes can also be shown at the beginning of words to show quantity or size, such as *macroeconomics*. Examples: *microwave, megabucks, hoodie, rockettes, booklet, nappie, suffragette*

11. *Paired-word sound play.* A "double word" is created in which the second word sounds like the first except for a change of vowel or opening consonant. The second vowel is usually produced lower in the vocal cavity. One of the two words may have an identifiable morpheme, but the second is just a phonemic variation of the first. There may be a slight onomatopoetic association (it sounds like the action it is describing), but not always. Examples: *hip-hop, mishmash, wishy-washy, wiggle waggle, humdrum*

12. *Multiple processes.* A combination of the above processes forms a new word. Examples: *deli* is borrowed from German (*delicatessen*) and

then clipped; *snowball* is compounded from two free morphemes to form a noun, then converted into a verb (the event *snowballed*, etc.); *cyberbullying* is a compound of the root *cyber* and the lexical morpheme *bully*, which is then converted to a verb, and then converted to a gerund (noun) by adding the suffix -*ing*.

English is constantly in motion. Here are two interesting examples.

I didn't know what "to TP a house" meant. My students had to explain it to me. I learned that it is an abbreviation of "toilet paper," which is then converted into a transitive verb. The house is the unfortunate object of the verb, when it is "decorated" with dozens of rolls of toilet paper in the middle of the night.—TENENA

My teenage daughter and her friends often use the new word "ish." "Ish" was originally a derivational suffix. As we know, when it is added to a root or stem, it modifies a characteristic, like "greenish," starting an event at "12-ish," or "newish" for "kind of new." Now it has been clipped and the suffix has become a root, forming a new word. When I ask her if she had a good time at a party, she may shrug her shoulders and answer "Ish!" in an offhanded way. It means "I had a moderately good time."—KRISTIN

When teachers combine their knowledge of morphemes with their metalinguistic awareness of new word formation in English, they can transform this knowledge into an exciting, word centered classroom for English language learners and native speakers alike.

Using Cognates

Depending on the other languages known to the English language learners, cognates may be a rich source of information for word study in English, and therefore we will give this strategy special attention.

A *cognate* is a word with a common or similar meaning in two languages and which comes from the same root. The word may or may not look or sound the same in both languages, depending on the language distance. English derives about 60% of its words from Latin or Greek origins (Freeman & Freeman, 2004), and the percentage of Latin and Greek words in other languages is also high.

Cognates from Greek and Latin can be found in science, philosophy, mathematics, and the social sciences in most of the Indo-European languages. ELLs can benefit dramatically from studying cognates if their first language is an Indo-European language. Cognate words with English can be found in languages as widely dispersed as Spanish, Romanian, Polish, Bosnian, and German. There is also a whole different set of cognate words shared with English from languages of Germanic origin, such as Dutch, German, Swedish, Danish, Norwegian, Frisian, Afrikaans, and others.

Cognates with Latin and Greek tend to be academic language. If we examine words in English and Spanish as an example, we can see that the words shared by both languages tend to be academic vocabulary words. Jim Cummins (2007) put it succinctly: "English is a romance language when it comes to academic language, just like Spanish and Romanian." The fact that CALP words in English look like common words in Spanish gives Spanish-speaking ELLs an enormous potential boost in developing their academic language, but only if these words are highlighted in the classroom. Here are some examples of academic verbs used in English classroom settings, for example, and their Spanish cognate words:

examine	*examinar*
discuss	*discutir*
explain	*explicar*
analyze	*analizar*
maximize	*maximizar*

In addition, many English words with Germanic roots correspond to Spanish words that are cognates with a more academic, CALP-language word in English. For example:

get	*obtener*	(obtain)
fix	*reparar*	(repair)
keep	*retener*	(retain)
breathe	*respirar*	(respire)

We use Spanish for an example, but these similarities occur across the languages with Latin origins. Words that look and sound similar to the words *photosynthesis, velocity, botany,* and *hydroelectric,* for example, can be found in many Latin or Greek-influenced languages. Even when the full word is not found in a learner's first language, there may be clues in the morphemes, such as *hydro* being related to water.

ELLs are excited when they are encouraged to think of their first language as a resource to help shine light on unknown vocabulary in English. Students feel like detectives! Appendix 6.1 offers a chart that can be used to generate English or Spanish words from a common Latin root.

Beware of *false cognates, cross-linguistic homophones,* and *cross-linguistic homographs!* False cognates have the same appearance or sound as a word in another language, but carry a different meaning. Examples of false cognates are *molestar,* which means *to bother* in Spanish, unlike the much more serious meaning of *molest,* or *sexually violate,* in English, or *passer un examen* in French, which means *to take an exam,* but not necessarily to pass it, unlike the English *pass an exam,* which means *to have a passing grade.* Appendix 6.2 lists some of the most notorious false cognates between English and Spanish.

*Imagine my surprise when I received a card on the last day of class, signed by all of my Hispanic ELLs, which read "In Deepest Sympathy." I didn't dare tell them that it was a card we use to comfort someone at the death of a loved one. They meant to tell me that they found me very nice and kind!—*LEAH

False cognates share a root but have different meanings. In addition, words that sound or look the same in two languages but do not share a common root can also cause many misunderstandings and amusing situations for learners. Cross-linguistic homographs share common letters, and cross-linguistic homophones share common sounds. An example of a cross-linguistic homophone is the Persian word pronounced as *party.* It means *clout,* which is not at all like the English definition of a party (although people with clout may give or attend a lot of them!). An example of a cross-linguistic homograph would be *pie,* which means *foot* in Spanish but has the same spelling as *a sweet dessert* in English.

Collocations: Phrasal Verbs, Idioms, and Listemes

English vocabulary words whose meanings cannot be understood through single words alone are referred to as *collocations.* Pinker (1999) defines collocations as "a string of words commonly used together" (p. 290). He also notes that collocations "are remembered as wholes and often used together" (p. 24). Part of learning to break text into "chunks" while reading is learning to keep collocations together as a single chunk.

Although these common groupings of words are encountered in all reading materials, they are overlooked in targeted vocabulary, usually in favor of teaching nouns. Therefore, part of vocabulary development requires teaching these groups of words as whole units. Collocations are pervasive in written and spoken English and can be found in many academic contexts as well as social settings. However, these collocations are often not introduced and taught explicitly to English language learners. Zwiers has identified a number of "academic idioms," which teachers tend to use. They include:

> . . . Phrases such as *all boils down to, the gory details, that answer doesn't hold water, a thin argument, a keen insight, crux of the matter, on the right track,* and *dissect the article.* Many of these academic idioms serve to describe cognitive processes and school tasks. (Zwiers, 2007, p. 108)

We describe three kinds of collocations in English—phrasal verbs, idioms, and listemes—and give suggestions about how to introduce them.

Phrasal Verbs

Phrasal verbs are verbs composed of a verb and a preposition or occasionally a verb and an adverb. If someone asked you to make a list of verbs in English, starting with the most common ones, you would quickly find that many of them are phrasal verbs such as *get up, sit down, get in, go into, pick up,* or *put down.* You can see that the "integrity" of the verb's meaning is lost if we take away its preposition—both words are part of the meaning of the verb. You will also notice that phrasal verbs tend to be a combination of short words that are not cognates with Latin-based words. (For a list of Latin-based equivalents of some common phrasal verbs, see Table 6.1.)

Because phrasal verbs are so common in spoken English, many ELLs will acquire them through their social language development. However, when ELLs read phrasal verbs with meanings that are not obvious, comprehension can be affected. For example, when Isho, a fourth-grade Iraqi ELL, reads a story in a basal that includes "The workers *picked up* the pace," he may have difficulty understanding the meaning of the phrasal verb because it has a different meaning from that of the base verb and the preposition alone and it also has multiple meanings, like many other phrasal verbs. For example, *pick up* means *speed up* in the previous sentence, but it can also mean *lift,* as in *pick up a grocery bag,* or *gather,* as in *pick up the pieces.*

If ELLs choose the wrong prepositions when they write phrasal verbs, it can throw off the meaning of a sentence or make it awkward. For example, it is common to see errors such as "He put it in the table," for "He put it on the table," "The plane left of Chicago" for "The plane left from Chicago," or "I ate a snack to tie me up until dinner" for "I ate a snack to tide me over until dinner." These are often caused by interference from patterns of preposition use in the learner's first language.

**TABLE 6.1. Selected Phrasal Verbs
and Their Latin-Based Equivalents**

Phrasal verbs	Latin-based synonym
ask about	inquire
call up	contact (by phone)
come across	project
come over	visit
cook up	create, invent
find out	discover
fix up	repair, rehabilitate
get over	recover, surmount
get on	board
get up	awaken
go away	depart
hand out	distribute
help out	assist
keep on	continue
look over	review
make up	reconcile, invent
pick up	transport
run into	encounter
set up	plan, organize
show up	arrive
take away	subtract
think up	invent, create
try out	experiment, audition
turn up	increase

Idioms

Idioms are metaphorical expressions whose meanings cannot be discerned by looking at the individual words (Pinker, 1999). Often colorful and humorous, idioms give insights into the cultural underpinnings of English speaking societies. For example, *straight from the horse's mouth* comes from the historical idea that the stable boy in close contact with a racehorse is most aware of its overall condition; it has come to mean "coming from the highest possible authority." All of the extra interest created by a colorful idiom enhances its communicative power tremendously, in both speaking and writing.

There are thousands of idioms in English, just as in every other language, and learning them is part of the fun of learning a new language. It's important to teach them explicitly. Pictures, skits, and jokes can all help.

> *These word combinations are always evolving. You might hear one meaning of an idiom, which is then extended into a new area through song lyrics or something in the news. Idioms can acquire new meanings all the time, and that's what makes them so interesting. They also bear careful instruction, however, because so many of them pick up sexual connotations.*
> —LEAH

When idioms are taught, it's important to reference the literal meaning of the idiom first and then demonstrate its metaphorical meaning. For example, when we say "Don't put the cart before the horse," we need to evoke the image of what it looks like when a cart is put in front of a horse—it can't go anywhere, because the horse is behind it! Then we can extend its meaning to the situation in which the idiom is being used, explaining that it means "Do the most important things first."

Another feature of idioms is that they are often only partially spoken or written by native speakers, who expect listeners or readers to fill in the rest of the idiom and then catch the meaning. Often giving the first part of an idiom is a way of making a humorous commentary (see Table 6.2 for examples). ELLs must be able to process a fragment of an idiom rapidly enough to get the point of a joke, and this is no small feat!

TABLE 6.2. Examples of Partial Use of Idioms

"Let the chips fall . . ." in the food section of a daily newspaper

The headline is over a picture of different kinds of potato and vegetable chips in midair. English readers know that the full idiom is "Let the chips fall where they may," meaning "Accept the minor consequences and keep going." The idiom comes from advice given to lumberjacks whose axes created chips on the ground while they were chopping down a tree. In the context of the article, it gives the idea that the other chips are just as acceptable as potato chips.

"It's six of one . . ." in a group of people discussing two options.

The phrase is the beginning of the idiom "It's six of one, half a dozen of the other," which means "they're equal" or "they're the same." To understand the idiom, we need to know that a dozen consists of 12, so a half dozen is six, and those are the same size.

"In one ear . . ." in a teacher's lounge

The phrase is half of "In one ear, out the other" which means, "It was heard but not remembered or learned." To understand this idiom, we have to picture an empty head that ideas flow right through. The idea is that there is no brain in the middle to process the information!

Listemes

Listemes are words that commonly appear together. In addition to phrasal verbs and idioms, there are numerous expressions that contain words in a fixed order that have to be memorized. We can call these expressions by the general term collocations, but a more precise term is listemes. Some examples of these fixed expressions are "up and down," not "down and up," "salt and pepper," not "pepper and salt," and "the whole wide world," not "the whole big world" or "the entire wide world." Other listemes, like paired words "mumbo-jumbo," "helter-skelter," and "wishy-washy" are bound by their ease of pronunciation (Pinker, 2000).

Collocations can be confusing for ELLs because very simple words may be combined in ways that are not at all simple, as can be seen in Figure 6.1.

Learning to recognize and use the collocations of English is an integral part of learning to read and write. The more collocations we know, the better we are able to comprehend spoken and written English. In turn, the more collocations we can use in our speaking and writing, the better we can develop our unique language styles and self-expression.

FIGURE 6.1. An English collocation. Reprinted with permission from Martha Rosenberg.

HOW DOES THIS LOOK IN THE CLASSROOM?

Playing with Words Is the Fun Stuff of Language Learning

Wordplay uses the kind of thinking that builds vocabulary through uproarious fun. Between morphemes, cognates, and diverse word formation processes, there are many ways to get students excited about words, and these are but a few.

Taking Cameras into the Community

Using cameras to hunt for the ways words are used can be a wonderful project. The photos can be turned into photo essays, either by individuals or the whole class, and then printed out or uploaded to a website. In addition to analyzing environmental print, it also gives students an opportunity to talk about their neighborhoods. It can also be fun to look at signs in other languages posted in ethnic neighborhoods, and the same word formation processes can be seen. An example of some Spanish word formation processes can be seen in Figure 6.2.

Idiom Calendars

To practice idioms, high school ELL reading teacher Barb Willson uses something she calls idiom calendars, a calendar displayed in the room featuring a different student-illustrated idiom every week. After it comes up on the calendar, students practice the idioms through dialogues and skits. When ELLs share idioms from their L1, it is also a great way to enjoy linguistic comparisons while teaching metalinguistic concepts.

Song Lyrics

Pop songs and country songs are chock full of phrasal verbs, idioms, and listemes that reflect common speech. Analyzing and singing along with song lyrics is a natural way to practice using these expressions effortlessly. Songs also help ELLs express their feelings and develop shared cultural experiences (Lems, 2001, 2002).

Pulling out Phrasal Verbs

Pulling out phrasal verbs as they are encountered in different kinds of texts, including songs, fiction, poetry, and Readers' Theatre scripts, is one way to highlight them. Sometimes phrasal verbs may be overlooked as the "easy words" in a text, but they carry rich associations worth explaining

FIGURE 6.2. Examples of Spanish word formation processes.

explicitly. For example, when a high school ELL at the Developing level chose to do a presentation about the mysterious song "Hotel California" by the Eagles, he did not recognize the irony of the line "living it up at the Hotel California," because he didn't know the idiom *to live it up*. The placement of that idiom in a song about being mentally trapped heightens the song's power. Collocations should be introduced and practiced as they appear in groups, not word by word. They should be put on the wall or included in vocabulary notebooks, just like individual words. Polysemous words can be represented on a graphic organizer that allows each meaning of a word to be represented in its own section. For the word *will*, for example, the word can be put in a middle of a semantic map (sometimes called a spider map). One branch can show the definition of *will* as a verb signaling future tense, while another branch can show the definition of *will* as a document people create to distribute their possessions after their death, and a third branch defines *will* as determination. To support learners at a lower proficiency level, the semantic map's definitions can be filled in by the teacher, and the students are asked to identify the word and write it in the center.

Studying Etymology

Etymology is a great history project. While learning about content, students can also explore the etymology of words that relate to that content, and talk about how those words are created. For example, what is the origin of the word *bankrupt*, and what morphemes can be seen in it? Students can easily research the origins of words they are learning and share them with the class.

Creating New Product Names

Advertising copywriters create new words all the time as they try to come up with new products and company names to entice the buying public. For example, "Bubblicious" is a blend that is the brand name of a successful product. When we see its name on the gum package, we know that it is *bubble gum*, and we also get an association with the word *delicious*, and that combination makes us want to buy it.

First, have students find several products in the store or somewhere else and break their product names into morphemes, analyzing how the morphemes are combined to create a certain effect. Evaluate how well the created names sell the product, then have students create a new product name for one of these products: toothpaste, soap, a pair of gym shoes, a car, a "smart pill" or other products, and create an ad for the product. Discuss what word formation processes students used to create their product name. If appropriate, have students vote on the best product name created in the class.

Create a Matching Game with Idioms

Split idioms in half and scramble them, and ask students to match them. When students have put the idioms together, ask them to define them in their own words, and use them in a skit. For students at a lower proficiency level, the teacher can provide a scrambled list of definitions that the students match with the idioms. Here is a sample to get you started. (*Note:* Idiom-matching games only work with idioms that are full sentences—and many are not!)

Too many cooks	and into the fire.
One swallow	spoil the broth.
It's out of the frying pan	doesn't fall far from the tree.
The apple	does not a summer make.

QUESTIONS FOR FURTHER STUDY

1. If you had to choose three important ideas from this chapter, which would you choose? How can you apply these ideas to your larger knowledge of teaching English as a new language?

2. Pick one of the following polysemous or homographic words and prepare a lesson to teach its multiple meanings, including its occurrence in idioms and, if possible, ways it might also be used as a verb. Words: bass, tip, wind, right, lead, game, bill

3. Words and phrases are always entering English. Can you think of some new ones you might have read in the newspaper or online or heard on TV or the radio? If you teach, what do you hear your students saying lately? After jotting them down, write a short definition and share with others.

4. Look at the new words on the signs in Figure 6.3 and classify them according to the word formation process(es) involved. (Note: Not all of the word formation processes are found in these photos.) Do some of the new words these businesses have created seem more "successful" than others? Do some of the words seem awkward? Analyze why certain company names work better than others.

5. With a partner or alone, classify these words by the word formation processes listed in the chapter. If the word is from the "multiple processes" category, describe the specific processes that go into the mix.

Jumbotron	ecocide	supersize	grandfather in (phrasal verb)	
topsy-turvy	MRI	e-book	danceathon	newbie
stagehand	ciao	gen-Xer	POTUS	skybox
FYI	spybot	spam	videographer	rubberize

FIGURE 6.3. Examples of English word formation processes.

FIGURE 6.3. *(cont.)*

FIGURE 6.3. *(cont.)*

6. If you have studied another language, make a list of some cognates you are aware of. How do you use these cognates to remember new words? Have you ever found any false cognates? If you have any stories about this, share them with others. If not, ask around to find stories from others.

7. Classify the following puns as based on homophones or polysemous words:
   a. Q: What is the best fruit for studying history?   A: Dates.
   b. Q: What two animals go everywhere you go?   A: Your calves.
   c. Q: What is the strongest day?   A: Sunday because all the rest are week days.
   d. Q: What letter is never in the alphabet?   A: The one that you mail.
   e. Q: What should be looked into?   A: A mirror.
   f. Q: Why did the Palmers name their cattle ranch "Horizon?"
      A. Because that's where the sons raise meat (sun's rays meet).

   Find some other jokes that are based on polysemous meanings or homophones of words. Better yet, do this with your students!

8. Idioms have rich cultural resonance. With a partner or alone, see how many idioms you can think of about one of the following topics: baseball, cooking, travel, weather, or a topic of your choosing. Try to do it from memory!

9. Choose two of the idioms you found in the previous question and think about their literal meanings. How could you best teach the literal meaning of some of these idioms?

10. Make a list of 10 listemes and share them with others. Listeme test: It's a listeme if another person can easily finish the second half for you.

11. Pick one of the following verbs and see how many phrasal verbs you can create with it. Look at Appendix 6.3 and take note of the numerous phrasal verbs possible with the verb "get." Make a table and write the definition of the phrasal verb next to it. Do some or all of them have a common meaning? Verbs: *come, go, make, write, pick, think*

12. Match the phrasal verbs on the left with their equivalent word on the right. Notice that one of the phrasal verbs is listed twice because it is polysemous. Which column of words contains more Latinate roots?

1. _____	run into	a. initiate
2. _____	talk about	b. tolerate
3. _____	think over	c. sacrifice
4. _____	make up	d. contemplate
5. _____	put up with	e. encounter
6. _____	give up	f. invent

7. _____ get out   g. reconcile
8. _____ make up   h. discuss
9. _____ start up   i. depart

13. Continue the list above with some additional phrasal verbs on the left and their Latin-based equivalents on the right. If you're stuck, look at Table 6.1 again for ideas.

14. Look at the three pictures in Figure 6.4, based on wordplay, and explain the puns in them.

FIGURE 6.4. Examples of English word formation using wordplay.

Ways to Generate Words in English and Spanish from a Common Root

Spanish word	Related Spanish word	English word	Related English words	Root meaning
primo	primero primavera primitivo primeramente	primary	primal primarily prime primordial primitive	*prim* (Latin, first)
servicio	servible servidor servilleta	service	subservient serving self-serving servitude serviceable	*serv* (Latin, servant)
escribir	escritorio escrito escribano	script	inscribe describe description scribble nondescript scripture	*scribere* (Latin, to write)
solo	soledad solamente soltero/a	solitary	solitude soloist soliloquy	*solo* (Latin, alone)
centímetro	centígrado	centimeter	centennial centenary cents centipede	*cent* (Latin, one hundred)
círculo	circulación circular	circle	circus circumference circumlocution circumnavigate circumflex circumcise circumfix	*circulus* (Latin, ring)
vacante	vacar vacación	vacant	vacate vacuum vacation vacuity evacuate	*vacare* (v) (Latin, to empty) *vacuus* (n)

Using a common root, found in the right column, Spanish ELLs can generate words in both Spanish and English. This chart is a good template for using L1 Spanish word knowledge in a classroom of Spanish ELLs. It can be adapted for other first languages.

Selected False Cognates between English and Spanish

English word	Spanish word that looks/sounds similar to English word	Meaning in Spanish
embarrassed	embarazada	to be pregnant
constipated	constipado	to have a head cold
deception	decepción	disappointment
excited	excitado	sexually aroused
groceries	groserias	saying vulgarities or gross things
effective	efectivo	cash
qualifications	calificaciónes	grades
success	suceso	event
actually	actualmente	at this time
support	soportar	put up with
assist	asistir	attend
attend	atender	take care of
carpet	carpeta	folder
realize	realizar	achieve
fabric	fábrica	factory
exit	éxito	success
mascot	mascote	pet

The Many Meanings of *GET*

Most learners of English as a foreign language would probably agree that the little verb *get* is one of the most difficult words in the language. Not only does it have several meanings by itself; it also combines with a number of particles to form phrasal verbs with idiomatic meanings. And, to make matters worse, many of these phrasal verbs themselves have multiple meanings.

For many learners, even when its meanings are learned, *get* tends to remain a part of their passive rather than their active vocabulary: whenever possible, they will use a synonym for it. This is especially true of the phrasal verbs. Experience has shown us that in most cases such substitution works pretty well: the speaker's meaning is communicated. To the ear of a native speaker, however, wholesale avoidance of two-word verbs, and of *get* in its various meanings, results in stilted, unnatural-sounding speech.

The following facts about *get* are offered for whatever use the teacher or learner may wish to make of them. The basic meanings of *get* as a single-word verb are:

receive *(Did you get a good grade on the exam?)*

win *(Mary got first place in the competition.)*

obtain *(Add up the scores and see what you get.)*

acquire *(She got a new hat to wear to the party.)*

reach *(When will we get to San Francisco?)*

make contact with *(The operator is trying to get Paris now.)*

go and bring *(Please get my coat when you go upstairs.)*

catch *(My sister had a contagious disease, but I didn't get it.)*

become *(How did you get sick?)*

understand *(I'm sorry, I didn't get your name.)*

influence or persuade *(Do you think you can get him to do it?)*

own *(I've got 20 books on that subject.)*

cause to be *(Why don't you get your hair cut?)*

cause to arrive *(Can you get him here by three o'clock?)*

take away *(Get that dog out of here!)*

be sentenced to *(The criminal got 10 years in prison for stealing the car.)*

prepare *(I'll get breakfast for you.)*

take revenge on *(slang) (I'll get you for that!)*

Among the more common phrasal verbs containing *get* are:

get about: to move from place to place; to go to many social events; to be active *(He doesn't get about much anymore.)* (also *get around*)

get across: to clarify or explain convincingly; to communicate *(He tried to get his meaning across to them, but they didn't understand.)*

get ahead: to succeed; to prosper *(He is working hard because he wants to get ahead in his profession.)*

get ahead of: to excel, surpass, do better than *(This group got ahead of all the others because they worked diligently.)*

get along: to proceed, make progress *(She's getting along quite well with her studies.)*; to agree, be compatible *(How does he get along with the other students?)*; to succeed or be fairly successful *(He doesn't make much money, but he's getting along all right.)*; to become old *(My uncle is getting along in years.)*; to leave, go away *(Get along, now; it's time to go to school.)*

get around: to avoid or circumvent (something) *(He managed to get around that rule by taking the course the following year.)*; to influence or gain favor by flattery *(He knew just how to get around his teachers so he wouldn't have to do any extra work.)* (see *get about*)

get around to: to deal with after a postponement *(I just got around to rewriting the paper.)*

(cont.)

From *English Teaching Forum* (January 1987).

get at: to ascertain or uncover *(We finally got at what he was trying to tell us.)*; to reach *(Standing on a ladder, I was able to get at the birds' nest.)*; to lead up to a conclusion *(I don't understand what you're getting at.)*; to apply oneself to *(Now let's get at this problem and see if we can solve it.)*

get away: to escape *(The thief got away before we could catch him.)*; to leave *(Get away from that machine!)*; go away, as on vacation *(We're going to try to get away for two weeks this summer.)*

get away with *(informal)*: to successfully avoid punishment or discovery of something done *(It's amazing what the children get away with in that class.)*

get back: to return *(She got back from her trip last Thursday.)*; to regain *(She got back all the money that had been stolen.)*

get back at *(informal)*: to take revenge against *(He could hardly wait to get back at the big boy who had embarrassed him.)*

get by: to pass *(There was hardly enough room for one car to get by.)*; to pass by without being discovered or punished *(He got by us without our even hearing him.)*; to manage or survive *(She is just barely able to get by on the salary that she is paid.)*

get down: to descend, dismount *(He had a hard time getting down from the roof.)*

get down to: give full attention to, begin to act on *(Now let's get down to work.)*

get in: enter or be allowed to enter *(Can all these people get in?)*; to arrive *(We called the airline to see what time the plane would get in.)*; to inject, put in (as in a conversation) *(I finally managed to get a couple of words in.)*; to receive *(The store just got in a shipment of ties.)*

get it: understand *(I don't get it; what are you trying to do?)*; *(informal)* to be punished or scolded *(When my father finds out what I did, I'm really going to get it.)*

get nowhere: to make no progress, accomplish nothing *(I've worked on this paper for three hours, and I've gotten nowhere.)*

get off: to get down from or out of *(How is he going to get off the roof?)*; to leave, go away *(Pack your suitcase as quickly as possible so that we can get off before noon.)*; to write and send, as a letter *(I want to get off a letter to Aunt Martha today.)*; to escape, as punishment *(He got off with a very light sentence: just 30 days in jail.)*; to remove *(I hope I can get this stain off of my sleeve.)*; to help someone to escape from punishment *(That lawyer can get you off if anybody can.)*; start, as in a race *(After two false starts, they still haven't gotten off.)*

get on: to climb up onto or into *(Do you know how to get on a horse?)*; to get along (q. v.), to grow older *(He looks young, but he's really getting on.)*; to proceed, make progress *(How are you getting on with your project?)*

get out: to go out or away *(He got out of the house as fast as he could.)*; to take out *(She got the stain out with some cleaning fluid.)*; to become public, as news *(They tried to keep that story from getting into the newspapers, but somehow it got out.)*; to publish, as a newspaper *(We get out a new issue of The Forum every three months.)*

get out of: to derive or draw *(She gets a lot of satisfaction out of helping those people.)*; to escape from or avoid *(Houdini got out of a lot of tight spots.)*; to go beyond (range, sight, earshot, etc.) *(The dogs ran so fast they got out of sight in two minutes.)*; to help someone to escape *(His friends got him out of prison in just a few days.)*; to find out from *(At first he wouldn't tell me, but I finally got it out of him.)*

get over: get across (q.v.); recover from (illness, grief, etc.) *(He got over it in just a few days; now he's fine.)*

get there *(informal)*: to succeed, attain one's goal *(I've set high goals and I don't know if I'll ever get there, but I'm going to try.)*

(cont.)

get through: to finish or complete *(Do you think you can get through that big pile of letters this afternoon?)*; to undergo and survive *(That was a hard experience to get through, but we certainly learned a lot from it.)*

get through to: to make contact with *(I've called several times, but I haven't been able to get through to him; the line is always busy.)*; to make understandable to *(I've told him that several times, but it just doesn't seem to get through to him.)*

get to: to have the opportunity *(I hope I get to go to the mountains this summer.)*; to reach *(The climbers should get to the summit by tomorrow morning.)*; to annoy *(slang)* *(His students' cruel remarks are getting to him.)*

get together: to come together, assemble (esp. socially) *(When can we get together for lunch?)*; to collect or assemble, put together *(I can't get these two parts of the puzzle together.)*; to come to accord, agree *(As soon as we can get together on this one point, we can finish the report.)*

get up: to arise *(I have to get up early tomorrow morning.)*; to climb up *(You can reach it if you get up on a chair.)*; to create, invent *(She couldn't get up the courage to do it.)*; *(informal)* to dress elaborately *(She got herself up like a princess.)*; to advance, make progress *(You're really getting up in the world!)*

get with *(slang):* to become up to date *(Get with it, man! You're way out of date.)*

CHAPTER SEVEN

"The Same, but Different"

Reading Fluency in English as a New Language

New Vocabulary in This Chapter: fluency, automaticity theory of reading, independent level, instructional level, frustration level, word retrieval, cognitive load, chunking, parsing, prosody, phonological loop

Fluency: No Signs of Cooling Down

Every year, the International Reading Association takes the pulse of its thousands of members by asking them to check off on a survey "what's hot and what's not" in reading topics and issues. For the past several years, reading fluency has among the top choices for "what's hot." The concept of fluency, measured by means of oral reading, has indeed been increasingly "hot" in the past few years, since the National Reading Panel validated it as a key reading competency in its report to the nation in 2000. It has continued to appear as a category in a comprehensive review of ELL literacy research by the National Literacy Panel (August & Shanahan, 2006).

A Working Definition of Fluency

The National Reading Panel defined fluency in the following way: "The fluent reader is one who can perform multiple tasks—such as word recognition and comprehension—at the same time" (National Reading Panel, 2000, 3.8).

Samuels (2007) puts it even more simply: "In order to comprehend a text, one must identify the words on the page and one must construct their meaning" (p. 564). Thus fluency is the part of the reading developmental process in which readers move beyond word recognition to beginning to stitch together meanings across words. Because of this linking function, it is sometimes called a "bridge" between decoding of words and comprehension of connected text.

In this book, we define *fluency* as the ability to recognize words and simultaneously construct meaning from connected text. Therefore, comprehension is a component of fluency.

Frequently, fluency is defined by performance metrics such as rate, accuracy, or prosody. All three of these measures may produce misleading readings for ELLs, however, because those three skills develop differently for ELLs than they do for native speakers. Rate is likely to be slower, accuracy lower, and prosody unnatural-sounding. At the other extreme, some ELLs have learned to perform an oral reading with speed, accuracy, and expression, yet may have no idea what they have just read. This common phenomenon has been noted by students in all of our classes over a period of several years.

In the field of ESL and foreign language learning, the word *fluency* carries a completely different meaning from the one used in the reading field. In language learning, when we say a person is *fluent*, we mean to say that he or she has native-like proficiency in a new language. It is unfortunate that these two different meanings of fluency are usually used interchangeably. In fact, other definitions of fluency are found in literature as well, and clarification is needed about which meaning of the word is in use. In this chapter and throughout the book, we use *fluency* to refer to a reader's ability to simultaneously decode and comprehend a written text.

Oral reading, on the other hand, is the means by which the unseen and elusive competency of fluency is best measured. Oral reading fluency as a measure of reading comprehension was first proposed as a valid classroom-based assessment in 1985 by Stanley Deno, a researcher in the special education field. He found that the way a young (L1 English) reader performed an oral reading from texts used in the actual classroom could tell teachers a lot about that reader's level of reading comprehension on other passages at a similar level. The information that could be derived from the *rate* and *accuracy* of the student's oral reading gave teachers a handy way to identify books at an appropriate level for the student, keep track of student progress, and provide additional help when indicated.

Also, oral reading was sensitive enough to show subtle improvements in reading—when reading comprehension went up, so did oral reading fluency scores (Deno, 1985).

Deno's proposal to use curriculum-based oral reading to assess reading progress was not the only research to show a strong correlation between oral reading and reading comprehension. Other studies showed strong validity for using oral reading as a measure of reading comprehension (Hintze, Shapiro, & Conte, 1997). Deno, Mirkin, and Chiang (1982) found high correlations between oral reading tasks and standardized reading comprehension tests; in another study, curriculum-based oral reading samples were able to distinguish students with learning disabilities from students from impoverished socioeconomic backgrounds and students in general education (Deno, Marston, Shinn, & Tindal, 1983). Fuchs, Fuchs, and Maxwell (1988) found stronger correlations between oral reading scores and standardized tests of reading comprehension than between standardized tests and question answering, oral recall, and written cloze. Jenkins and Jewell (1993) found oral reading to correlate strongly with reading comprehension activities. Hintze et al. (1997) and Fuchs and Deno (1992) found oral reading to be an equally robust measure of comprehension regardless of the kind of reading curriculum used. A confirmatory study by Shinn, Knutson, Good, Tilly, and Collins (1992) found that oral reading "fits current theoretical models of reading well and can be validated as a measure of general reading achievement, including comprehension" (p. 476). This compelling research led people in the reading field to take a closer look at fluency.

ELLs and Fluency Research

Although there is some research about fluency and reading comprehension for young ELLs, much of it is buried in titles and keywords that don't reveal the presence of ELLs in the sampled student groups. Baker and Good (1995) found the correlation between an oral reading fluency measure and a commonly used measure of reading comprehension in second-grade Spanish ELLs to be comparable to that of their L1 English peers. The study also noted that "[curriculum-based oral] reading in English may be a better measure of English reading proficiency than English oral language proficiency for bilingual students" (p. 573). In other words, the processes involved when ELLs read aloud resemble their silent reading more than speaking does. As noted elsewhere in this book, an ELL's oral proficiency in English may not reflect his or her level of academic language, whether it be reading or writing. In another study, Ramirez (2001) found that there were higher correlations between fifth grade Spanish ELLs' oral reading fluency and several measures of reading comprehension than there were with any other measure, including simple decoding.

The Automaticity Theory

The high correlation of rapid and accurate oral reading and silent reading comprehension corresponds well with the *automaticity theory*, a key reading theory that was posited by reading researchers LaBerge and Samuels in 1974. They hypothesized that readers learned to read better when they were able to move from effortful decoding of words, which took all of their attention, to unconscious and automatic decoding, which allowed them to pay attention to constructing meaning while reading. In effect, readers who could not process text fluently didn't have enough mental energy "left over" for understanding a text. Another way to frame fluency is to think of it as developing "processing efficiency" (Koda, 2005). When it is difficult to process text because decoding is very cumbersome, mental attention cannot be devoted to reading comprehension.

The reason for the delay in using oral fluency to measure reading comprehension was that many teachers questioned its validity because it did not seem plausible. They assumed it meant that oral reading and reading comprehension would take place at the same time, using the same text, and that just didn't make sense. Teachers knew from their classroom experience that when students are involved in reading out loud in class, it reduces their ability to construct meaning at the same time. They are too busy pronouncing the text to be able to comprehend it deeply. To give an analogy, it would be like taking Karima, a new driver, out on the road for a road test and then at the same time judging her on her posture!

However, the original research and the confirmatory research were not structured to combine the oral reading with an assessment of comprehension; actually, the correlations between oral reading fluency and silent reading comprehension were established using different texts at different times.

Oral reading fluency checks were proposed as a handy, cost-free assessment that could tell the teacher something about a student's reading level without a costly standardized reading test, in a fraction of the time and with much less stress. It was never meant to replace other reading comprehension assessments, nor to substitute for the silent reading that should occur in classrooms on a daily basis. Keeping track of oral reading fluency was more like taking a "snapshot" of a student's reading progress, using a certain text, at certain moments in time, to assess the need for reading intervention and for flexible grouping for guided reading (Blachowicz, Sullivan, & Cieply, 2001).

Fluency Instruction

Another key work, called "The Method of Repeated Readings" (Samuels, 1979), found that when students reread passages up to four times, their comprehension of not only that passage but other passages improved dramatically. The repetition of the words and word patterns made them able to be retrieved more automatically so more attention could be paid to meaning making. The method of repeated reading, whether oral or silent, did not take hold on a widespread basis until fluency became highly regarded as an assessment method. Ironically, what was originally a handy, low-stress way to measure reading comprehension has morphed into a tool to improve reading itself—a true case of assessment informing instruction.

Components of Fluency Instruction

Fluency instruction includes one or more of the following characteristics: (1) some kind of reading repetition or practice; (2) modeling by an expert or more proficient other; and (3) some kind of progress monitoring (Rasinski, 2003). Now, many kinds of fluency instruction are being implemented in the classroom, with impressive results. Fluency instruction includes such diverse techniques and methods as Readers' Theatre, poetry performance, lyric singing, paired reading, timed repeated reading, simulated TV broadcasts, podcasts, choral reading, and more (Rasinski, Blachowicz, & Lems, 2006).

In some fluency programs, the reading levels of striving readers have been boosted by several grade levels in only a few months. There is also widespread anecdotal evidence that students enjoy these activities, too, and that they increase students' motivation to read. In addition to the more automatic retrieval of words, fluency instruction ensures that striving readers are reading more words than they otherwise would. For ELLs, this is even more important: "It is clear that if fluent reading is to be developed by English language learners," warned Hiebert and Fisher (2006), "the amount of exposure to texts that students have in classrooms needs to increase" (p. 291).

There is evidence that fluency instruction delivers results for ELLs. Hiebert and Fisher (2006) found that first-grade ELLs benefited from daily fluency interventions that included repeated reading and modeling by the teacher, whether they were reading highly decodable books or those with more high-frequency, high-imagery vocabulary. Pluck (2006) implemented an audiotape-assisted reading fluency intervention in New Zealand and found almost double the level of progress in word recognition, accuracy, comprehension, and spelling in ELLs compared with native

English speakers. Koskinen et al. (1995) used tape-assisted book reading as part of a home–school literacy program with first-grade ELLs, and both the teacher and parents noticed a marked increase by the children in daily conversations about books and increased motivation to read. In addition, children became able to read more difficult books.

Fluency instruction has many benefits for ELLs, but it is important to separate fluency assessment from fluency instruction, for reasons we discuss below.

Text Difficulty Levels

At one time, oral reading was a central component of the American classroom (Allington, 2002). Oral reading with accompanying comprehension questions was used as a basis for evaluating students' reading skills, and Betts (1946) established three different standards based on the percentage of words students read correctly. Students were considered to be reading at the *independent level* for a given text if they read it with 99% accuracy and 90% comprehension; they were considered to be at the *instructional level* with 95% accuracy and 75% comprehension, and the *frustration level* at below 95% accuracy and 50% comprehension. Reading specialists still use these designations or variations of them when they assess students' oral reading levels for placement, for small group assignments, to match students with the right text difficulty level, and as the basis for reading intervention when needed. The independent level, which varies for each student and changes across time, is used to select texts for extensive reading and for fluency instruction because it will be a satisfying and successful reading experience. The instructional level is the focus of classroom instruction because it addresses students at the edge of their knowledge and challenges them to move to a higher level with support. The frustration level, as its name indicates, can frustrate students and cause them to give up. Many students who fail in school were given reading material that was beyond their instructional range. For ELLs, finding these ranges is very important, and teachers need to design reading activities for maximal enjoyment and challenge.

Why Oral Reading Does Not Assess ELLs Fairly

Despite the strong case for fluency instruction with ELLs, using oral reading as an assessment of ELLs' reading comprehension is problematic (Birch, 2007; Helman, 2005; Lems, 2005; Riedel, 2007) due to several key issues.

The Foreign Accent Factor

First is the "foreign accent factor": ELLs may mispronounce a word because some of the sounds do not exist in their first language and they have not learned to say them in English, or because the letters they are trying to pronounce map to different sounds in their native language. As a result, raters may mark miscues (mistakes) in the reading performance even though the reader knows the meaning of a word. For example, native speakers of Persian (or Farsi, the language of Iran) may pronounce the letter *w* as a /v/ in English because the closest equivalent to the *w* in English is pronounced as a /v/ in Persian. Therefore, a Persian ELL might read the word *went* as /vent/, and a rubric would classify it as a substitution error and mark it as a miscue even though the reader may have recognized and understood the word. The foreign accent issue becomes even greater when ELLs start their study of English in adolescence or beyond, when their foreign accent is more likely to be set in place.

The flip side of the foreign accent issue is that ELLs may struggle a long time trying to pronounce an unknown word correctly, and thus score at a lower fluency rate than their real comprehension level. In particular, proper nouns, such as place names and family names, are especially opaque—that is, likely to have pronunciation that isn't easily decodable. As a result, ELLs may spend a long time trying to sound them out.

> *When I was studying adult ESL oral reading for my dissertation I found that the students made far more miscues on proper nouns in the passage than native speakers would have made; for example, most of the Chinese ELLs in the study were stopped cold by the word* Indianapolis *in the passage and tried to pronounce it many times, mostly coming to an unsuccessful conclusion. They lost several seconds in their reading rate just from that one word, and the miscue was deducted anyway.*—KRISTIN

Being assessed at a lower level because of oral reading also affects L1 learners with problems of *word retrieval* (quickly retrieving and pronouncing a word from long-term memory). They may know a word by sight but have trouble pronouncing it rapidly, and as a result they are sometimes placed in lower reading groups than is warranted (German & Newman, 2007). These learners, and ELLs who take a long time to pronounce words, are likely to be misclassified and may be given less challenging reading as a result.

When oral fluency snapshots by ELLs are rated on fluency charts based on samples of L1 English children, the scores are likely to be misleading at some points of development. As Thomas and Collier (2002) have noted, it takes 5 to 7 years for ELLs to achieve a level of English proficiency on a par with native speakers of English, so this will be reflected in fluency scores for some time. A score below the mean for a certain time of year at a certain grade level may not warrant the concern that would be raised for a native speaker of English because the student is learning an additional language. By extension, making high-stakes decisions about students or schools based on an ELL's oral reading scores alone is problematic for the previously mentioned reasons.

ELLs and Word Calling

Another issue of reading fluency concerning ELLs is word calling, or decoding a text without comprehending it. If ELLs do decode and pronounce the words accurately, they may still not have the words in their English listening vocabulary, and thus may not comprehend the text. Word calling, famously dubbed "barking at print" by researcher Jeanne Chall, can occur with L1 English speakers, but research tends to support the notion that it is not commonplace. Students who are slow and inaccurate oral readers are also weak in answering comprehension questions that are at grade level (Markell & Deno, 1997). Also, researchers found that teachers who consider their students to be word callers may be using subjective criteria (Hamilton & Shinn, 2000).

However, word calling may be a real phenomenon in the oral reading of some ELLs. Helman (2005) notes that Spanish ELLs she studied in Arizona struggled with comprehension questions in an oral reading assessment and warned, "A classroom teacher may make the assumption from hearing students reading out loud that comprehension is occurring. This assumption is less likely to be true for English learners, who may have adequate accuracy and fluency on lower-level passages, but may not understand the vocabulary and content" (p. 221). A longitudinal investigation of 261 Spanish ELLs from first through sixth grade revealed that although their word decoding stayed on pace for the norm, their reading comprehension scores began to fall behind, starting in the third grade (Nakamoto, Lindsey, & Manis, 2007).

Samuels also mentions this concern: "As Riedel reports in his research, about 15% of the students who take the Oral Reading Fluency test [of the DIBELS] get misidentified as good readers, when, in fact, they have poor comprehension. These misidentified students are often English-language learners who have vocabulary problems that interfere with comprehension" (Samuels, 2007, p. 564).

Of course, the ability of ELLs literate in their L1 to read aloud swiftly and accurately is influenced by the linguistic proximity of the L1 writing system to the English writing system. One study of literate adult ELLs from mixed language backgrounds found a significant correlation between English oral reading and silent reading comprehension for Spanish or Polish speakers, a lower correlation for Ukrainian or Bulgarian speakers, and no correlation for students whose L1 was Chinese, even though the students did equivalently well on measures of reading comprehension (Lems, 2005). The results appear to be related to orthographic distance because Spanish and Polish have the same basic alphabet as English, unlike Ukrainian and Bulgarian, which use the Cyrillic alphabet, or Chinese, which is logosyllabic. The students from languages with more written linguistic proximity to English, like Spanish and Polish, found it easier to decode words in English because it looked more like their native language than those from linguistically distant orthographies, like Cyrillic or Chinese.

Because of the complicated nature of cross-linguistic influence and the diverse orthographic backgrounds and experiences ELLs bring to the classroom, oral reading may be a less valid measure of reading comprehension than it is for L1 English speakers, at least when learners are at the Entering, Beginning, or Developing levels of English proficiency (Lems, 2005.

Even when ELLs decode well and know the words they are reading, the *cognitive load*, or mental engagement, required is considerably heavier because the words are not in their first language. When the mental requirement of reading in a new language is compounded by the need to pronounce words accurately and rapidly, it's no wonder oral reading by ELLs might not match their reading comprehension. At the least, they should not be evaluated on the same benchmarks as those used for native speakers (Birch, 2007). On the other hand, monitoring progress in an individual student over time can still be meaningful because increases in oral reading scores reflect increases in reading level for both L1 English learners and ELLs (Fuchs, Fuchs, Hosp, & Jenkins, 2001; Lems, 2005).

Fluency Instruction for ELLs: Great, but for Different Reasons

Unlike oral reading assessment, fluency instruction can be highly recommended for ELLs, not only for all the reasons it benefits native English speakers, but because of special benefits it confers, benefits that go well beyond those derived by a native speaker. Six main benefits of fluency instruction for ELLs are listed below.

Fluency Instruction Gives Practice in Chunking and Prosody

In addition to increasing rate and accuracy of word recognition, fluency instruction gives ELL readers practice in developing two important reading competencies: *chunking* and *prosody*. Chunking (which is sometimes called *parsing*) is the ability to separate or combine written text into meaningful phrase or clause units. It requires knowledge of syntax, and it develops unconsciously for native speakers as they learn the patterns of a language through listening to it and speaking it. When they start to learn to read, they apply the auditory memory of how words cluster together when they are spoken, and apply that to the stream of words across a line of text.

For Ann, a native speaker of English, developing the chunking skill is closely related to her auditory memory of the sounds of the words, so it is natural that the fluency field closely associates chunking with prosody— the vocal patterns and inflections that people use when speaking and reading aloud. For example, when Ann "reads the punctuation" of a sentence, by pausing at periods or changing intonation patterns for questions, she is showing that she can chunk the phrases or clauses of a sentence correctly.

However, prosody goes well beyond the ability to chunk the words in a sentence. It includes interpretive features such as "getting into character" for reading certain texts by speaking more loudly, using variation in intonation, or pausing for emphasis. When working with ELLs, we should reckon that these additional oral reading skills might come considerably later than chunking skills, or may not come at all. Because of their developing oracy in English, ELLs may have limited knowledge of how a written text might sound in terms of its expressive features. Therefore, for ELLs, we should expect knowledge of chunking to precede expressive reading, and it may be premature or unrealistic to expect ELLs to read expressively. Nonetheless, practicing both chunking and prosody are important ways to boost reading comprehension, and they can be practiced together.

Fluency Practice Aids Expressive Reading

Expressive reading can assist in comprehension. It is usually thought to include both vocal interpretation of the words and of the punctuation, and includes pausing, intonation patterns, and word lengthening. Johnson and Moore (1997) found a moderate but significant relationship between the reading comprehension scores of ELLs and how "native-like" their pausing behaviors were when reading English text aloud. Seeing how prosody looks and hearing how it sounds are very useful for ELLs, and fluency practice gives them a chance to do both at the same time. In English, the most important words in a text are longer, louder, and higher-pitched, which underscores their importance. Reading along silently with a text that is being read aloud helps students create these associations. Oral reading practice probably has positive washback in ELLs' pronunciation and speaking fluency too, but this has not been verified.

Kathleen McColaugh, a Spanish teacher at Addison Trail High School in Addison, Illinois, says about oral reading:

Whenever I have to read aloud in front of an "audience" I never comprehend what I am reading. The weird thing is, though, when I don't understand something that I have read silently, I read it aloud. As I am reading it aloud, I accentuate the words of importance and then I understand. This seems odd to me since I would classify myself as a visual learner. Even when I write, I usually speak aloud as I write. It really helps me to hear and see what I am trying to understand.

Oral Reading Is a Way to Practice Phonological Decoding

Pronouncing written words, or phonological decoding, is a vital skill for beginning readers. The ability to decode and pronounce words is one of the most powerful predictors of reading success, even as early as first grade (Bowers, Golden, Kennedy, & Young, 1994; Share & Stanovich, 1995; Torgeson & Burgess, 1998; Wagner, Torgeson, & Rashotte, 1994). It has been found that this ability crosses many languages, including those with other kinds of orthographies. Koda (2005) puts it at "number one": "Phonological decoding is perhaps the most indispensable competence for reading acquisition in all languages" (p. 34). That is because, even for mature readers, having a good phonological representation of a word helps retrieve it from working memory. It is a core literacy skill (Koda, 2005, p. 185).

When we see or hear a written word that we know, we retrieve it from our long-term memory and move it into our short-term memory for use. How does the word get there to begin with? It is stored through a process called the *phonological loop* (Baddeley, Gathercole, & Papagno, 1998, p. 1158; Birch, 2007). When we encounter a new word for the first time, the phonological loop converts the visual or audio stimulus of the word into a sound-based "phonological image." The brain in turn, creates a short-term "slot" to hold the word, which can be filled with a semantic association at that time or later, at which time we have learned it. The phonological loop is like a messenger who takes the information and moves it into auditory memory. The loop moves data from the eyes or ears into short-term and then long-term storage. Rehearsal solidifies the word in long-term memory through visual and auditory repetition.

What ELLs do not have available in their long-term memory is that reservoir of remembered words, the listening vocabulary, that native speakers build up through the natural, automatic process of acquiring our first language. As a result, it's really important that ELLs have enough exposure to a word to secure it in memory through the phonological loop, and fluency practice provides that exposure. In fact, ELLs in a repeated reading study cited repetition as one of the factors contributing to their reading comprehension progress (Taguchi, Takayasu-Maass, & Gorsuch, 2004).

Fluency Practice Builds Stamina for Reading Connected Text

In addition to vocabulary growth, fluency practice helps build stamina in the key skill of reading connected text. Hiebert and Fisher (2006) note that there are reports of sharp discrepancies in the ability of first-grade Spanish ELLs to read individual words from a list compared with reading connected text (p. 291). Reading comprehension requires moving swiftly and accurately through connected texts in many genres, and fluency helps students build the endurance to keep moving and bring text processing up to speed.

Fluency Practice Boosts Confidence and Builds Motivation

An additional benefit of fluency practice is that children who have the opportunity to listen to or practice passages multiple times, whether for a performance, a home–school program with audiotapes, or through partner reading, develop more self-confidence and independence as readers (Koskinen et al., 1995) in a setting with a low affective filter.

Repeated Reading Increases Reading Rate

The rate at which people read in a second language is slower than that of their first language, and below a certain rate, it is impossible for readers to keep up with an academic curriculum (Birch, 2007; Rasinski, 2000). ELLs benefit from opportunities to learn techniques to increase their reading rate so that they can function successfully academically. These might involve timed repeated readings (oral or silent), charting progress on a graph, or repeating reading until reaching a certain target rate (Anderson, 1999).

Evidence of Success in Fluency Instruction for ELLs

Research has shown impressive results for ELLs in fluency programs. For example, ELLs gained an average of 2 years in their reading comprehension level from a tape-assisted reading program offering 15 weeks of daily fluency instruction for one hour a day (Pluck, 2006). The students read short, high-interest stories along with a tape, repeating their practice until they could perform the reading on their own. The program from which the study came, Rainbow Reading, is now widely used in New Zealand and increasingly in other English-speaking countries. Li and Nes (2001) studied Chinese ELLs who received weekly English language paired reading activities at grade level, led by a skilled adult. The children made impressive gains in accuracy and fluency, even during the maintenance period, when the sessions became less frequent and then ceased. In another case, McCauley and McCauley (1992) successfully used teacher-led choral reading to promote language learning by ELLs and confirmed its success. Kozub (2000) discovered that Readers' Theatre was very effective with her ELLs. Lems (2001) and others have used poetry performance in adult ESL classrooms. Initially, the language instructor can model the text with exaggerated stress and intonation to highlight its prosodic contours. Practicing the prosody while preparing for a poetry or drama performance allows students to develop the expressive features so important to the development of L2 oral fluency and adds a positive social dimension to the practice.

HOW DOES THIS LOOK IN THE CLASSROOM?

Segmenting Text

Segmenting text into lines that break at natural phrase endings, or by marking with slashes, is a great technique for ELLs. In one study, segmented text produced better comprehension in young readers than conventional text (O'Shea & Sindelar, 1983). This technique was validated in research comparing it to other techniques that used only repeated reading (Hoffman, 1987). Of course, poetry naturally segments phrases into different lines, and lines of a skit or Readers' Theatre show the breaks of different partners in a conversation. All of these are good places to start to look for authentic text that is naturally segmented. Rasinski (1990) proposed an alternate method of checking chunking knowledge, not by having students read aloud, but by having them mark the text themselves, with a pencil. To be sure there was high reliability, Rasinski first had skilled readers mark the texts. A correct score for the students consisted of a check made by at least 50% of the skilled readers. To see an example of these two ways to segment text, see Appendix 7.1.

Trying Out a Creative Fluency Program:
Choral Reading, Echo Reading, or Popcorn Reading

Many fine fluency instructional programs are now available, and some, such as Read Naturally, include activities that make reading aloud and repeated reading part of an authentic integrated experience. Choral reading, with the instructor in the lead, works very well for very new ELLs who do not know the sounds of words and do not want to be singled out. Echo reading allows for a little more individual performance but still safely shadows the model speaker. Popcorn reading can be done in small groups, where ELLs take turns reading a short passage, then stop when they feel like it and pass the reading on to the next person. This works in a sheltered classroom but can be embarrassing for some students in a classroom mixed with native speakers.

Using Audio-Assisted Oral Reading

Many reading programs now have audio-assisted versions that ELLs and others can use to practice reading aloud. Whether it's in the form of audiobooks on tape or CD, an audio track in a classroom or computer lab, or singing along with a musical recording, audio-assisted tracks are an excellent method for modeling language for ELLs and providing access to the sounds, appearance, and meanings of English. One caution: Passages read by a voice synthesizer, and some Internet audio samples, do not have natural prosody, and therefore may not assist students in acquiring natural language.

Building the Comprehension Habit

Professor Yvonne Gonzalez, a specialist in bilingual special education at Texas Women's University, checks comprehension as her ELLs read aloud by asking them to read a sentence for her, then stopping them halfway through and asking them to finish the sentence. "If they are really constructing meaning while they read," she says, "they will be able to finish the sentence with a logical sentence ending" (personal communication, 2008). Another way of checking comprehension is to ask students to retell the gist of each paragraph to a partner.

Avoiding Oral Reading in High-Stakes Assessment

Oral reading should not be relied on as a significant measure of ELL reading proficiency in the beginning or intermediate levels of achievement. Instead, think of it as an additional source of data in a one-on-one setting for a snapshot of classroom progress. Oral reading assessments, after all, do not resemble real reading experiences because their goal is not comprehension. When using fluency assessments with a comprehension component, allow ELLs to read a text silently more than once, do not impose an arbitrary speed limit, and be sure to let students clearly understand that there is a comprehension component before beginning the activity.

Creating Classroom Fluency Norms

Establishing fluency norms makes sense because native speaker fluency rates do not always reflect rates of ELLs. If you work in a setting with many ELLs, we suggest creating local norms by collecting students' reading fluency scores over time and building the database as more students are assessed. If school fluency measures are already taken, disaggregate the scores for ELLs, and be prepared to expect somewhat lower scores from students whose native languages are orthographically distant from English.

Any Balanced Literacy Program Needs Silent Reading

Make sure that classroom practice in oral reading doesn't deprive learners of that critical silent reading experience, which may not be possible for them to get at home. Some students depend on the school to learn how to do silent reading and to get a chance to practice it every day. Reading can be a social activity, but most of all, it is an individual one. Make sure both take place every day.

"Pacing and Racing" Can Be Fun—but Only to a Point

Students who read text very slowly cannot keep up with their schoolwork, and that means that ELLs need to achieve a comparable reading rate to that of their L1 peers over time. Timed repeated reading and other fluency rate practices can help students increase their reading rate and can serve as motivators. When doing repeated reading to increase rate, passages should be at the students' independent reading level so that the focus can be on processing text more rapidly rather than guessing the meanings of unknown words. A set of instructions for one way to carry out timed repeated reading is provided in Appendix 7.3.

Some computer-based programs can also help build reading rate. However, it shouldn't be the main point of fluency practice, or even of repeated reading practice (Zutell, Donelson, Bevans, & Todt, 2006, p. 270). When students practice in order to build their reading rate, they are not building the habit of reading for comprehension. Although a rate increase may apply to other reading passages, the reading done in timed settings is not likely to yield high levels of comprehension. Of course, this is exactly what so much high-stakes testing asks students to do: it forces them to rush through unknown passages and answer comprehension questions with little time for reflection or rereading. If we know that's not good in the classroom, why is it used for so many standardized tests?

QUESTIONS FOR FURTHER STUDY

1. If you had to choose three important ideas from this chapter, which would you choose? How can you apply these ideas to your larger knowledge of teaching English as a new language?

2. With a partner, practice reading the passage provided in Appendix 7.2 aloud for 1 minute. Repeat four times. Plot your rate, using the procedure and scoring charts in Appendix 7.3. What differences did you note?

3. If you are able to listen to the oral reading of ELLs, jot down notes about their reading performances. Did anything surprise you?

4. Did you read aloud in school as a child? How did you feel about it? Share with a partner. How might that influence how you would plan oral reading activities?

5. Have you ever read a text aloud without understanding a word of it? Talk about it.

6. Look at the three ways the sample text is presented in Appendix 7.1. If possible, find three different people and ask each one to read the text in one of the three ways: unmarked, marked, or separated by lines. Compare the performances. Which way of presenting the text would be most appropriate for English readers at the Entering or Beginning level? Developing, Expanding, or Bridging? Reaching level? Did you notice differences in rate, accuracy, phrasing, or expression with the different presentations? Talk about it.

7. Do you know people who read well, but cannot read aloud expressively? Do you think reading aloud expressively is an important quality for teachers, or optional? Do certain kinds of teachers need to read expressively more than others?

8. Looking at the quote from Kathleen McColaugh, do you feel that hearing your own voice as you read helps or hinders you? Why? Relate your discussion of this answer to the main ideas of this chapter.

Two Ways to Mark Text for Oral Reading

A. Original text

Salty food may seem like the least of your worries, especially if you're among the 40% of people who mindlessly shake salt on every dish. An extra dash here, a few sprinkles there—what's the big deal?

A lot, when you consider the fact that a mere teaspoon of the stuff contains all 2,300 milligrams (mg) of your recommended daily allotment. Yet daily salt consumption is on the rise in the United States—from 2,300 mg in the 1970s to more than 3,300 mg today. And according to Monell Chemical Senses Center researchers, 77% of that sodium intake comes from processed-food purveyors and restaurants. Their motivation: Pile on the salt so we don't miss natural flavors and fresh ingredients.

Why is that a problem? With ever-expanding portion sizes, supersalty foods are displacing fresh fruits and vegetables, which are rich in potassium. And a 1:2 ratio of dietary salt to potassium is critical for your health. Studies show that a high-sodium, low-potassium diet is linked to a host of maladies, including high blood pressure, stroke, osteoporosis, and exercise-induced asthma (Murrow, 2008).

B. Text divided into phrases, retaining punctuation marks

Salty food may seem like the least of your worries,
especially if you're among the 40% of people
who mindlessly shake salt on every dish.
An extra dash here,
a few sprinkles there—
what's the big deal?
A lot,
when you consider the fact
that a mere teaspoon of the stuff
contains all 2,300 milligrams (mg)
of your recommended daily allotment.
Yet daily salt consumption
is on the rise in the United States
from 2,300 mg in the 1970s
to more than 3,300 mg today.
And according to Monell Chemical Senses Center researchers,
77% of that sodium intake
comes from processed-food purveyors and restaurants.
Their motivation:
Pile on the salt
so we don't miss natural flavors and fresh ingredients.
Why is that a problem?
With ever-expanding portion sizes,
supersalty foods are displacing
fresh fruits and vegetables,
which are rich in potassium.

(cont.)

And a 1:2 ratio of dietary salt to potassium
is critical for your health.
Studies show that a high-sodium,
low-potassium diet
is linked to a host of maladies,
including high blood pressure,
stroke,
osteoporosis,
and exercise-induced asthma.

C. Text divided by notches, with/for "half stop" (pause) and // for "full stop" (longer pause)

Salty food may seem like the least of your worries,/ especially if you're among the 40% of people/ who mindlessly shake salt on every dish.// An extra dash here,/ a few sprinkles there/—what's the big deal?//

A lot,/ when you consider the fact/ that a mere teaspoon of the stuff/ contains all 2,300 milligrams (mg) of your recommended daily allotment.// Yet daily salt consumption is on the rise in the United States//—from 2,300 mg in the 1970s/ to more than 3,300 mg today.// And according to Monell Chemical Senses Center researchers,/ 77% of that sodium intake/ comes from processed-food purveyors and restaurants.// Their motivation://
Pile on the salt/ so we don't miss natural flavors and fresh ingredients.// Why is that a problem?// With ever-expanding portion sizes,/ supersalty foods are displacing fresh fruits and vegetables,/ which are rich in potassium.// And a 1:2 ratio of dietary salt to potassium/ is critical for your health./ Studies show that a high-sodium,/ low-potassium diet/ is linked to a host of maladies,/ including high blood pressure,/ stroke,/ osteoporosis,/ and exercise-induced asthma.//

Instructions for marking text

1. Read the text aloud, preferably with another colleague marking text as you read in a natural, relaxed manner. If you do not feel fully confident in your judgment of pauses, ask a highly proficient colleague to read it aloud while you mark the text.
2. Mark a full stop (//) between any two sentences or after a colon.
3. Mark a half stop (/) after a comma, between items in a list and between long subjects and the prepositional phrases or predicates that follow them.
4. Note: Educators not experienced in marking oral reading tend to place too many breaks in a text, creating an interpretation which does not sound natural. A fluent oral reader has fewer pauses than one would predict, and the pauses are not very long. Of course, interactive read-alouds and dramatic passages heighten the speaker's pauses and features of intonation more than reading informational text.
5. Before having ELLs read a marked text aloud, it is a good idea to model several times, allowing students to hear the natural pauses of a proficient speaker of English.
6. Students can mark these texts themselves after they are sufficiently experienced in reading and listening to oral texts.

Numbering Text for Timed Repeated Readings

	Salty food may seem like the least of your worries, especially if you're among
15	the 40% of people who mindlessly shake salt on every dish. An extra dash here,
32	a few sprinkles there—what's the big deal?
39	A lot, when you consider the fact that a mere teaspoon of the stuff contains all
55	2,300 milligrams (mg) of your recommended daily allotment. Yet daily salt
66	consumption is on the rise in the United States—from 2,300 mg in the 1970s to more
83	than 3,300 mg today. And according to Monell Chemical Senses Center researchers,
96	77% of that sodium intake comes from processed-food purveyors and
107	restaurants. Their motivation: Pile on the salt so we don't miss natural flavors and
122	fresh ingredients.
123	Why is that a problem? With ever-expanding portion sizes, supersalty foods
136	are displacing fresh fruits and vegetables, which are rich in potassium. And a 1:2 ratio
152	of dietary salt to potassium is critical for your health. Studies show that a high-
167	sodium, low-potassium diet is linked to a host of maladies, including high blood
180	pressure, stroke, osteoporosis, and exercise-induced asthma (Murrow, 2008).
Total:	
187	

Guidelines for numbering text for timed repeated reading practice:

- Put number to left of text, matching number with first word of the line.
- Do not count titles or subheadings, and tell students not to count them.
- Count each number as a word.
- Count each hyphenated word as two words.
- Teach students to count their own timed passages by starting from the left of the line up to the last word read.

Procedure and Scoring Charts for Timed Repeated Reading

PROCEDURE

Preparing the reading:

1. Ensure that the reading is at the independent or instructional reading level of the student (there should be very few unknown words). When possible, use a reading that has the word count already marked. Many commercially produced materials come with numbered lines, and some word-processing programs also allow for automatic line numbering. If not available, prepare your own numbered readings using the instructions in Appendix 7.2. Take care that the passage is clean and easy to read, preferably with double-spaced lines. Since students are learning to count their own words, the numbers should be included next to the text, unlike teacher-administered fluency assessments in which the student does not see the number of words he or she has read.

2. Keep a file of readings at a wide range of reading proficiency levels. A fluency instructional unit should have a sufficient number of readings for students at a number of proficiency levels, enough to last the duration of the unit. Try to include passages from a number of genres, including informational and narrative text. As students' proficiency increases, so should the length of the passages.

3. Provide copies of the two charts in this appendix for each student to use. Students must have a copy of the first chart, "Chart for a Single Reading," for each new passage they read. The second chart, "Chart for a Set of Readings," is used across a series of different passages. The top count from each individual repeated reading is entered into the second chart each time students complete a new passage.

4. Make sure students understand the purpose and the procedure for doing the readings before beginning the project. Clarify that this is a targeted exercise focusing on reading rate, not comprehension. For ELLs, it is useful to take everyone through a "dry run" with the whole class, modeling the procedure, before starting to use the charts.

5. Decide whether you will conduct the timed fluency practices as a whole class, in pairs, or individually, and keep to that format. If using pairs, train the timer to carefully report the words read to the reader. This may take some practice. It is important to create a low-stress, noncompetitive atmosphere, so pairs should be thoughtfully assigned. It is also possible to let students choose their own partners in some situations.

The reading procedure:

1. Students read the passage for 1 minute, then count the number of words they read and plot it in the first column of the chart.

2. Without discussion, start the clock to read the same passage a second time, and ask students to mark in the second column the number of words read correctly.

(cont.)

3. Repeat a third and fourth time, marking the number of words read on the chart.
4. Ask students to draw a line graph connecting the oral readings, then to calculate the difference between the fastest reading and the slowest one and write it in the space at the bottom of the graph.
5. The first two or three times students perform repeated readings, bring the class together and ask students to discuss the experience. How did their oral performance change as they reread the passage? How did their understanding of the passage change by reading it?
6. The next time students do timed readings, they will use the "Chart for a Set of Readings" to track their best performances over time. Take care that the texts being compared are at the same reading level. The best performances will very probably show improvement over time. When students are ready to move to a higher reading level, have them start a new tracking sheet.
7. The "Chart for a Set of Readings" may use different minimum and maximum numbers of words per minute, depending on the proficiency level of the student.

Note. This timed repeated reading method is not a reading comprehension activity. Its purpose is to build automaticity through rehearsal. It doesn't strive to cultivate expressive reading or performance. It can be done on a regular basis, but for very short periods of time, and never as a substitute for comprehension building.

(cont.)

CHART FOR A SINGLE READING

340				
330				
320				
310				
300				
290				
280				
270				
260				
250				
240				
230				
220				
210				
200				
190				
180				
170				
160				
150				
140				
130				
120				
110				
100				
90				
80				
Title of passage:	First reading	Second reading	Third reading	Fourth reading
Slowest score	Fastest score	Difference:		

(cont.)

CHART FOR A SET OF READINGS

340						
330						
320						
310						
300						
290						
280						
270						
260						
250						
240						
230						
220						
210						
200						
190						
180						
170						
160						
150						
140						
130						
120						
110						
100						
90						
80						
Best score from each passage	Name of passage:	Name of passage:	Name of passage:	Name of passage:	Name of passage:	Name of passage:

CHAPTER EIGHT

Achieving Comprehension in L2 English Reading

New Vocabulary in This Chapter: *reading comprehension, reading comprehension strategy, frontloading, keyword method, punctuation, inferencing, signal words, transitions, and connectors, graphic organizers, semantic map, T-chart, Venn diagram/H-chart, content frame/semantic feature analysis grid, text structure, visualization, audio imaging, metacognition, think-alouds, literacy advantage, extensive reading, drop everything and read (DEAR), sustained silent reading (SSR), free voluntary reading (FVR)*

In the previous chapters, we reviewed some of the components that are needed to create a "syndrome of success" for an ELL reader—proficient oracy, decoding, an understanding of morphemes, word formation processes, cognates and collocations, and the attainment of reading fluency. This chapter focuses on how these work together to actually bring about *reading comprehension*, the ability to construct meaning from a given written text. Reading comprehension is not a static competency; it varies according to the purposes for reading and the text that is involved. When the prerequisite skills are in place, reading becomes an evolving interaction between the text and the background knowledge of the reader. This is accomplished through use of strategies, both cognitive and metacognitive.

Comprehending Connected Text in a New Language Is Hard!

Even if an ELL is an able decoder in English, the level of effort required to read for meaning in real time academic situations can be a monumental task. Look how author Richard Rodriguez (1982) describes his own reading in English as a new language:

> Most books, of course, I barely understood. While reading Plato's Republic, I needed to keep looking at the book jacket to remind myself what the text was about. (p. 64)

One might ask how Rodriguez could be reading a book at such an advanced level in English but still not reading with comprehension. How could he read and yet not read? And what is it that makes reading in a new language so overwhelming? Perhaps part of the answer can be found in the less extensive listening vocabulary upon which ELLs can draw when reading written words they have never seen before. When we read words that we haven't heard, we don't get the advantages of the phonological loop, the cycle that helps us retrieve words from long-term memory by means of phonological information. Perhaps it is partly due to the opacity of English orthography, which makes it harder to "hear" the way unknown words look on the page. Part of it may result from incomplete knowledge of the syntax and grammar patterns of English. But it is surely also the limits of working memory. When we struggle with sentences in a new language, reading takes a great deal of cognitive energy. As a result, retaining the gist of the previous sentences in a paragraph or of previous paragraphs in working memory is hard to do as we move through a text.

Even when decoding is no longer very effortful, it is still much harder to move along through a text and construct meaning from it as we read in a new language. We might describe this as a real-time "delay." When the rate of processing meaning from text can't "catch up" with the rate of our decoding, the result may be the strange phenomenon of decoding but not comprehending, as lamented by Richard Rodriguez above. Native speakers experience this phenomenon, too, and reading teachers have developed many strategies, such as highlighting text or reading and retelling to a partner, to help them build the comprehension habit as they read.

These techniques work for ELLs too, and strategies are even more necessary—if such a thing is possible! If Sara, a 10-year-old ELL from Peru, develops the comprehension habit when reading "easy" chapter books, it will be less overwhelming for her later, when texts become denser and longer. If texts become overwhelming, the struggle associated with reading makes it become unpleasant, and then a vicious cycle develops. In it, the student avoids reading and begins to fall further and further behind. Stanovich compares the phenomenon to the Bible story of the Parable of the Talents, which can be paraphrased to mean "the rich get richer, and the poor get poorer" (Stanovich, 1986).

Making the transition from general vocabulary, both oral and written, to the content-specific language of the classroom is hard even for native speakers, but it is especially challenging for ELLs. Often ELLs are mainstreamed from bilingual and sheltered English programs just at the exact moment content reading and writing are becoming much more intense, and they are not prepared to perform the needed new academic activities in English. For this reason, developing strategies to cope with academic language is a must, and teachers need to guide ELLs in learning strategies that they can use independently both inside and beyond the classroom.

Good ELL readers are able to orchestrate a repertoire of strategies that serve them as they read different kinds of texts for a variety of purposes. It is important to remember that these strategies are performed in combination while reading. For example, when we read an editorial in our local newspaper last week, we activated background knowledge about a politician in one part of the text, identified a text structure using a direct quotation by the politician in the next paragraph, visualized a humorous scenario proposed by the editors within the next paragraph, and chuckled at a pun in the punchline. Proficient readers employ all of these strategies and many more as they move through text at a comfortable clip.

Strategy Use by L1 Learners

Reading comprehension requires the use of *strategies* before, during, and after reading. In the context of reading comprehension, strategies can be defined as deliberate actions that readers take to establish and enhance their comprehension (Jimenez, Garcia, & Pearson, 1996; Pritchard & O'Hara, 2008). As we learn to read in our first language, we create a collection of working strategies that we apply to different reading purposes. Once we know how to activate and effectively use a set of strategies, we can apply them to new texts and new tasks.

Better readers in any language use more strategies and use them better. A study of resilient and nonresilient ELLs found that resilient ELLs employed more successful strategies while reading (Padrón et al., 2000). Schoonen, Hulstijn, and Bossers (1998), in a study of middle school and secondary Dutch ELLs, found that vocabulary and use of reading strategies were decisive factors in their successful reading comprehension in English.

Pritchard and O'Hara (2008) noticed that the strategies L1 Spanish ELLs used in reading texts in their first language were not the same as those they used in reading English, even though they were proficient readers in both languages. They were able to use analytical and critical strategies in Spanish, their native language, but used more sentence-by-sentence analysis in reading English. Fitzgerald (1995) did a meta-review of research on L2 academic reading and came to the conclusion that in academic tasks, the more proficient an ELL reader becomes, the more his or her processing strategies resemble those of a proficient L1 reader, both in amount and choice of strategies used. Other studies lend credence to this view (see Fender, 2001; Jimenez et al., 1996). August and Shanahan (2006) echo the idea, saying, "Strategies of various types are unlikely to help students who do not have the requisite language proficiency to comprehend the text" (p. 355). This research lends support to the threshold theory (see Chapter 2), which holds that students cannot benefit from certain levels of instruction until their L2 language proficiency is at a sufficient level.

Students need to see how strategies work through modeling and support, and they need many chances to practice them. We should not expect students to figure out all the various reading strategies in a new language by themselves. It is like putting someone in a kitchen for the first time and asking them to produce a banquet! We need to introduce the tools and show how they work with the text through careful guidance. Only then can we truly "cook!"

In the following section, we introduce some key strategies that fit with best practices for ELLs. Many vocabulary strategies were introduced in the previous two chapters. Here, we move from a focus on single-word strategies to longer discourse-level strategies, using the following organizational format: developing word-learning strategies, phrase- and sentence-level strategies, paragraph- and discourse-level strategies, and metacognitive strategies. We fold these strategies into the body of the chapter in lieu of citing classroom practices at the end.

Developing a Set of Word-Learning Strategies

Because learners, whether native speakers or ELLs, need to learn such a colossal amount of vocabulary during their academic lives, it is impossible to teach all of the words that they need to know. In addition, there is no consensus about a best method for teaching vocabulary to all learners (Beck & McKeown, 1991). However, vocabulary learning cannot be left to chance (Nagy, 1985); therefore, a set of explicit vocabulary learning strategies are needed.

Vocabulary learning is best when it's treated as a cumulative process in which subsequent meanings of words are built upon over time. For ELLs, it is especially important to receive ample exposure to new words so that they can reach a comfort level in trying them out. The best way to ensure that ELLs will be vocabulary learners over the long haul is to help them master those strategies and skills that can be used throughout and beyond their years of schooling to achieve success in school and in life.

All of the following vocabulary-learning strategies can be used in an all-English environment, but they can be powerfully used in referencing the L1 language resources of learners as well.

Preteaching Vocabulary

Preteaching vocabulary (Bamford & Day, 1997) is a proven method of enhancing knowledge before reading a new text, as well as introducing cultural aspects of a text, using pictures, film, or a field trip. Previewing text in this way is sometimes called *frontloading*. Preteaching vocabulary is a way of clearing up the unknown vocabulary through oral activities so that by the time it is found in the reading, it is already familiar (Hoyt, 2002). Freeman and Freeman (2004) said learning new vocabulary "involves learning about something, talking about it, wondering about it, and then reading and writing about it" (p. 198).

> *If you think of vocabulary as a classroom resource that you can help provide, rather than a "gotcha" guessing game, you can save ELLs a lot of time and grief.*—KRISTIN

Saying It with Pictures

If new words are introduced with both pictures and sentences showing the words in context, it helps ELLs enormously. Internet-based image and video banks make it easy to provide visual support for new vocabulary. If students are also given the opportunity to draw the word, say it, write it down, or even physically demonstrate it somehow, the odds go up that students will truly understand and retain the word.

Word Cards/Word Banks/Word Rings

Using a simple set of index cards can generate hours of effective practice. ELLs can write a new word on one side of an index card and a picture, its L1 translation, and a definition of the word on the other. For bilingual learners, the word can also be defined using words from the L1. The cards can be kept in a box and sorted according to different criteria. They can also be hole-punched and slid onto a big key ring—something students enjoy. The kinesthetic aspect makes it more likely that an ELL will recognize and understand the word. Nation (2001) says, "There is thus plenty of evidence that, for the simple word form–word meaning aspect of vocabulary learning, direct learning from word cards is an efficient and highly effective practice" (p. 299). In fact, there is some evidence that L2 vocabulary is retained best by using a simple L1 or L2 synonym (Fraser, 1999). Variations of the word card technique abound, and can include having students use the word in a sentence, finding its opposite, writing synonyms, and so on. The word cards can be grouped using many systems, including color coding by part of speech or thematic unit, or by structural characteristics of the word.

Word Walls and Labeling

If teachers have their own classrooms, they can create word walls. Word walls come in many varieties. They are most often arranged alphabetically, but can just as easily be arranged by concept or topic, bilingually, or by characteristics of words, such as blends or endings. Pictures can also be included next to words. Sight words, the words that are hard to decode, are often put up on word walls as an aid to memory for emergent readers. For Entering and Beginning learners, putting labels on common classroom objects around the room is a natural way to enrich the print environment.

The Keyword Method

The *keyword method* is another route. Using the keyword method, the teacher encourages students to form a mental image connected to the meaning of a new word, often through its sound (Baumann & Kame'enui, 1991). This combined auditory and visual memory aid is often effective for hard-to-learn words.

> *When I was learning the word* pool *for swimming pool, I made a mental image of a hen, which is* poule *in French, the language in which I studied in school in Ivory Coast, flapping around in a swimming pool. Picturing that hen in the water allowed me to remember the word* pool.—TENENA

Making Sure There Are Enough Repetitions

Hiebert et al. (2004) found that words are repeated much less frequently in beginning reading series than they once were. This is a problem because ELLs who are at the Entering or Beginning levels using beginning reading books often do not encounter the words frequently enough to learn to decode and comprehend them. The authors propose "an emphasis on a handful of familiar yet compelling categories [of new words] across a set of texts" as opposed to having "different categories of items in every text" (Hiebert et al., 2004). In other words, new words can be "bundled" into high interest categories or topics. These high-interest categories, along with an opportunity to interact with the things the word represents, will help ELLs construct background knowledge as they learn new words. For example, all of the vocabulary involved with maintaining a fish tank in the classroom will allow for many conversations that are built on repetitive vocabulary.

Making Daily Use of Dictionaries

Dictionaries are an indispensable resource for ELLs but must be introduced and used properly for full effect. Please see Appendix 8.1 for some observations about dictionary purchase and use.

Phrase-and Sentence-Level Reading Strategies

Punctuation

What's the use of those little specks all over the text? Do they convey any meaning? *Punctuation* is an incomplete attempt to codify the ways words are spoken aloud. We can call them the "traffic signals" of language—they tell us "to slow down, notice this, take a detour, and stop" (Truss, 2003, p. 7). English punctuation, like other aspects of English, is language-specific, but it also shares commonalities with punctuation in many other languages. For example, English shares PCI with Chinese regarding the period, or full stop, at the end of a sentence. This marker will transfer effortlessly when learning English as a new language—but for Chinese speakers, the dot is floating in the middle of the line, not sitting on it! However, other punctuation features may cause interference when they are not the same in the two languages. For example, in French months or days of the week are not capitalized, and French-literate ELLs will need to learn to do that.

Punctuation can make a tremendous difference in the meaning of sentences. Take these sentence pairs, for example:

A woman without her man is nothing.
A woman: without her, man is nothing.

Of course, when we read these two sentences aloud, there is no problem distinguishing their meanings. Our voices provide the clue to meaning through our intonation and our pausing, which represents the punctuation. To help ELLs understand the meaning functions of punctuation, it is important that they hear text read aloud as they look at it. In this way, when they see and hear the punctuation at the same time, they will develop a sense of how punctuation contributes to the meaning of words.

Inferencing

When we speak of someone who is not very perceptive, we often say that they "take things too literally." We value a person's ability to read "between the lines" and see the hidden dimensions of situations. Knowing how to make inferences is an abstract skill that is cultivated in settings in which it is valued. In reading, it is indispensable. *Inferencing* requires actively interacting with the words in a sentence and among sentences. It includes such subskills as:

- Pronoun reference (knowing what a pronoun in a sentence refers back to)
- Forming hypotheses about what is coming next in the text
- Guessing the meanings of unknown words or phrases
- Forming impressions about character motives and behaviors across multiple locations in a text
- Knowing the subtle connotations of words as they are used in particular contexts
- Understanding cause–effect relationships of events mentioned at different times in a text
- Drawing upon background knowledge in order to fill in gaps within a text

ELLs can begin to be inferential in their thinking even before they are reading. Inferencing can be developed through interactive dialogue and conversations about texts. A question as simple as "What do you think the author might be trying to say here?" can help an ELL begin the process of learning to infer.

One of the ways I try to foster inferencing with advanced learners of English is to read them daily mysteries aloud from the book series "Two-Minute Mysteries" (Sobol, 1967). I read the mystery three times slowly, without interruption, and at the end, the students try to figure out "whodunit" on the basis of the clues in the story. Their listening and inferencing abilities get better and better as they get accustomed to the format. It's a great way to boost reading between the lines, and interest is always high.—KRISTIN

Signal Words, Transitions, and Connectors

Has anyone ever responded "Yes, but . . . " to your great idea? That sentence is a kind of "shorthand" telling you that the person really doesn't agree and is planning to object. Both words are powerful, and their meanings clash. The connector *but* tells us that the thought is taking a turn toward the negative. Just like traffic signals, connectors tell the reader what's coming up and where to go. Connectors can be tremendously useful in providing road signs and keeping readers moving along in a text even if they are missing some vocabulary words. If we know the rhetorical device represented by a certain connector, we can stay on track even when we're not quite sure what's around the bend.

Signal words, transitions, and connectors use a baffling variety of syntax patterns and punctuation, and these can prove challenging to ELLs. What form does the verb take after that preposition? Do I need a subject in the second clause of the sentence? Learning to use connectors in writing can take a long time; however, their semantic purposes can be learned at an earlier stage, through reading. For example, even though they are punctuated differently, the words *but, although, nevertheless, regardless,* and *despite the fact that* all have the same general meaning, that of contrast. Teachers need to point out these relationships explicitly to students.

Paragraph- and Discourse-Level Reading Strategies

Four Graphic Organizers

Graphic organizers are, in a sense, the visualization of the way we store the knowledge we keep in our brains and the methods by which we organize new information. They are useful organizing tools for ELLs and all students because they can help manage a great deal of information in a concise way. When teachers carefully choose the appropriate graphic organizer for a reading assignment, they are making the reading task more manageable for their ELLs. Teachers can also provide graphic organizers to help ELLs gather and sort information and to give them a framework to prepare for writing full-fledged compositions.

Many wonderful books in the literacy field contain detailed sets of graphic organizers and guidance in their use in order to help learners read and write (e.g., Buehl, 1995; Essley, 2008; Zwiers, 2008). We encourage you to make use of them. We highlight only four graphic organizers we have found to be particularly effective with ELLs in both their reading comprehension and writing. A small model of each of the four organizers can be found in Appendix 8.2 at the end of the chapter.

Semantic Map

A *semantic map* is a graphic organizer used to connect a word with many associations. On an unlined piece of paper, learners create a "map" with the word or concept in the center and associations with the word branching out from it in various directions. Often the result looks like a spider web. Semantic mapping especially helps activate a student's prior knowledge for reading and for brainstorming before beginning to write.

T-Charts

T-charts can provide an entrée into listing the characteristics of two separate things before discussing how they are related. This helps ELLs organize information they find in content reading.

Venn Diagrams or H-Charts

The overlapping circles of the *Venn diagram* are widely used to help students learn how to compare and contrast two ideas or items. However, teachers note that the "overlapping" part doesn't give students enough room to write in the commonalities. A slight variation of the Venn diagram is the *H-chart*, with two overlapping long rectangles. It provides students with much more room to write the common features, while still preserving the visual display of comparison and contrast. H-charts are a great way to support developing the ability to read and write about contrasts.

Content Frames (Semantic Feature Analysis Grid)

The *content frames* chart allows students to list and compare attributes of several items with respect to a number of different characteristics. For example, different animal names can be placed along the left column of the organizer, and qualities animals possess, such as hair, warm-bloodedness, kinds of appendages, can be listed in the top row of the chart. Students look at the intersection of each animal with each characteristic and fill the box by checking, writing *yes* or *no*, or adding detailed information. To scaffold less proficient learners, some of the boxes can be filled in beforehand.

A grid like this can also be used as a knowledge rating for vocabulary. Across the top are categories of familiarity with a word: 0—don't know the word; 1—have seen it or heard it; 2—think I know it; and 3—know it well. Vocabulary is listed in the left column. Students assess their vocabulary knowledge of keywords before reading. They return to the same words after reading and reassess (Cobb & Blachowicz, 2007).

Text Structure

Text structure refers to how different kinds of writing can be organized. It affects the length of a text and the sections in it, how it is subdivided by headings, how material is summarized through indexes, glosses, glossaries, or subheadings, and even what a paragraph looks like. Text structures are related to genres but focus more on the organization than the content. The text structure of an informal letter, for example, looks very different from the text structure used for a letter of recommendation, or a science article in a journal, or an editorial in the newspaper. Each has its own conventions, and they are culturally specific. ELLs need to be exposed to many text structures and be able to analyze them. Later, they need to learn to write in several text structures.

As students become aware of the way different kinds of written texts are structured, it helps them both as readers and as writers. Research indicates that readers use knowledge of text structure to store, retrieve, and summarize information they read (Meyer, Brandt, & Bluth, 1980). As learners become more familiar with these forms, they create mental templates that make it easier for them to access future texts that contain the same structures.

Students can apply their awareness of text structures in three specific ways that involve both reading and writing:

- When they preview a text by looking at its text structure
- When they are taking notes as they read, and
- When they are practicing writing in different text patterns.

When students are preparing to read an informational text, it is very helpful to preview the text by walking through the headings and subheadings to get an idea of what will be coming. This is very helpful to ELLs, who work best with "no surprises." Students can also make use of their awareness of text structure when they learn to take notes that follow the structure of a text as they read. Doing so creates active involvement with the text while it creates a memory aid and study guide for later use. Similarly, when students learn to write compositions using different kinds of text structures, such as comparison and contrast, problem-solution, or process compositions, they are practicing the organizing skills that will help them recognize those structures when they read. In other words, learning text structure organization "has a profound effect on comprehension and memory" (Peregoy & Boyle, 2005, p. 321).

Teaching text structure has value for both L1 learners and ELLs. It's even more valuable for ELLs because it provides another cueing strategy that can provide a frame while other vocabulary knowledge and sentence-level reading skills are still developing.

Visualization or Audio Imaging

Visualizing allows us to see in our heads the events that are occurring in a story. Although most strongly applied in language arts classrooms, *visualization* can also help learners "see" chemical processes, mathematical shapes, or dramatic moments in history. Strategies that use visualization are excellent for ELLs because they build L2 oracy when they involve oral reading or performing, and they serve as aids to memory as well. Asking students to create a visual representation of something they have seen or read is both an authentic way to check comprehension and a bridge to writing.

Audio imaging can also enhance comprehension. Television shows have musical motifs that have come to signal certain situations, such as the opening of the vintage show *Twilight Zone*, a motif that denotes "something mysterious is going on." Today's ELLs are heavily exposed to media and the audio inherent in it, so this can be a real source of information and an additional cueing system. Kids can even take the lead in choosing or obtaining these sounds.

It's also possible to add sound effects while stories are being read aloud.

> *When one of our teachers did a read-aloud to students with the story of Balto, the heroic Alaskan dog that saved a town in Alaska during a blizzard (Kimmel, 1999), she put on a sound effects tape with the sounds of a violent snowstorm. Some of the children began shivering just from the sound!*—KRISTIN

Metacognitive Strategies

Metacognition is conscious awareness of our own thinking and learning process. It is part of our human heritage and can be found in people with no formal schooling. However, it becomes much more highly developed as we obtain more education, and it has a demonstrable influence on reading and academic success. Metacognition is usually divided into three categories of planning, monitoring, and evaluating one's own comprehension (before, during, and after performing a task). In the beginning, the metacognitive skills may be very conscious, but as they become more facile, they tend to become less conscious and more automatic. When we read, metacognitive strategies help us prepare for a reading task, monitor the task as we go along, and then evaluate it when we have completed it (Grabe & Stoller, 2002).

Metacognitive reading strategies include "fix-up" strategies used when comprehension breaks down, such as rereading, using graphic organizers, looking for pronoun references and transition words that connect thoughts within and between sentences, and much more. Writers use metacognitive strategies when they make careful word choices or use rereading or editing strategies.

Some metacognitive strategies rely on language-specific qualities, and others are more universal. Teachers of ELLs should carefully analyze the language requirements for performing different metacognitive tasks. Learners can't perform metacognitive tasks in a new language if they don't know the words that cue the task. For example, even if Hussein realizes that he needs to find a way to keep notes on a text as he reads it so that he can go back and reread it later, he has to know what it means when the teacher says to "mark" or "highlight" in class. If he doesn't know the words, he cannot implement his burgeoning metacognitive insights.

Monitoring Comprehension

When good readers realize that their comprehension has broken down, they do several things to get it back on track. The most obvious and universally used is rereading. We also employ such strategies as retelling, paraphrasing, looking for alternative explanations, looking for a connection to our own experiences, looking forward or backward in a text, checking the illustrations, or stopping and asking ourselves questions. We can also search our prior knowledge to see if a hint to meaning might be hidden in something we already know. *Think-alouds*, or verbal reports (Anderson, 1999), are always a great way to help students become metacognitive learners. A think-aloud is a technique in which teachers orally explain for students how they figure out and execute a certain task as they are performing it. It might involve asking oneself questions or ruminating on what to do, often in a conversational and informal style. After this demonstration, students are given opportunities to try practicing think-alouds in small groups or pairs.

When teachers model think-alouds for ELLs on a regular basis, ELLs will have a well-rehearsed strategy to use when they are trying to comprehend text on their own. Think-alouds are useful in three important ways:

1. They build metacognitive awareness.
2. They give the teacher a window into the thinking processes of the learner.
3. They give ELLs opportunities to practice using academic language orally.

Strategies Kick in at Different Times in L1 and L2

It is important to note that some learners may be able to use both cognitive and metacognitive strategies while reading in their L1 and yet not be able to use them in English because they don't have the requisite language to perform the strategies at that time (Alderson, 1984, 2000). ELLs may not have enough reading skills to be able to read a certain English text, and their L1 literacy knowledge about how texts are put together may be "waiting in the wings" to be activated once they reach an adequate level in English. We call their first language literacy the *literacy advantage*, and it is enormously important in the syndrome of success for reading in a new language. Bernhardt's L2 reading model (see Figure 2.1) depicts L1 literacy as accounting for fully 30% of L2 reading comprehension.

As described earlier with regard to the threshold theory, L1 reading skills and strategies are very important but cannot always be fully implemented until learners reach a certain threshold of proficiency in the new language. That proficiency is built on the "bottom-up" skills that must be working smoothly before the cognitive and strategic processing skills can be fully activated. Schoonen et al. (1998), for example, found that metacognitive knowledge contributed to reading in English among secondary school–age Dutch ELLs only when those learners reached a certain threshold of proficiency. Once a learner recognizes the meaning of certain connecting words in English, such as *therefore, in addition,* or *nevertheless,* for example, it is then possible to apply PCI they have reading in their first language to figuring out the meaning of the English text.

To make an analogy, let's imagine a good cook from Greece is trying to use an English-language cookbook to make banana bread for the first time. Even with Costas's good background knowledge about cooking, he will still have to be able to read the names of the ingredients, the abbreviations for the measuring units in English, and the meaning of the descriptive verbs, such as *whisk, fold,* and *spoon.* His background knowledge and metacognitive strategies—such as sniffing the kitchen to detect whether something is nearly cooked, or sticking a fork in the bread to see if it's done, will come into play when he can execute the recipe by knowing the English vocabulary needed to accomplish it.

Extensive Reading Develops All of the Strategies

There is no doubt that extensive reading is the best global method to help all learners consolidate their reading comprehension. *Extensive reading,* which can be defined as reading a large amount of text for general comprehension (Anderson, 1999), helps with vocabulary acquisition, content knowledge, familiarity with syntactic structure, knowledge of genres, and reading rate. Strategies that are taught and practiced in the classroom must then be followed up, almost like learning to drive a car in a driving class followed by a great deal of time "behind the wheel." That is where extensive reading comes in. However, one cannot count on outside reading to do the trick when there is limited silent reading time in the classroom. Hiebert says, "[I]f students are not reading voraciously in their classrooms, it is hard to expect that they would read voraciously at home, especially when language and cultural patterns differ in the two contexts. If English language learners are to read voraciously at home, they also need to read voraciously at school" (Hiebert & Fisher, 2006, p. 291). Therefore, ELLs need to read "voraciously" during the school day and as part of their homework as well.

A good "reading workout" involves both intensive and extensive reading. Like an exercise program, one activity alone will not build overall strength and fitness. A good workout for ELLs gives opportunities to do many kinds of reading on a regular basis, especially reading for pleasure. Like any other disciplined activity, it helps "build muscles." Programs for extensive reading abound in schools, and they are cornerstones of good literacy practice. Some examples follow.

Daily Silent Reading

Whether it's *DEAR (Drop Everything and Read)*, *SSR (Sustained Silent Reading)*, *FVR (Free Voluntary Reading)*, or another format, ELLs deserve chances to do daily silent reading of their choosing throughout the school year and into the summer. During silent reading, teachers also model the technique by reading and refraining from circulating or grading papers. When a teacher reads and values reading, it is contagious. After silent reading, ELLs can also benefit by sharing what they have just read with a buddy. Interactive dialogue about books builds oral language as well as social and academic skills.

Reading Buddies

Many schools bring together older and younger children to read on a regular basis. There are several formats for these visits. In the most common two, the older children may bring picture books to read with the younger children, or the younger children can practice reading as their older counterparts listen to them. Such partnerships allow rich possibilities for literacy development and community building. ELLs benefit from reading buddy programs, whether they are older children or younger children. It gives older children a chance to feel a sense of mastery of the book they prepare to read to the younger children, and they enjoy the admiration younger children naturally feel toward their older peers. It gives younger ELLs enjoyment to experience the attention and mentorship of an older student. A couple of tips for cross-age groupings with ELLs:

1. Any assignment involving a reading performance should be given well in advance, so that students can practice their parts as much as needed.
2. The reading activity should involve a text that is within the ELL's instructional level.

Book Bags

Good classroom libraries can circulate home with the students through a book bag system. Teachers obtain durable, waterproof book bags, enough for each member of the class, and allow students to check out books to bring home. A log sheet in the book bag gives students or their parents a place to report on their home reading. For younger students, parents can be asked to initial the sheet to verify that reading has taken place. A variation of book bags is to involve parents or caregivers in reading with the child at home. For ELLs, the best way to make sure this happens is to have a number of titles in the native languages of each student in the classroom. Even though some parents and caregivers may not be able to read in any language, it is more likely that they will be able to read in their L1 than in English. When families are involved with home reading activities organized by the teacher, they are led in the direction of initiating other home reading activities.

Public Library Programs

Especially in the summer, public libraries have many reading incentive programs. Offering entertainment, prizes, friendly competition, and a comfortable place to read, public libraries are a core resource for families with ELLs. Whether it's a field trip to the library or a letter home to parents about the library's activities, teachers of ELLs should build libraries into their orientation procedures for families and children. A weekly visit to the school library makes it easier for children to expect the same thing of their public library, especially during the summer months. Some large fast-food chains also have reading incentive programs.

With all of the supports available, an extensive reading workout is easy and important to do.

Additional Ideas for Developing Classroom and School Resources

Seeking Out Bilingual Titles

When they are available, it's great to pick books that ELLs can already read in their L1 and to provide an English version of the book next to it. Whether it's two separate books or a book with bilingual text on the same page or on opposing pages, it can increase vocabulary in both languages. When ELLs have already read the Harry Potter books in their native language, for example, they will already have many concepts, words, and features of plot available to them when they read the series in English. Bilingual text can be as good a support as pictures if a learner is literate in his or her L1.

Middle School and High School Libraries Need Picture Books

Virginia Runge noticed this problem in her middle school ESL classes.

> *When introducing a lesson, one of my strategies is to use tradebooks to teach background knowledge with which my ESL students can connect. Unfortunately, my junior high is lacking in this area and I must rely on the elementary schools or public libraries to loan me picture books to facilitate more meaningful learning.*—VIRGINIA RUNGE, middle school ESL teacher

Using Many Kinds of Print Sources

Comic books (Rankin, 2008), graphic novels, newspaper and magazine articles, letters, recipes, advertisements, and websites are all potential sources from which ELLs can and should have reading experiences. This will also improve their ability to write in different genres.

QUESTIONS FOR FURTHER STUDY

1. What are some ways teachers can make vocabulary learning "multisensory"? What are some ways vocabulary could be tied in with speaking practice, the arts, graphic art, or other methods of self-expression?

2. In your experience, what graphic organizers have been useful or not useful for certain kinds of strategic tasks? Explain why some work better with certain kinds of content.

3. Look at the list of metacognitive strategies on pp. 181–182 and apply them to yourself as a reader. Which of these are you aware of using on a regular basis? Are there other metacognitive strategies that you find useful? Describe them.

4. How do you think text structures have changed due to the growing influence of the Internet?

5. How would you describe the text structure of this book? Look at the different elements of the book. Do you consider this to be a classic textbook format? If so, how, and if not, why not?

6. What experiences have you had with extensive reading programs, whether as a student or as a teacher? Have you known anyone in a book

club? What effect do you think it has had on the person who took part in it?

7. How can the multimedia available to today's students work in favor of their greater involvement in extensive reading? In what ways does it work against it?

8. Think of some "messages" given by society about reading. Do you think pleasure reading as described in the "reading fitness program" is a harder sell for children than it once was? How can reading among ELLs be encouraged in school settings?

Some Observations about Dictionaries

No book about reading in English as a new language would be complete without some discussion about the key role of dictionaries in building reading and writing skills. It is true that every classroom with ELLs should include multiple copies of good dictionaries. Teachers should spend time examining dictionaries, not just reading about them in catalogues, before ordering them for the classroom. These might include: two-way bilingual dictionaries; dictionaries for an ELL target audience; picture dictionaries; a "good old-fashioned" English dictionary, perhaps on a wooden stand, that includes etymologies and multiple examples of words used in sentences; a content-area dictionary; a thesaurus; and a dictionary that includes the insights from corpus linguistics. Teachers should consider dictionaries not only for their students' use, but for their own. It is a good idea to model and scaffold dictionary use early in the school year, using the following guidelines:

1. *Bilingual dictionaries* can be a great resource in a bilingual or dual-language classroom and can also scaffold students in a sheltered or grade-level classroom. They can help language development in both directions. However, after a certain point, the English language development of students will benefit if they transition to English-only dictionaries. English dictionaries can increase vocabulary acquisition.

2. *Overreliance on dictionaries* is likely to be more common in those whose languages have a different orthography from English, such as Chinese learners. Word-by-word translation is not an effective long-term strategy for either reading or writing and may result in a failure to develop comprehension of longer chunks of text. As students become more knowledgeable about English morphemes, word formation processes, and etymology, their probabilistic reasoning and guessing strategies will also develop. For students who have less experience with the roman alphabet and English etymology, a corpus-based dictionary, either in paper form or on online, will help them develop probabilistic reasoning.

3. *Picture dictionaries* are a great way to help ELLs learn a cluster of vocabulary words around a chosen topic. Some of them arrange words and images on a page by theme or by topic. Others have small images for each word along the margin and are listed in alphabetical order. Each kind has its uses. A beginning-level classroom benefits from a picture dictionary in alphabetical order, whereas more advanced content-centered classes can benefit from thematically arranged picture dictionaries or a content-based dictionary such as *The Oxford Picture Dictionary for the Content Areas*. Probably each classroom should have both kinds. Oxford University Press has an outstanding set of picture dictionaries that span the grade levels, from K–3 to the content picture dictionary for upper elementary to a high school–level picture dictionary all the way to an adult literacy picture dictionary. There are also Internet picture dictionaries available at no cost, including the *Internet Picture Dictionary*.

4. *Online dictionaries* are handy, but some of the no-cost versions lack the editorial rigor of paper dictionaries. If you are allowing students to use them, preselect the dictionary sites you trust.

(cont.)

5. *Alphabetical order.* Students need explicit instruction in dictionary use and regular practice in using them. Automaticity in sorting by alphabetical order is a must for word recognition and for study skills—at the beginning of the year, fun "drills" can be created to help students develop speed in looking things up or filing them in folders.

6. *Pronunciation.* Teachers can include pronunciation of new words that ELLs find in dictionaries by asking students to read sentences including the word. Many dictionaries now include a CD-ROM that pronounces all of the headwords (main entries) in the dictionary. Saying a word as part of a phrase also helps, since the sounds of English words may change depending on the sound coming before or after them.

7. *Dictionaries of idioms* can also be found, and are good to have on hand.

We recommend having multiple copies of English dictionaries that include word origins in the classroom. Our favorites include: *The American Heritage Dictionary of the English Language, The Oxford English Dictionary, The Longman Dictionary of Contemporary English, The Longman Advanced American Dictionary,* and *The Cambridge Advanced Learners Dictionary,* which is built on corpus linguistics.

Four Useful Graphic Organizers for ELLs

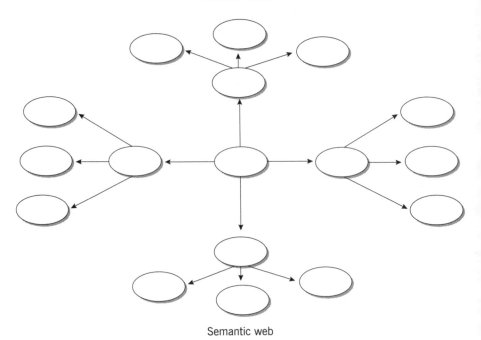

Content frame

Semantic web

(cont.)

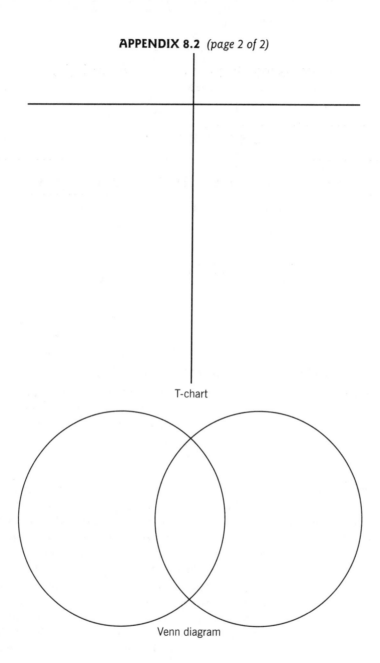

T-chart

Venn diagram

CHAPTER NINE

Writing to Learn in English across the Curriculum

New Vocabulary in This Chapter: *expressive writing, expository writing, redundancies, process writing, writing workshop, independent writing, revising and editing, publish, telling versus composing, responsive writing, focus on form (FoF), recasts, uptake, linguistic complexity, vocabulary usage, language experience approach (LEA)*

Writing is one of humanity's greatest inventions and is one defining feature of a civilization. It is a way to compress, organize, store, and transmit vast amounts of information. It is also a path to understanding ourselves and others. When we engage in *expressive writing*, it allows us to share our thoughts, feelings, and dreams with people we have never met, and when we read another's words, we can experience that person on a deep level. Writing gives us the ability to respond to situations, too, and alter their outcomes through our written efforts. We can fill out an application to gain acceptance to a program, or write a letter of protest about a bill, for example. We also do a wide range of *expository writing* to explain, analyze, and influence the world around us. As we do these many writing activities, we address a multitude of readers.

It is also clearly the case that if there weren't writers, there would be nothing to read! Writers create the material that makes all reading possible. Good writers make reading pleasurable; bad writers make reading difficult. Both readers and writing teachers know this!

Interactions between Reading and Writing

There is a close and complex relationship between writing and reading, close enough that our book about reading could not be complete without a chapter on writing. Table 9.1 lists some of those similarities. Both reading and writing are core competencies for achieving academic success, and both can be thought of as "drawing from a common pool of cognitive and linguistic operations" (Kucer, 1985, p. 331).

Although the reading skills and writing skills do not necessarily develop in parallel, even for L1 speakers of a language, a good case can be made for combining them in the classroom. Tierney and Shanahan (1990) did an exhaustive review of the reading–writing connection and found, "Writing and reading together engage learners in a greater variety of reasoning operations than when writing and reading are apart or when students are given a variety of tasks to go along with their reading" (p. 272).

Although reading and writing were taught separately in the past, views on this approach changed as people became aware of the interactions between them (Kucer, 2001; Tierney & Pearson, 1983, 1985; van Dijk

TABLE 9.1. Similarities between the English Reading and Writing Processes

- Both activities are centered around written language and do not exist in languages that are unwritten.
- Both reading and writing consist of a wide variety of genres with which students need to be familiar in order to succeed in school settings. These genres vary in formality, complexity, and breadth of vocabulary, as well as discourse structures.
- Both require an understanding of the relationship of phonemes and graphemes that make up words.
- Both are complex activities with many component processes enfolded in them.
- Both reading and writing are a way of creating, selecting, and organizing information that can be stored for later use.
- Academic vocabulary expectations for both reading and writing become more challenging as students move up through the grade levels.
- Both are context reduced. Meanings are able to be communicated through words alone.
- Both reading and writing may use English structures that are more complex and lengthy than oral speech and lack the redundancies and clarifications of spoken English. Written sentences can be longer than sentences in oral English.
- Reading and writing vary according to different purposes, audiences, and contexts.
- Reading and writing are the cornerstones of academic success.

& Kintsch, 1983). The reading field, in fact, has reconfigured itself in the past couple of decades to highlight the key role of writing in literacy development. Students agree: "Nearly everything you do in school you write about," says one (Protherough, 1993, p. 125). By using writing as a tool to learn, students can process their academic knowledge more thoroughly, remember it better, and enhance their reading comprehension (Craik & Lockhart, 1972; Oded & Walters, 2002).

Of the five domains of language learning (listening, speaking, reading, writing, and communicative competence), writing requires the conscious "orchestration" of the largest number of skills. Whether it's for a language arts, social studies, science, or math class, students are expected to use their "CALP language" to report on their understandings of the material they're studying, and to share in print their reasoning processes, experiences, feelings, reactions, and beliefs. As children advance through the school system, writing becomes more and more closely connected to overall academic success. Because of that, writing practice with ELLs needs to start right away.

Written Language—Not Just Frozen Speech!

In Chapter 3 we talked about the grammar of oral language and the ways oral grammar can be decoded through *redundancies*, or repetitions of the same material in slightly different ways, and through clues in the environment. Writing, on the other hand, requires more formal grammar and relies more on the organization of the words themselves. Writing lacks the gestures or expressive qualities of human speech, and what's more, the listener/reader is usually not there to give immediate feedback. Therefore, "writing requires a double abstraction: abstraction from the sound of speech and abstraction from the interlocutor" (Vygotsky, 1986, p. 181). Because of its inherently abstract nature, writing is the hardest domain to do well, for native speakers and ELLs alike.

Written language, and especially academic language, is distinct from oral language in several important ways that take on added meaning in the context of teaching writing to ELLs. These warrant a closer look. Some of these differences will remind you of the discussion about BICS and CALP in Chapter 2.

• *Written sentences are longer* and use such structures as passive voice, embedded clauses, conditionals, ellipsis, and other features that aren't normally found in spoken English. Because of the limits of our working memory, we cannot keep track of long, complex sentences when they are spoken aloud. Written English, on the other hand, does not have this restriction because we can always go back and reread the text. For the same reason, long introductory phrases and clauses are likely to be found in written English but are rare in spoken English because it's too hard for the listener to keep the introductory information in working memory.

As an example, let's look at this sentence in a magazine ad for a watch: *From the sweeping second hand to the illuminated numerals on the unique ivory-colored face, every detail has been carefully reproduced.* In spoken form, we would say something like "They copied every detail from the sweeping second hand to the lighted numbers . . . " We made four distinct changes when we turned it into spoken text: (1) we changed the order of the phrases, moving the subject up to the front of the sentence and putting the introductory phrase after it; (2) we changed the verb *reproduced* to *copied* and from passive to active voice; (3) we changed the tense from present perfect to simple past; and (4) we changed several words to conversational BICS language. The written form was able to create a more dramatic effect by means of the words and word order. When spoken, our vocal expression would do that instead.

Students become familiar with these written language forms by encountering them through reading or listening and then practicing them in writing. As they become familiar with more written patterns over time, it becomes easier to learn to use them in writing. The more patterns they see and understand, the more they will later feel comfortable using them.

- *Written texts use a much wider range of vocabulary words,* both in content words and function words such as connectors. Written text includes more low-frequency or even rare words, more concept words in noun form (Fang, 2008), and connectors not found in contemporary spoken English. For example, the connector "hence" is found in written language, but it is rarely spoken. In spoken English, we would be more likely to say the words "therefore" or "so" to express the same meaning as "hence."

- *Punctuation takes on critical additional meanings* in written English. Fluency instruction can help students learn to "read" punctuation with vocal expression and understand the functions of periods, some commas, question marks, quotation marks, and exclamation points. However, other punctuation marks cannot be rendered by reading aloud because they show subtle relationships among words in the text that can only be understood in written form. The more "academic" punctuation marks include semicolons, apostrophes, colons, parentheses, and hyphens. All of these abound in academic writing. The semicolon, for example, can be placed in many of the same places that a period is placed, but writers choose it to indicate a close relationship between the words before and after the semicolon. Look at this sentence: "The raft was ready for release; they lowered it into the water." The semicolon tells us that these actions came in close succession. The semicolon allows us to dispense with a connector like "then." Academic writing is full of these "shortcuts," and good writers use them a lot.

Change in the Philosophy of L1 Writing

In the early 1960s, researchers as well as teachers began to consider new approaches to writing instruction. Graves (1973), researching the classroom environment, concluded that the writing curriculum, with its focus on correctness and lack of authentic purposes, did not encourage students to become actual writers. Educators such as Marie Clay (1968), Lucy Calkins (1984), Nancie Atwell (1987), and Ralph Fletcher (Fletcher & Portalupi, 1998; Portalupi & Fletcher, 2001) examined writing as a thinking process. In so doing, they helped bring about a major overhaul in the way writing was taught in schools. These understandings are still in use today.

This paradigm shift supports the belief that helping students develop the love of writing is as important as helping them develop their skills and confidence in it. In this integrated view of writing, there is no reason to wait for a certain level of readiness; writing activities can be set in motion very early in a student's education and can continue through all the school years, right into adult life.

In the new model of writing, teachers are encouraged to view themselves as writers, through professional development programs like the National Writing Project. The idea is that when teachers like to write, their students are more likely to as well, so the first place to address improving student writing is to get teachers writing. The notion that has emerged is that writing is a tool not just for written products but part of a process of self-discovery and learning, and it is now widely accepted that writing, in combination with reading, is indispensable for every kind of class, from language arts to physical education.

Math teachers, for example, now expect students to be able to jot down the steps they used to arrive at an answer, and sometimes the written description of the process receives as much credit as the answer itself. In many classes, teachers ask students to keep learning logs, summarizing what they have learned or have questions about; reading logs, used during or after reading to help students apply comprehension strategies; or notes that they share periodically with the teacher. All of these journaling activities help students develop metacognitive skills and use writing as a learning strategy. Using writing so often and in so many ways also helps students overcome anxiety about writing and makes it easier to pick up the pen or pencil or tap away at the keyboard, thereby developing the writing habit.

Process Writing and Writing Workshop

The *process writing* model breaks the writing curriculum into steps. The most widely used model of process writing is *writing workshop* (Calkins, 2006; Fletcher & Portalupi, 2001).

Writing workshop consists of four main stages: prewriting, independent writing, editing/revising, and publishing. Students may be in any one of these four processes on a given day and cycle through them as they undertake new writing. Writing occurs 3 to 5 days a week, on a reliable basis. Writing workshop usually starts off with short mini-lessons the teacher presents to the whole class (Calkins, 2006). Mini-lessons teach writing skills explicitly, beginning with making a connection to the students' experiences, followed by modeling or making a teaching point, often by means of a think-aloud or a demonstration.

During prewriting, students brainstorm ideas through many different kinds of stimuli: scribbling, pictures, memories, dialogues, semantic maps, or even a set of prompts, or suggested writing topics, from which they can choose. Prewriting helps students find personally meaningful topics and details. During *independent writing*, students are shown strategies for developing their ideas in conferences with the teacher and produce a rough draft, analyze their own text, and comment on the writing of others. In the stage for *revising and editing*, others help guide writers as they refine their ideas. These could be peers, the teacher, tutors, or others. In this stage students develop the discipline and stamina to create multiple drafts. The process differs in length for each student and should not be rigidly timed. Finally, students *publish* their work by sharing it with an audience. It may be through creating a book or by reading for their classmates in the "author's chair" (Graves & Hansen, 1983). Students have the satisfaction of sharing a finished product with peers and experiencing their appreciation.

Writing Workshop and ELLs' Writing Needs

Several aspects of the process writing model coincide with research findings about how ELLs learn best:

- There is extensive classroom time given to develop writing skills—students are not expected to learn them at home or on their own.
- The writing atmosphere is relaxed, lowering the affective filter.
- Students choose their topics, which gives ELLs a chance to validate their prior experiences and write to their strengths.
- Each student has the opportunity to write at his or her own level. Even labeling of drawings is acceptable in writing workshop when

ELLs are at the Entering or Beginning level. Calkins and others also point out that writing in one's L1 may be accepted in some contexts and at some stages (2006, p. 89).

- Working closely with peers in collaborative settings is of particular value for L2 acquisition (Waxman & Tellez, 2002).
- The predictable routine of writing workshop can be comforting for an ELL getting adjusted to many new classroom routines.
- There is an opportunity to share finished writing with peers, building relationships and mutual respect.

On the other hand, writing workshop is not a perfect fit for ELLs. Following are the reasons that the process writing model may come up short for ELLs.

ELLs Need Closer Guidance from Teachers

In order to perform the cognitively demanding task of "generating meaningful text in a second language" (Myles, 2002, p. 4), ELLs need considerable teacher guidance. In a process writing model, ELLs may be left in a small group without guidance from an expert peer or adult. Teachers are needed to guide ELL writers in topic selection, vocabulary selection, sentence structure, paragraphing, editing, spelling, and punctuation, all areas in which ELLs need explicit teaching. Even for college-level ELLs, Silva (1993) found that when they revised their own work, the editing tended to be at a superficial level and required guidance from the teacher.

Peer Editing Requires a Language Proficiency Threshold

Before ELLs are able to benefit from peer discussion and peer editing, they need two things: a sufficient level of reading comprehension to be able to read, appreciate, and provide relevant comments on each others' writing, and enough language proficiency to be able to understand and benefit from feedback given by other students, who may not be very articulate or clear. These are high-level, nuanced skills, and moving ELLs into peer editing when they are not at a proficiency level to benefit is not a good use of time for either member of the pair. Several studies of peer editing by ELLs failed to show improvement in their writing quality (Shanahan & Beck, 2006, pp. 434–435).

Academic Writing Encompasses both Telling and Composing

Myles (2002) points out that writing in academic contexts does not just involve *telling*, or narrative writing, but the more difficult skills of *composing*. Composing requires taking information about a subject, gathered from a variety of courses, and "transforming or reworking" that information. Writing workshop works best in helping learners create narrative pieces, and it is usually done during language arts time. These experiences are very important for creating a welcoming environment and developing a child's identity, but ELLs also require a great many opportunities to learn to create the expository prose needed to perform academic tasks, and this may not receive enough attention. Composing can take years to learn and needs careful scaffolding, especially since it requires utilizing ever-increasing content knowledge vocabulary.

Coherence

Writing rubrics usually consider "coherence"—consistency across paragraphs or sections—a valued attribute, but ELLs may not know enough about discourse patterns of English to know how to manipulate information across paragraphs. If they are not very familiar with the writing structures they are expected to produce, their text may appear incoherent above the sentence or paragraph level. Coherence requires mastering many discourse connectors in English (conjunctions, connectors, transition words, etc.), and these take a long time to learn. It is necessary to practice them extensively. Very often, these many connectors are not taught very "coherently," making it even harder. They may require more explicit, direct instruction than the minilessons in process writing allow for.

Zwiers (2007, 2008) has "unpacked" the language requirements that comprise academic tasks faced by ELLs. He characterizes academic language as a "dialect that describes cognitive processes, complex relationships, and abstract concepts" (2007, p. 96). This academic "dialect" is often understood implicitly by its speakers (teachers and students from educated and/or prosperous backgrounds), but is not clearly explained or taught to "outsiders," including ELLs. Teachers need to examine their own academic processes and conventions and then clearly explain what they're doing so that ELLs can emulate it. This is not easy! For example, Zwiers points out that in the process of providing comprehensible input for ELLs, teachers may simplify complex content temporarily to clarify it for ELLs but then neglect to figure out how to move the students back up to the level of complexity the content requires. If that doesn't occur, providing comprehensible input may just end up enabling failure. ELLs need to be shown exactly how to acquire the skills needed and be challenged to work on them.

Instructional Settings

Even for native speakers, the writing instruction provided by teachers at the same grade level and across grade levels can be contradictory and confusing. For ELLs, the inconsistencies in what they are asked to do in writing can be even more bewildering. For example, McCarthey, Garcia, Lopez-Velasquez, and Shumin (2004) took a look at writing opportunities for ELLs at the fourth- and fifth-grade levels in several programmatic settings, and found the writing tasks and requirements to be both complicated and "fragmented." They also found that interactive dialogue about the writing was uncommon.

On the other hand, an 8-year longitudinal study in 13 secondary schools in a California school district showed encouraging results for ELL students whose teachers implemented a cognitive strategies approach in a learning community (Olson & Land, 2007). When they were exposed to a rigorous language arts curriculum, which included the development of writing strategies and metacognitive strategies, there was significant improvement in their academic writing for 7 consecutive years. In addition, their grade-point average exceeded a control group, and they performed better on standardized tests and in high-stakes writing assessments. The findings reinforce the importance of teaching critical thinking strategies and having high expectations for ELLs, exposing them to a rigorous language arts curriculum, and involving them in a learning community.

A Framework for Analyzing School Writing Tasks

We have developed a framework to help analyze the varying writing demands on ELLs and others in the school settings and come up with ways to meet them. We have broken them into three broad levels: expressive writing, responsive writing, and expository writing. Table 9.2 provides a description of each level, common writing assignments likely to occur at each level, and activities teachers can use to develop and bridge the levels.

Expressive Writing

This level is usually found in learners at the Entering, Beginning, or Developing levels of English proficiency. Expressive writing has a minimum of formal language and doesn't interact much with classroom content. It may be used at all stages of language proficiency, but it is the only kind of writing low-proficiency students will be able to do in class. When ELLs have only limited oral English, their writing will probably look like their oral English. It will use the same words, and the words may look like a transcription of their speech. Here is an example of expressive writing, written by a ninth-grade Spanish ELL as a caption to a drawing:

> *What I like to improve was my Inglish because I don't speke to much.*

TABLE 9.2. Three Levels of Formality and Complexity in English Writing

Level of writing	Description of writing demands	Examples of common writing assignments in this type of writing	Scaffolding to help ELLs at level and to prepare to advance to the next level
Level I: Expressive writing TESOL Proficiency Level: Entering, Beginning, Developing	• Drawing representational drawings • Labeling • Drawing and labeling • Describing lived experiences • Describing familiar people, places, and things • Writing simple and compound sentences • Writing a short paragraph • Filling out a simple form	• Labeling • Drawings people, objects, and events • Drawing cartoons depicting events • Stories • Poetry • Diaries • Journals • Personal narratives • Songs • Fantasy • Friendly letters • Captions for a photo essay or cartoon	• Teacher modeling of sentences and stories • Language experience approach • Shared writing—each student contributes a sentence, all transcribed by teacher and coherence, connectors are talked about • Paired writing with more capable peer, tutor, teacher, adult • Sentence walls • Retelling fieldtrips, holidays, etc., and creating a class book with illustrations • Performing written compositions for parents, the class, others • Providing kid-friendly rubrics to remind ELLs of what good writing looks and sounds like • When doing interactive read-alouds, pausing to discuss author techniques and discussing ways to apply them to one's own writing • Having lots of writing and drawing materials on hand to encourage creative expression • Allowing and encouraging native language writing resources • De-emphasizing "correctness" in favor of developing writing comfort

(cont.)

201

TABLE 9.2. (cont.)

Level of writing	Description of writing demands	Examples of common writing assignments in this type of writing	Scaffolding to help ELLs at level and to prepare to advance to the next level
Level II: Responsive writing TESOL Proficiency Level: Developing, Expanding	• Using connectors to create complex sentences • Using transitions to connect paragraphs • Creating topic sentences • Giving examples • Describing less familiar topics • Making judgments • Giving opinions • Using academic vocabulary • Explaining steps in a process • Indicating topic through a title • Making comparisons • Making recommendations • Giving reasons for preferences • Rereading and revising three-paragraph compositions, five-paragraph themes • Developing a sense of voice and point of view in differing writing tasks	• Filling in simple forms • Writing responses to readings • Learning logs • Dialogue journals • Interviews • Recipes • Book reports • Movie reviews • Reports on an event, person, or place • PowerPoints showing main points • Short compositions based on information in a graphic organizer • Peer editing and peer review • Filling in graphic organizers • Writing about the same event from multiple perspectives • Notetaking • Blogs	• Modeling specific skills involved in the writing process to the whole class, in small groups, and one on one • Teaching academic language to describe the processes writers use, using ample examples • Sharing journals in small groups • Including writing workshop in the literacy program • Doing interactive readalouds of nonfiction and discussing author technique • Author studies and practice writing in that author's style • Using a wide variety of writing activities for all units of the curriculum • Working with ELLs in centers during guided reading • Setting up process writing procedures • Training students to do regular peer editing, using a written rubric • Modeling editing and revising with sample papers • Modeling reflective skills through think-alouds • Encouraging writers to enhance reader comprehension of compositions using supportive illustrations such as clip art and graphic organizers

| Level III: Expository writing TESOL Proficiency Level: Expanding, Bridging, Reaching | <ul><li>Creating a thesis statement and support over a longer composition</li><li>Reporting on research obtained from several sources</li><li>Creating a formal essay</li><li>Showing formal voice through word choices</li><li>Showing conventions of formal writing in paragraphing, citing, or quoting</li><li>Creating a summary based on reading</li><li>Creating a summary of an experiment</li><li>Explaining cause–effect relationships</li><li>Providing written interpretation of information on graphs</li></ul> | <ul><li>Creating graphic organizers</li><li>Research reports</li><li>Writing for school publications</li><li>Timed writing on high-stakes standardized tests</li><li>Essays submitted for college admissions</li><li>Final reports for content classes</li><li>Science lab reports</li><li>Comparing key points of several documents on the same topic</li><li>Writing an in-depth analysis of a work of fiction</li><li>Preparing note cards, summary sheets, or graphic organizers for writing or speaking tasks</li></ul> | <ul><li>Having rubrics for writing on the classroom walls and alluding to features of good writing throughout the curriculum</li><li>Allowing and encouraging use of native language vocabulary as appropriate</li><li>Providing exposure to different text structures, including nonfiction</li><li>Involving library staff and aids in teaching research writing and referencing skills</li><li>Modeling how to integrate information into a common composition, using very easy texts as a model</li><li>Modeling how to integrate information into a common composition, using small excerpts of challenging texts</li><li>Breaking writing into smaller sections and discussing ways to recombine</li><li>Focusing on using larger range of connectors and transition words</li><li>Developing editing skills and metacognitive skills for self-editing and peer editing</li><li>Planning timetable for completion of challenging writing assignments</li></ul> |

We see that she is writing what she would say in English. She is unsure of the verb tenses and spelling: she is writing down her BICS language. This is a starting point for writing narrative essays and short paragraphs. As the student develops her English vocabulary and reading base, she will learn to make sentences that use more CALP language and more formal conventions.

Responsive Writing

We call the second level *responsive writing* because it is usually created in response to something else occurring in the instruction. It might be responding to a reading, movie, or class lecture; it might be part of a project or report, like the "composing" skills described earlier. At this stage, writers increasingly learn to use academic language and formal features of writing; now, writing no longer simply resembles speech. Writing genres begin to be introduced, and the connectors and language needed for formal presentation of ideas become more important. Students at the Developing and Expanding proficiency levels need a great amount of modeling and guidance in this kind of writing. During this stage, students are introduced to many different kinds of writing genres, including writing tasks in each content area, and they develop skills needed to use writing as a learning tool. Learning journals and note taking are some of the many ways to develop responsive writing.

Expository Writing

The third and highest level, expository writing, uses the language of the content areas to demonstrate academic knowledge and skills. It is strictly CALP language. Vocabulary is specific to the writing genre and the content area, and formal elements need to be in place. This is the area in which ELLs struggle the most. Even when they are deemed capable of exiting an ESL instructional program, ELLs tend to lag behind in writing expository language. The demands of expository writing increase dramatically throughout the grade levels, and by high school, students are asked to perform many complex and challenging writing tasks. If they aren't fully prepared for the transition to expository writing, it can come as a great shock and capsize their academic aspirations. All too often, the writing activities taught in expressive and responsive writing do not provide a bridge to expository writing. Learners may believe they are strong writers only to discover that the qualities they developed in narrative and essay writing did not prepare them for the new demands of expository writing. Teachers must ensure that this doesn't happen by building ELLs' expository writing every step of the way.

The Need to Foreground Expository Writing

Current instructional writing programs often do not adequately ready students to produce expository writing. That is unfortunate because weakness in this one key area can bring about discouragement or poor grades that may result in failure to graduate from high school. Therefore, a good program for ELLs must build in a strong expository writing component.

Errors in ELL Writing

There are many reasons that ELLs might make errors in writing: they may overgeneralize language rules, be unsure of rhetorical or text structures, be unclear about what they want to say or lack the vocabulary to say it, or experience L1 interference. All of these may manifest as mistakes. Writing mistakes dog many a dedicated ELL writer, and the stubborn persistence of errors even after a mistake has been explained, demonstrated, or practiced in class can be exasperating both for the student and the teacher.

Cronnell (1985) found that error patterns of ELL writing could be predicted by their first language, but overall writing quality was not connected to the error patterns themselves. In other words, good writing is more than just "correct" writing. On the other hand, too many grammar errors can impede meaning. All of us who have studied or taught another language are probably aware of the differences between the structures of various languages. In particular, syntax differs from one language to another, and it is very easy to use our L1 syntax when we write in a new language. The problem is that when we are using our L1 syntax, we do not notice that it is wrong until we have internalized an understanding of the new syntax.

The *focus on form (FoF)* approach (Doughty & Long, 2003; Doughty & Williams, 1998) is an approach to error correction that was developed for ESL students in higher education settings but has been used with some school-age learners. In FoF, teachers guide ELLs in the direction of noticing and correcting errors by means of *recasts*. Recasts consist of restating or rewriting the incorrect form generated by the student into a grammatically correct form. When students accept and use the recast, it is called *uptake*. This attention to form, or grammar accuracy, "often consists of an occasional shift of attention to linguistic code features—by the teachers and/or one or more students—triggered by perceived problems with comprehension or production" (Long & Robinson, 1998, p. 23). The important goal of FoF is building self-monitoring strategies in learners that they can use outside of formal academic settings.

ELLs learn to self-monitor their written errors as they practice through carefully targeted techniques. A combination of careful scaffolding with strongly practiced metacognitive skill development is likely to increase editing skill and lessen errors, but the goal should be effective writing with a minimum of mistakes, as opposed to error-free writing.

Cultural Aspects of Writing in English

Expressive writing involves self-revelation and self-discovery through journaling, peer editing, and the like. Revealing oneself in print may be alienating or even threatening to ELLs from cultures in which writing is not used that way. For one thing, issues of privacy differ among cultures, and being asked to write down one's challenges or personal experiences may seem like prying to some families. For another, some face issues regarding legal status that could prove devastating if revealed to the wrong persons. To avoid self-disclosure, students may feel compelled to produce "formulaic" compositions with many platitudes. They may also fabricate stories.

Peer editing is sometimes questioned by ELL families, who may feel uncomfortable with the idea that their children are judged by peers rather than by the teacher. ELL families are eager for their children to have expert models. In classrooms that contain native speakers and ELLs, there is also a valid concern that peer editing of an L1 writer by an ELL with less language knowledge can create a stressful situation for both.

Cultural considerations also influence vocabulary choices in writing. For fear of writing a wrong word, language learners often choose to "play it safe" by writing only the words they are absolutely sure of, making for a very dull read. Building metalinguistic awareness of language will help ELLs develop the courage to go out on a limb and try to use unique words and phrases—even if they don't pan out the first few times. By the way, praise by teachers helps a lot!

Understanding Plagiarism

In addition, cultural aspects defining copying and plagiarism differ dramatically among cultures, and concepts of plagiarism in the U.S. school system are often confusing or obscure. Some ELLs may not clearly understand what plagiarism really is; many teachers rush through this at the beginning of the year, and others do not cover it at all. Few reinforce it during the year. Also, insecure ELLs looking for a model from which to write may think that wholesale imitation of a valued writer is the best way to be a good student. They may have no idea what the teacher is looking for, so they provide the writing they think is most likely to please the teacher. Problems with plagiarism have multiplied a thousandfold in this era of digital technology and the Internet.

Spelling Is Just a Recoding Skill

ELLs are likely to have more spelling errors than L1 writers because of less developed probabilistic reasoning (see Chapter 4) about the graphophonemic system of English or interference from their L1 sound and writing systems. Although spelling is correlated to some extent with good reading, it is not an important component of good writing, in the same way handwriting is not very important. Spelling and handwriting can be thought of as "accessories"—they can beautify or distract, but they are not the main garment!

All too many writers, both native speakers and ELLs, believe they cannot write well simply because they have spelling problems. Spelling can be checked in the final stages of editing, during proofreading. Let's face it—opaque English is a "spelling problems" language, so we need to keep spelling in perspective!

Guidance from the ELP Standards

The TESOL/WIDA writing standards, found in Appendix 9.1, summarize the writing skills needed across all the grades of school according to three categories: linguistic complexity, vocabulary usage, and language control. *Linguistic complexity* refers to the ability of a writer to create complex sentences and paragraphs that are well-organized, coherent, and varied. *Vocabulary usage* refers to knowing and choosing words and phrases that best express a wide variety of ideas and purposes while keeping the reader's interest. Language control, an issue of special concern in teaching ELLs, refers to having enough grammatical accuracy in writing that errors do not impede comprehensibility of the written text. These three areas can be used as a yardstick for checking on the growth of ELLs' writing skills, whether they are involved in expressive, responsive, or expository writing.

HOW DOES THIS LOOK IN THE CLASSROOM?

We separate out suggestions about writing activities into three divisions: intensive writing activities, which are skill based and structured; extensive writing activities, which are more open ended and designed to address the affective rewards of writing; and writing for learning activities, that are useful mainly as a support for academic learning.

Good writers do all three of these kinds of writing, which are both overlapping and complementary. Extensive writing activities foster a love of writing, confidence about writing, and the writing habit, and they create the motivation to want to persevere at writing. Extensive writing activities for ELLs can be organized in almost the same way as those offered to L1 children.

Intensive writing activities, on the other hand, are targeted to specific writing needs faced by ELLs and others; they consist of all of the skill-building activities used in an L1 writing classroom along with a number of additional skills. These include the mini-lessons that are part of writing workshop, but they also include components of responsive and expository writing that allow students to be able to summarize, find supporting quotations, use formal language, and so forth.

Writing for learning activities, the third genre, include metacognitive activities like showing one's thinking process in finding a solution to a problem or using a graphic organizer to organize study notes. These activities are likely to be found in content-area classrooms, whereas the other two more often reside in the language arts classroom.

Whichever of the three modes of writing is used, it is important for teachers of ELLs to recognize the importance and value of writing, so that it is not just squeezed into the schedule as an afterthought, but woven into the fabric of every single school day, as well as in homework assignments. In addition to its other benefits, time spent doing content writing can ultimately save class time needed for review, because writing about content tends to help students remember it better (Tierney & Shanahan, 1990).

Intensive Writing Activities

Providing Sentence Frames

As ELLs are learning simple sentences, it helps to provide "fill-in-the-blank" sentence frames that they can modify with a single word or phrase. Even when ELLs are at an advanced level, sentence frames are a great way to lock in sentence patterns.

> *A sentence frame I've always enjoyed showing students is "He/she/it is as _____ as _____." I demonstrate several colorful phrases in English like "The wrestler is as strong as a lion," or "That joke is as old as the hills" and then ask students to think of their own. Often students have amusing phrases from their own cultures. My favorite is the Polish "He's as dumb as a doorknob." It's also a chance to talk about the roles animals play in different cultures. That also serves as a nice tie-in to folktales.*—KRISTIN

The Dictocomp: A Transitional Way to Summarize Main Ideas of a Text

One way to help build student learn summary writing while building listening comprehension is by having them respond in writing to an oral text rather than a reading. The technique is called a dictocomp. In a dicto-comp, a teacher preteaches a couple of ideas in the text he or she is about to read, explains to the students that they will be writing a response to the oral text, and then reads it out loud several times, at a relaxed pace. Then students are asked to write the main idea. A rubric that encapsulates the important points in the text can be designed in advance (Bailey, 1998, pp. 149–150). This is a good transition for ELLs who are not yet swift read-ers but still need to practice the vital skill of summary writing. In many states, students are asked to demonstrate comprehension of a text in sev-eral content areas, not just the language arts, and dictocomp helps to build this skill.

Getting out the Scissors

As students learn to organize and move around material, especially in their content-area writing, it helps to write on every other line. That gives them enough room to cut and move their written work around, trying out various potential organization patterns. Often inexperienced writers do include important examples or reasons in their writing, but they put them in the wrong place in the text, as an afterthought. Cutting sentences destroys the idea that any particular arrangement of words is sacrosanct, and conveys the idea that reordering sentences and paragraphs is a natural part of the editing process.

Expository Writing Can Begin in Middle Elementary Grades

There is no reason to hold back on expository writing until a certain age. Children can learn the principles of collecting and recording data on top-ics even before they are reading connected text or doing extensive writing. For example, the life cycle of butterflies can be charted using information gained from different picture books, movies, and measurements taken from the butterfly hatchery in the classroom. Then students can write a sentence or a paragraph describing their findings. ELL students should learn the foundations of expository writing by the time they are at the Developing level. When new skills are taught using topics with which they are already familiar, they can focus on the writing procedures; by the time the content is more challenging, the procedures have become part of their academic routine.

Filling in Comic Strips—a Way to Transition to Narrative Writing

To make the transition from sentence writing to writing a narrative, teach-ers can provide paper with empty cartoon strips with three, six, or nine boxes and ask students to fill them in with drawings about an event in their life. After drawing the comic, they then write captions for the story underneath the cartoon. When the drawings are taken away, students have the beginnings of a story, which can then be written again in full sentences, adding connectors.

Extensive Writing Activities

Dialogue Journals

Dialogue journals are a powerful way for students to use writing to communicate their thoughts and feelings. They can be arranged in different ways according to the teacher's classroom organization. Dialogue journals are kept in a separate notebook, not just on loose-leaf paper, and the entries are usually dated. They can be written in class or as homework. They may be turned in to a teacher, who may write comments and return the journal, or they may be shared with other students. Dialogue journals can even be kept in an online setting, as blogs.

Dialogue journals share these features:

- Topics are freely chosen.
- Journals are read for content, not form.
- Dialogue journals should not be graded, except perhaps for number of entries.
- Some sort of real dialogue occurs between the reader and the writer.

*When I taught low-proficiency adult immigrants, I assigned dialogue journals that could be done in written or oral form. If students felt they needed more writing practice, they wrote the journals. If they wanted more opportunity to practice their speaking, they could record dialogue entries on a cassette. Several students chose taped dialogue journals. Each week, I would take their tapes home and listen to the journals and then record a response at the end of their last entry. After listening to my responses, they would record their new entries over my responses. By the end of the class, students remarked that they could hear how much their speaking fluency had improved just by listening to their tape. The tapes also became a cherished artifact of their early efforts in English, to be listened to years later.—*KRISTIN

Language Experience Approach

The *language experience approach (LEA)* can be considered one kind of writing for learners at the Entering or Beginning level. In this technique, students narrate sentences or a story to a teacher, who writes it down and then asks the student to read it back. LEA can be a powerful bridge to writing when learners have something to say but have not mastered enough conventions of the writing system to encode it. When students realize that their spoken word can be turned into a written composition, it eases the transition into writing. Young ELLs can illustrate their LEA stories, and older learners can recopy the story the teacher has transcribed for practice in writing conventions.

Encouraging Students to Write in Their Preferred Languages

Giving ELLs the choice of what language to use can be very reassuring to students who are trying to project their identity onto paper. Although L1 writing can help achieve higher level writing goals, it is also true that writing about one's life in a new language can be quite liberating (Steinman, 2005). As their education proceeds, there may be a change in ELLs' language writing dominance. The long range goal of bilingualism and biliteracy, however, is always one to be supported.

Using a Multimodal Approach

Writing can emanate from many different sources and modes, and adolescents place a high value on music and movies. These can be used positively in learning situations. At least one finding has shown that high school ELLs benefit from writing activities that combine language and content with cooperative group activities that involve the media (Early & Marshall, 2008).

Writing for Learning Activities

Think-Alouds with Modeled Writing

The very best way to model writing conventions and techniques for ELLs is through the use of think-alouds. A teacher stands at an overhead projector, facing the class, and writes a paragraph on a transparency while thinking aloud through the process. This gives ELLs a rich insight into the writing process. They not only hear the thinking process that goes into such processes as creating a thesis statement, capitalizing letters, or choosing words and connectors, but they also see the text actually being created on the image in front of them. This kind of modeling fills in the gaps for ELLs and is a powerful form of real-time learning.

We know one teacher who used this technique every Friday, either in response to different writing prompts she provided or to construct summaries of what the students had learned that week. She modeled different genres, including friendly letters, book reports, and summary paragraphs. When the composition was completed on the overhead, students copied it verbatim into their writing notebooks. This continued for several months and provided a foundation upon which students could build their own writing, with the security that they knew what a good paragraph looked like. The students achieved impressive results on the writing portion of their annual test of English proficiency, well above students in a class that did not use this practice. The teacher pointed out that this seemingly prescriptive method actually helped students grow wings to write more creatively on their own because they had confidence about the fundamentals of what good writing should look like.

Reading Drafts Aloud

Reading drafts aloud, whether alone or to a partner, helps ELL writers become better editors of their work. Sometimes words might not "sound right" even when they look right on the page—a common phenomenon for all students, but especially ELLs from different L1 writing systems. For some learners, their ears are better developed in English than their eyes (and BICS skills generally precede CALP skills), so they can hear and correct mistakes when they listen to themselves read. Build this into the editing routine.

Graphic Organizers Help Writing, Not Only Reading

Graphic organizers help readers find main ideas, summarize, extract information from several sources, and more. Many of the strategies that help ELLs construct meaning from text while reading also help them construct meaningful text when they write. When students are at the Developing level of proficiency and are beginning to write paragraphs, semantic maps help them brainstorm and organize their ideas. During the writing and revising stages, writers can identify gaps in their organization by representing their main points on outlines, Venn diagrams, T-charts, and the like. They can check that they are following the structures of the genre in which they are writing by looking at graphic organizers for text structures, such as cause–effect charts or timelines. They can also make use of blank templates to make sure they are following the correct form, such as blank frames for friendly letters, lab reports, and so on.

After writing, rubrics and checklists can help students monitor their own writing by proofreading. Graphic organizers work best when they are displayed around the classroom and referred to frequently, so that students will naturally look at them for guidance.

Arlene Duval's unique use of woodland characters to accompany writing responses to reading can be seen in Figure 9.1.

Arlene Duval, a K–5 ESL pull-out teacher, uses a number of visual supports to support her students' reading and writing activities. Arlene has adopted a scaffold that she calls an "Owl of Many Questions." A bulletin board holds a laminated owl for each student attached by Velcro to the bulletin board. When students come in, they take their owl off the bulletin board. When they sit down to read in small groups, the first thing they do is to write the guiding strategy they are focusing upon on one wing of the owl. Then they formulate the questions they are going to use to guide their reading by writing questions on the owl's body with a marker. It sits by them as they read, reminding them what questions and strategies are guiding their reading. The owl's body can be dry-erased every time it is used, and students return the owl to the bulletin board after the day's lesson. Arlene says, "They usually couldn't wait to get them and were always excited when I told them we would be using them." The activity worked well for all grade levels.

To give students a chance to talk about books they have read, she and her coteacher, Amanda Raudebush, created a tree on one of the walls of the classroom. They wrote this poem and put it on the trunk:

Minds mature fed with reading
Leaves grow with lots of feeding
For every book you get to know
A new leaf will bud and grow.

When students finished a book, they wrote something about it on a "leaf" and added it to a branch of the tree. Arlene says that even students who didn't take easily to writing loved to fill out a leaf and add it to the tree.

Instead of a word wall, Arlene and Amanda put up "bee-loved words" on a hive hanging on the tree. The "bee-loved words" are words ESL students tend to overuse, such as "good" or "big." The overused word is written on the bee's body and students, in pairs, write synonyms (such as huge, enormous, gigantic, or vast) on the wings. When students did a writing activity, they referred to the words. "Since I only had room for one word wall and I had students coming in from several grade levels, I made the words for each grade level in a different color—pink for first grade, blue for second grade," Arlene explains.

Arlene Duval holding an Owl of Many Questions
and showing a photo of the bulletin board.

(cont.)

FIGURE 9.1. A tree, a beehive, and an "Owl of Many Questions."

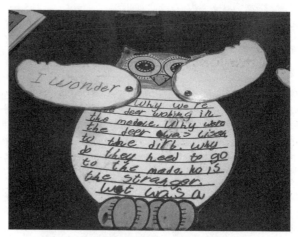

The "Owl of Many Questions."

Word tree, poem, and "Bee-loved" words in Arlene Duval's classroom.

FIGURE 9.1. *(cont.)*

QUESTIONS FOR FURTHER DISCUSSION

1. If you had to choose three important ideas from this chapter, which would you choose? How can you apply these ideas to your larger knowledge of teaching English as a new language?

2. Think about the writing instruction you received in elementary or high school. In what ways have those experiences influenced how you think about yourself as a writer?

3. Look at Table 9.2 and think about the areas in which you feel confident or less confident as a teacher of writing. Discuss with a partner.

4. If possible, analyze a writing program for ELLs with which you are familiar and see what kinds of experiences it provides students to produce expressive, responsive, and expository writing. Look at Table 9.2 and see which activities are included or missing from each of the three levels of writing. In what areas is the writing program strong? In which area(s) does it require strengthening?

5. Looking at the right column of Table 9.2, in which areas do you think ELLs require the same amount of scaffolding as L1 writers? In which do they require more?

6. What experiences have you had learning or teaching intensive, extensive, and writing for learning activities? What do you think constitutes a proper balance of the three?

7. Do you think handwriting is a skill ELLs should be taught? In what ways might handwriting practice enhance understanding of English reading or spelling, if any?

Writing Rubric of the WIDA Consortium Grades 1–12

Level	Linguistic Complexity	Vocabulary Usage	Language Control
6 Reaching	A variety of sentence lengths of varying linguistic complexity in a single tightly organized paragraph or in well-organized extended text; tight cohesion and organization	Consistent use of just the right word in just the right place; precise vocabulary usage in general, specific or technical language.	Has reached comparability to that of English proficient peers functioning at the "proficient" level in statewide assessments.
5 Bridging	A variety of sentence lengths of varying linguistic complexity in a single organized paragraph or in extended text; cohesion and organization	Usage of technical language related to the content area; evident facility with needed vocabulary	Approaching comparability to that of English proficient peers; errors don't impede comprehensibility
4 Expanding	A variety of sentence lengths of varying linguistic complexity; emerging cohesion used to provide detail and clarity	Usage of specific and some technical language related to the content area; lack of needed vocabulary may be occasionally evident	Generally comprehensible at all times, errors don't impede the overall meaning; such errors may reflect first language interference
3 Developing	Simple and expanded sentences that show emerging complexity used to provide detail	Usage of general and some specific language related to the content area; lack of needed vocabulary may be evident	Generally comprehensible when writing in sentences; comprehensibility may from time to time be impeded by errors when attempting to produce more complex text
2 Beginning	Phrases and short sentences; varying amount of text may be copied or adapted; some attempt at organization may be evident	Usage of general language related to the content area; lack of vocabulary may be evident	Generally comprehensible when text is adapted from model or source text, or when original text is limited to simple text; comprehensibility may be often impeded by errors
1 Entering	Single words, set phrases, or chunks of simple language; varying amounts of text may be copied or adapted; adapted text contains original language	Usage of highest-frequency vocabulary from school setting and content areas	Generally comprehensible when text is copied or adapted from model or source text; comprehensibility may be significantly impeded in original text

Note. Level 6 is reserved for students whose written English is comparable to that of their English-proficient peers.

From Teachers of English to Speakers of Other Languages (2006). Reprinted by permission.

Glossary

abbreviation: one of the processes for forming new words in English (e.g., *Mass.* for Massachusetts).

academic writing: writing involving complex composing tasks, such as synthesizing, analyzing, proving theses, etc., usually performed in academic situations.

acronym: one of the processes for forming new words in English (e.g., *ATM* [automatic teller machine], *radar* [radio detecting and signaling device]).

affect: emotional response, often characterized as being high, low, flat, and so on.

affective filter: emotional response to the language learning situation, characterized as either high or low.

affix: morpheme attached to a base, root, or stem to form words or change grammatical categories; prefixes and suffixes in English.

alphabet: writing system in which letters (*graphemes*) represent sounds (*phonemes*).

alphabetic orthography: writing system having a symbol or symbols representing each vowel and consonant sound.

assimilative motivation: incentive to learn a new language and construct a new personal identity in order to merge entirely into a group or community.

auding: interaction between active listeners and oral texts, active listening.

audio imaging: using sounds or music to prompt visualization in order to remember a word, event, or idea.

audiolingual method (audiolingualism): language teaching method in which oral skills (oracy) take precedence over reading and writing skills.

auditory comprehension: a synonym for listening comprehension (see comprehension of oral language).

automaticity theory of reading: theory claiming that learning to read better requires moving from effortful decoding of words to unconscious and automatic decoding of words. (LaBerge & Samuels, 1974).

backformation: one of the processes for forming new words in English (e.g., *televise* from *television*; *teach* from *teacher*).

balanced literacy: an approach combining discrete reading and writing skills within a framework of large meaning-based activities.

basic interpersonal communicative skills (BICS): primarily oral skills ELLs pick up in informal and social situations (Cummins, 1981).

borrowing: one of the processes for obtaining new words in English (e.g., *tortilla*, *pajamas*, *pecan*).

bottom-up skills: word-level skills required for decoding.

bound morpheme: morpheme that must attach to a base, root, or stem to make a word.

bound root: root that must attach to another root or affix in order to create a single morpheme (unit of meaning).

chunking (parsing): separating written text into meaningful phrase or clause units.

clipping: one of the processes for forming new words in English (e.g., *gym* from *gymnasium*; *auto* from *automobile*).

cloze: activity in which blanks are in the place of certain words of a text; oral or written.

cognate: a word having a similar form and meaning in different languages.

cognitive academic language learning approach (CALLA): prominent content-based instructional model (Chamot & O'Malley, 1986).

cognitive academic language proficiency (CALP): the academic language, oral and written, of school, professions, and other literate venues (Cummins, 1979, 1991, 2008).

cognitive load: amount of mental work required for doing a task.

coinage (neologisms): one of the processes for forming new words in English; "making up" words (e.g., *google, Tylenol, kleenex*).

collocation: words occurring together in a fixed order (e.g., listemes, phrasal verbs, and idioms); usually a memorized unit.

communicative approach: a teaching approach involving learners doing meaningful oracy activities with language.

communicative competence: the synergistic knowledge language learners use to make appropriate language choices for different social and academic purposes.

compensatory model of second language reading: L1 literacy, L2 proficiency, and various unidentified variables contribute to L2 reading (Bernhardt, 2005).

compounding: one of the processes for forming new words in English (e.g., *toothbrush, butterfly, snapdragon*).

comprehensible input theory (input theory): theory claiming that enormous amounts of spoken or written language facilitate the acquisition of a new language (Krashen, 1995).

comprehensible output theory (output theory): theory claiming that opportunities for producing spoken and written language are essential for acquisition (Swain, 2005).

comprehension of oral language: a synonym for listening comprehension and auditory comprehension.

concept of word: the ability to tell where words begin and end within the flowing stream of speech.

content area: subject area such as math, science, and social studies.

content-based instruction (CBI): a language teaching methodology in which students learn English while mastering content subject matter.

content frame (semantic feature analysis grid): graphic organizer with attributes of several items classified according to a number of separate characteristics; has a matrix format.

content word: noun, verb, adjective, adverb, and some prepositions.

context-reduced oral language: conversation lacking cues used to compensate for breakdowns in auditory comprehension.

contrastive analysis: predicting or understanding errors produced by learners of a new language based on the structure of their first language.

contrastive stress: changing normal stress patterns of phrases or clauses for emphasis.

conversion (category shift): one of the processes for forming new words in English (e.g., "Are we out of *butter*? Yes, George used all of it to *butter* the toast.").

cross-linguistic homograph: a word that shares the same letters and the same spelling in L1 and L2.

cross-linguistic homophone: a word that shares the same sounds and the same pronunciation in L1 and L2.

cross-linguistic influence: the action, conscious or unconscious, of applying features of a first language to the learning of a new language; often referred to as *transfer*.

decodable word: word having easy-to-match phonemes and graphemes.

decoding: recognizing the sound and meaning of words across a connected text.

deep orthography (opaque orthography): a writing system in which graphemes do not closely represent the phonemes of the language (e.g., Chinese, English).

derivational morpheme: prefix or suffix combined with a base, root, or stem to create words, change word meanings, or change grammatical categories.

dictation: technique in which students write down words or phrases spoken or read by a teacher or a recording; used for practicing listening comprehension, phonological awareness, and concept of word.

digraph: sound represented by two letters, such as *ph*.

discourse marker: conversation fillers, sounds, and paralinguistic cues that help listeners keep track of the speaker's course in an utterance at a given moment.

drop everything and read (DEAR): one sustained silent reading/extended reading technique.

ellipsis: missing words that proficient listeners or readers fill in from context.

English as a foreign language (EFL): term used for studying English in countries where English is not the primary language for communication or schooling.

English language learner (ELL): a learner of any age whose first language is not English.

English language proficiency (ELP): used when talking about level of English proficiency of an English language learner.

English as a second language (ESL): term used for studying English in countries where English is the primary language for communication or schooling.

etymology: the origin and history of a word.

explicit instruction: explaining or demonstrating how certain language features work.

expository writing: purposeful composing for presenting information about a given nonfiction topic.

expressive writing: the early stages of writing, usually narrative and descriptive, based on the writer's observations, feelings, and experiences.

extensive listening activities: getting the gist of oral texts through practice and strategies.

extensive reading: reading large amounts of text for general comprehension.

false cognate: words derived from the same roots but having different meanings in different languages.

fluency: the ability to recognize written words while simultaneously constructing meaning from connected text.

focus on form (FoF): learners and teachers paying in-depth attention to grammatical forms and their meanings in context.

free morpheme: morpheme that can stand by itself as a word; lexical morphemes are functional morphemes.

frontloading: preteaching vocabulary or other knowledge prior to reading a text or beginning a unit of study.

frustration level: the level of text difficulty at which a reader makes too many errors in accuracy and comprehension to be able to benefit from the reading; should be avoided.

function word: article, conjunction, auxiliary verb, pronoun, and some prepositions; also called *functional morpheme*.

functional morpheme: article, conjunction, auxiliary verb, pronoun, and some prepositions; also referred to as *function word*.

free voluntary reading (FVR): an extensive reading technique in which readers pick their own texts.

generative: producing many elements with a given set of rules, such as a generative grammar.

gist: the main idea of a text, either oral or written.

grammar translation approach: a language learning approach using texts to teach grammar with little or no attempt to build communicative competence.

grammatical category: classes of words having certain features in common, such as verbs or nouns.

grapheme: a written symbol that represents speech.

graphic organizer: a visual system for organizing information.

H-chart: graphic organizer with two long overlapping rectangles for representing common features; similar to a Venn diagram.

homograph: term used to describe two words with the same appearance but different sounds and meanings (e.g., "bass" for "bass fishing" or "bass guitar").

homonym: term used to describe two words that look or sound alike; the two kinds of homonyms are homophones and homographs.

homophone: word having the same sound but different meanings and spellings (e.g., *bear, bare; to, too, two*).

hypothetical model of the reading process: reading model focusing on activating an interaction between processing strategies and knowledge bases in order to process a text (Birch, 2007).

idiom: expression that cannot be understood from the meaning of the individual words; memorized as a unit (e.g., *straight from the horse's mouth, raining cats and dogs*); idioms are one kind of collocation.

independent level: the level of text difficulty at which a reader can read without assistance; best for outside reading.

independent writing: stage in process writing for developing ideas more fully.

inferencing: ability to read "between the lines" or make connections within a text, whether oral or written.

inflectional morpheme: morpheme (suffix) combined with base, root, or stem to change grammatical categories or functions of words.

input hypothesis (comprehensible input theory): theory claiming that enormous amounts of spoken or written language at a level learners can comprehend facilitate the acquisition of a new language (Krashen, 1995).

instructional conversation: questioning and sharing ideas and knowledge through dialogue.

instructional level: the level of text difficulty at which a reader can read with scaffolding; target level for classroom instruction.

instrumental motivation: the incentive to learn a new language for a specific purpose (e.g., school, work, relationships).

integrative motivation: the incentive to learn a new language in order to integrate completely into a community.

intensive listening activity: listening practice focusing on discrete features of an oral text.

interactive dialogue (collaborative dialogue): social and academic conversations to form and develop personality, beliefs, and relationships.

interactive process: a description of reading as a process combining bottom-up and top-down skills and strategies.

interactive read-aloud: a teaching technique using a picture book; readers stop at various points for discussion and to monitor comprehension.

interdependence hypothesis: theory claiming that knowledge of one language can be applied to the learning of another language (Cummins, 1979, 1981).

interference: features of the first or subsequent language negatively affecting acquisition of a new language.

intonation pattern: the vocal changes of pitch occurring in the normal course of speaking.

intrinsic motivation: the incentive to learn a new language or anything else "for its own sake."

keyword method: a technique based on forming mental images and connecting them to new words, often through the word's sound.

language distance (linguistic proximity): similarities or differences of features and characteristics shared by languages (e.g., phonemes, word order).

language-based theory of learning: theory claiming all learning is a linguistic process with three interconnected areas: learning language, learning content through language, and learning about language (Halliday, 1993).

language-specific: a linguistic feature occurring only in a given language.

language experience approach (LEA): an approach using a student's dictated stories for a text.

level of difficulty (listening): a percentage of unknown words causing comprehension to break down.

lexical morpheme: free morphemes making up the majority of words in a language; also called *content words*.

lexicon: the mental dictionary; all the words in a language.

lingua franca: a language used by speakers of diverse languages to communicate.

linguistic complexity: complex, organized, coherent, and varied sentences and paragraphs; a highly proficient composing skill.

linguistic proximity: *see* **language distance**.

listeme: a memorized string of words occurring in a fixed order (e.g., idioms); a listeme is one kind of collocation.

listening comprehension (comprehension of oral language or **auditory comprehension)**: the ability to understand spoken language.

listening vocabulary: the storehouse of one's remembered words; also referred to as *oral word bank*.

literacy: reading and writing and related activities.

literacy advantage: the knowledge and benefits that accrue to those literate in a first language; a critical foundation for creating a syndrome of success for reading in a new language.

logographic writing system: a writing system having characters which represent morphemes but may or may not contain phonological information (e.g., Chinese).

metacognition (metacognitive awareness): conscious awareness of one's own thinking and learning processes.

metalinguistic awareness: ability to think about, reflect on, and manipulate the forms and functions of language.

modal auxiliary verbs: verbs used to form moods; precede main verbs (e.g., can, must, should).

morpheme: the smallest linguistic unit of meaning.

morphology: units of meaning and the ways they combine to make new words.

morphophonemic: containing both phonemic and morphological information; a morpheme may have different pronunciations due to surrounding sounds in a word (e.g., *please, pleasure*).

motherese (caretaker speech): vocalizations such as rising and falling pitch contours, exaggerated rising pitch for questions, and slow, deliberate pacing used by adults with infants and beginning language learners to aid comprehension.

multiple processes: one of the processes for forming new words in English, combining other processes such as borrowing and clipping (e.g., *deli*, from the German *delicatessen*).

onset: the vowel or consonant(s) beginning a syllable.

opacity: the degree to which symbols or graphemes are in close correspondence with the phonemes of a language; a language can be classified as more transparent (a close correspondence) or opaque (not a close correspondence).

oracy: the combined skills of listening and speaking; used as a parallel to literacy.

oral proficiency: high level of achieved speaking skill.

oral text: words being spoken.

orthographic depth: *see* **opacity**.

orthographic distance: similarities and differences between two or more writing systems.

orthography: the written system of a language.

output hypothesis (comprehensible output theory): theory claiming that opportunities for producing spoken and written language are essential for acquisition (Swain, 2005).

paired-word sound play: one of the processes for forming new words in English; the second word sounds like the first except for a vowel or consonant (e.g., *hip-hop, wishy-washy, humdrum*).

paralinguistic feature or cue: linguistically and culturally specific non-word-based cue, such as a gesture or body language.

phoneme: smallest unit of sound having meaning; each language has a different set.

phoneme segmentation: breaking down phonemes of a word and putting them back together for reading and writing.

phonics: the letter–sound and sound–letter relationships and spelling patterns in a language; opaque alphabetic orthographies require more phonics practice.

phonological awareness: the ability to decode and pronounce words, a predictor of reading success.

phonological loop: taking visual or auditory data and transferring it into short-term and then long-term storage through repetition.

phonology: the sound patterns of a language and the rules governing how they combine; the distinct auditory identity of a language.

phrasal verb: the combination of a verb and one or more prepositions or occasionally a verb and an adverb (e.g., *get up, sit down*); these can be considered collocations.

polysemous word: word having the same spelling and pronunciation as another word, but with different meanings (e.g., *bank* [for money], *bank* [land at the side of a stream], *bank* [to tilt an airplane wing in order to turn], *bank* [safe place for storage]).

positive cross-linguistic influence (PCI): the facilitating effects of the first language on second language acquisition.

prefix: affix placed at the beginning of a word.

probabilistic reasoning: a cognitive skill developed by a reader through practice that a letter or combination of letters will likely correspond to a certain sound or a combination of sounds (e.g., the letter *b* will sound like /b/); also used in other cognitive tasks.

process writing: model focusing on the process of writing rather than the end product; stages include prewriting, drafting, revising, editing, and publishing.

prompt: an oral or written cue to which students are asked to respond in speaking or writing.

prosody: vocal patterns and inflections used in speaking or reading aloud; they are language-specific.

publish: sharing writing with an audience; a stage in process writing.

punctuation: written conventions representing oral speech (e.g., commas, periods, exclamation marks).

purpose for listening: clearly defined goals for a listening comprehension task.

reading comprehension: the ability to construct meaning from a given written text.

reading comprehension strategy: term used to represent numerous conscious and unconscious processes for understanding a written text.

realia: using "real" objects, such as children's clothing items, food items, seeds, leaves, flowers, etc., for building background knowledge.

recasts: creating a grammatically correct form by restating or rewriting an incorrect form.

recoding: representing spoken words in written form.

redundancies: the built-in overlap in oral and written texts that allows a person to discern a meaning even if some of his or her cueing is incomplete; there are more redundancies in oral text than written text to aid comprehension.

resiliency: ability to persevere to overcome obstacles.

responsive writing: writing, such as descriptions, directions, book or movie reviews, interviews, newsletter articles, reports, and summaries, that is made in response to something seen, heard, or read.

revising and editing: refining ideas and preparing text for publishing; a critical stage in the process writing model.

rime: in a syllable, the vowel and any consonants coming after the onset (e.g., *-ang* is the rime for *sang, bang*).

root: morpheme containing the primary meaning of a word; may be the base for attaching affixes.

scale change: one of the processes for forming new words in English; adding a prefix or suffix can show quantity, size or familiarity (e.g., *macroeconomics, minimart, hoodie, Bobbie*).

second-language acquisition (SLA): term used for the numerous components related to acquiring a new language (e.g., SLA theory, SLA research, SLA methodology).

semantic feature analysis (content grid): graphic organizer with attributes of several items classified according to a number of separate characteristics; has a matrix format.

semantic map: a graphic organizer used to connect a word with many associations; often used as a prewriting activity or for activation of prior knowledge; has a spider web format.

semantics: the meanings of morphemes, words, phrases, and sentences.

shallow orthography (transparent orthography): a writing system having symbols or graphemes that closely match the phonemes of the language (e.g., Spanish, Turkish).

sheltered instruction: subject matter content adapted to ELLs' language proficiency levels; used in CBI models.

sheltered instruction observation protocol (SIOP): research-based model used in sheltered instruction (Echevarria et al., 2004).

short-circuit hypothesis: theory claiming that high levels of second language proficiency are necessary for first language reading skills to facilitate second language reading (Clarke, 1980).

sight word: a word whose spelling pattern is not easily decodable and whose spelling has low frequency of occurrence.

signal words, transitions, and connectors: discourse signals conveying information at numerous levels in texts—for example, *because, additionally* (signal words), *thus, therefore* (transitions), *so, although, but* (connectors).

silent period: a prespeech stage focusing on listening to and understanding language.

simple view of reading: decoding times language/listening comprehension produces reading comprehension (Gough & Tunmer, 1986).

socially constructed: understandings based on social interactions to provide frameworks for learning.

specially designed academic instruction in English (SDAIE): program used in California for content-based instruction of English.

sustained silent reading (SSR): students and teacher reading silently on a daily basis; an extensive reading technique.

stem: a root plus one or more affix.

story grammar: predictable pattern of anticipated elements or events in a story.

stress pattern: audible differences in pronounced length, pitch, and volume of words or groups of words; they are language-specific.

suffix: affix placed at the end of a word.

syllabary: a writing system in which the majority of its symbols represent syllables (e.g., Cherokee).

syllabic writing system: a writing system in which each symbol represents a consonant–vowel combination (e.g., Japanese Hiragana and Katakana).

syllable: set of vowel–consonant patterns making up English words.

syndrome of success: seemingly disconnected factors, such as developing literacy and learning a new language, which work together for a positive outcome.

syntax: word order or arrangement of words forming phrases and clauses in a language.

T-chart: graphic organizer for organizing information with two charts of information alongside each other.

telling versus composing: using one's own experiences as a basis for writing (telling) versus using academic information (composing) as a basis for writing.

TESOL (Teachers of English to Speakers of Other Languages): professional organization of ESL experts and educators; author/publisher of the TESOL Standards.

text structure: organization of texts by genre (e.g., fiction, nonfiction, drama, research paper, editorial); reading strategy focusing on the specifics of text organization.

think-aloud/verbal report: orally modeling the ways vocabulary and ideas are understood or tasks are completed; also, an informal assessment of comprehension.

threshold hypothesis: theory claiming that high levels of first and second language proficiency provide cognitive benefits (Cummins, 1976, 1979).

threshold theory: theory claiming L2 proficiency, not L1 literacy, determines reading and writing proficiency in the second language (Alderson, 1984, 2000).

top-down skills: analytical and cognitive skills needed for reading comprehension.

total physical response (TPR): listening comprehension strategy having students respond to language prompts with movements.

transfer: the ability of first language skills to assist in acquiring particular second language skills; a synonym for interdependence hypothesis.

transparency: a close match between phonemes and graphemes.

transparent orthography (shallow orthography): writing systems having a close match between phonemes and symbols (e.g., Spanish, Dutch).

uptake: accepting and using recasts in which students correct their own grammatical errors.

Venn diagram: graphic organizer with overlapping ovals for representing features, such as similarities and differences; can be used to guide reading or writing. *See also* H-chart.

visualization: forming a visual image in the mind in order to remember or evoke a word, event, or idea.

vocabulary usage: the use of a repertoire of words for reading and composing.

word calling: decoding words of a text aloud with little or no comprehension of their meaning.

word recognition: various ways of recognizing and accessing individual words.

word retrieval: quickly retrieving and pronouncing a word from long-term memory.

writing workshop: name used for well-known process writing method; emphasizes collaboration and support during all stages of composing.

zone of proximal development (ZPD): learning and developmental level at which learners can perform independently, but require assistance to progress to a higher level (Vygotsky, 1986).

References

Alderson, J. C. (1984). Reading in a foreign language: A reading problem or a language problem? In J. C. Alderson & A. H. Urquhart (Eds.), *Reading in a foreign language* (pp. 1–24). London: Longman.

Alderson, J. C. (2000). *Assessing reading.* Cambridge, UK: Cambridge University Press.

Allington, R. (2002). Oral reading. In P. D. Pearson, R. Barr, M. L. Kamil, & P. Mosenthal (Eds.), *Handbook of reading research* (pp. 829–864). Mahwah, NJ: Erlbaum.

The American heritage dictionary of the English language (4th ed.). (2000). Boston: Houghton Mifflin.

Anderson, N. (1999). *Exploring second language reading.* Boston: Heinle & Heinle.

Asher, J. (1988). *Learning another language through actions: The complete teacher's guidebook.* Los Gatos, CA: Sky Oaks.

Atwell, N. (1987). *In the middle: Writing, reading, and learning with adolescents.* Portsmouth, NH: Heinemann.

Atwell, N. (2002). *Lessons that change writers.* Portsmouth, NH: Heinemann.

August, D., Calderon, M., & Carlo, M. (2002). *Transfer of skills from Spanish to English: A study of young learners. Report for practitioners, parents, and policy makers.* Washington, DC: Center for Applied Linguistics.

August, D., & Shanahan, T. (Eds.). (2006). *Developing literacy in second-language learners: Report of the National Literacy Panel on language-minority children and youth.* Mahwah, NJ: Erlbaum.

Baddeley, A., Gathercole, S., & Papagno, C. (1998). The phonological loop as a language learning device. *Psychological Review, 105,* 1158–1173.

Bailey, K. (1998). *Learning about language assessment.* Pacific Grove, CA: Newbury House.

Baker, S. K., & Good, R. (1995). Curriculum-based measurement of English reading with bilingual Hispanic students: A validation study with second-grade students. *School Psychology Review, 24*(4), 561–578.

Bamford, J., & Day, R. R. (1997). Extensive reading: What is it? Why bother? *The Language Teacher, 21*(5), 6–8, 12.

Bartlett, B. J. (1978). *Top-level structure as an organizational strategy for recall of class-room text.* Unpublished doctoral dissertation, Arizona State University, Tempe, AZ.

Baumann, J. F., & Kame'enui, E. J. (1991). Research on vocabulary instruction: Ode to Voltaire. In J. Flood, J. J. D. Lapp, & J. R. Squires (Eds.), *Handbook of research on teaching the English language arts* (pp. 604–632). New York: Macmillan.

Bear, D. R., Templeton, S., Helman, L., & Baren, T. (2003). Orthographic development and learning to read in different languages. In G. Garcia (Ed.), *English learners: Reaching the highest level of English literacy* (pp. 71–95). Newark, DE: International Reading Association.

Beck, I. L., & McKeown, M. G. (1991). Conditions of vocabulary acquisition. In P. D. Pearson, R. Barr, M. L. Kamil, & P. Mosenthal (Eds.), *Handbook of reading research* (pp. 789–814). Mahwah, NJ: Erlbaum.

Benczik, V. (2001). *Language, writing, literature: A communication theory approach.* Unpublished doctoral dissertation, University of Kansas, Lawrence, KS.

Bernhardt, E. B. (2000). Second-language reading as a case study of reading scholarship in the 20th century. In M. Kamil, P. B. Mosenthal, P. D. Pearson, & R. Barr (Eds.), *Handbook of reading research* (Vol. 3, pp. 791–811). Mahwah, NJ: Erlbaum.

Bernhardt, E. B. (2005). Progress and procrastination in second language reading. *Annual Review of Applied Linguistics, 25,* 133–150.

Bernhardt, E. B., & Kamil, M. (1995). Interpreting relationships between L1 and L2 reading: Consolidating the linguistic threshold and the linguistic interdependence hypotheses. *Applied Linguistics, 16,* 15–34.

Betts, E. A. (1946). *Foundations of reading instruction.* New York: American Book Company.

Biemiller, A. (1970). The development of the use of graphic and contextual information as children learn to read. *Reading Research Quarterly, 6,* 75–96.

Biemiller, A. (1999). *Language and reading success.* Cambridge, MA: Brookline Books.

Birch, B. M. (2002). *English L2 reading: Getting to the bottom.* Mahwah, NJ: Erlbaum.

Birch, B. M. (2007). *English L2 reading: Getting to the bottom* (2nd ed.). Mahwah, NJ: Erlbaum.

Blachowicz, C. Z., Sullivan, D. M., & Cieply, C. (2001). Fluency snapshots: A quick screening tool for your classroom. *Reading Psychology, 22,* 95–109.

Block, C. C., & Pressley, M. (Eds.). (2002). *Comprehension instruction: Research-based best practices.* New York: Guilford Press.

Bouffard, L. A., & Sarkar, M. (2008). Training 8-year-old French immersion students in metalinguistic analysis: An innovation in form-focused pedagogy. *Language Awareness, 17*(1), 3–24.

Bowers, P., Golden, J., Kennedy, A., & Young, A. (1994). Limits upon orthographic knowledge due to processed indexed by naming speed. In V. W. Berninger (Ed.), *The varieties of orthographic knowledge, I: Theoretical and development issues* (pp. 173–218). Dordrecht, The Netherlands: Kluwer.

Brazil, D. (1995). *A grammar of speech.* Oxford, UK: Oxford University Press.

Breen, M., & Candlin, C. (1979). Essentials of a communicative curriculum. *Applied Linguistics, 1*(2), 90–112.

Breen, M. P., & Candlin, C. (1980). The essentials of a communicative curriculum in language teaching. *Applied Linguistics, 1*(2), 89–112.

Britton, J. (1988). Writing, learning, and teacher education. In D. Sheridan (Ed.), *Teaching secondary English: Readings and applications* (pp. 131–148). New York: Longman.

Brown, D. (1950). "And having ears, they hear not." *Journal of the National Education Association, 39*, 586–587.

Brown, G., & Yule, G. (1983). *Teaching the spoken language: An approach based on the analysis of conversational English.* Cambridge, UK: Cambridge University Press.

Brown, H. D. (2001). *Teaching by principles: An interactive approach to language pedagogy* (2nd ed.). White Plains, NY: Longman.

Bryson, B. (1990). *Mother tongue: English and how it got that way.* New York: Harper-Collins.

Bryson, B. (1994). *Made in America: an informal history of the English language in the United States.* New York: Morrow.

Buehl, D. (1995). *Classroom strategies for interactive learning: A monograph of the Wisconsin State Reading Association.* Schofield, WI: Wisconsin State Reading Association.

Calderon, M. (2006). Quality instruction in reading for English language learners. In K. Tellez & H. Waxman (Eds.), *Preparing quality educators for English language learners* (pp. 121–144). Mahwah, NJ: Erlbaum.

Calkins, L. (1984). Learning to think through writing. In A. Jagger & M. T. Smith-Burke (Eds.), *Observing the language learner* (pp. 190–198). Newark, DE: International Reading Association.

Calkins, L. (2006). *A guide to the writing workshop.* Portsmouth, NH: Heinemann.

The Cambridge advanced learner's dictionary (3rd ed.). (2008). Cambridge, UK: Cambridge University Press.

Canale, M. (1983). From communicative competence to communicative language pedagogy. In J. Richards & R. Schmidt (Eds.), *Language and communication* (pp. 2–27). New York: Longman.

Canale, M., & Swain, M. (1980). Theoretical bases of communicative approaches to second language teaching and testing. *Applied Linguistics, 1*, 1–47.

Carlisle, J. F., Beeman, M. B., & Shah, P. P. (1996). The metalinguistic capabilities and English literacy of Hispanic high school students: An exploratory study. *Handbook of the National Reading Conference, 45*, 306–316.

Carrier, K., & Tatum, A. (2006). Creating sentence walls to help English-language learners develop content literacy. *The Reading Teacher, 60*(3), 285–288.

Carver, R. P. (1981). *Reading comprehension and auding theory.* Springfield, IL: Charles C Thomas.

Chall, J. S. (1996). *Stages of reading development* (2nd ed.). Fort Worth, TX: Harcourt Brace.

Chamot, A. U., & O'Malley, J. M. (1986). *A cognitive academic language learning approach: An ESL content-based curriculum.* Wheaton, MD: National Clearinghouse on Bilingual Education.

Chamot, A. U., & O'Malley, J. M. (1994). *The CALLA handbook.* Reading, MA: Addison-Wesley.

Chaney, C. (1992). Language development, metalinguistic skills, and print awareness in 3-year-old children. *Applied Psycholinguistics, 13*(4), 485–514.

Chen, L., & Mora-Flores, E. (2007). *Balanced literacy for English language learners, K–2.* Portsmouth, NH: Heinemann.

Cherry, M. (2008, March–April). *The Humanist* interview: Emel Gokcen. *The Humanist, 68*(2), 24–26.

Chitirri, H. F., & Willows, D. M. (1997). Bilingual word recognition in English and Greek. *Applied Psycholinguistics, 18*(2), 139–156.

Chomsky, N. (1965). *Aspects of the theory of syntax.* Cambridge: The MIT Press.

Chomsky, N. (1972). *Language and mind.* New York: Harcourt.

Clarke, M. A. (1980). The short-circuit hypothesis of ESL reading—or when language competence interferes with reading performance. *Modern Language Journal, 64*(2), 203–209.

Clay, M. (1968). A syntactic analysis of reading errors. *Journal of Verbal Learning and Verbal Behavior, 7,* 434–438.

Clyne, M., Hunt, C. R., & Isaakidis, T. (2004). Learning a community language as a third language. *International Journal of Multilingualism, 1*(1), 33–52.

Cobb, C., & Blachowicz, C. (2007). *Teaching vocabulary across the content areas.* Alexandra, VA: Association for Supervision and Curriculum Development.

Comrie, B., Matthews, S., & Polinsky, M. (Eds.). (1996). *The atlas of languages.* New York: Facts on File.

Craik, F. I. M., & Lockhart, R. S. (1972). Levels of processing: A framework for memory research. *Journal of Verbal Learning and Verbal Behavior, 11,* 671–684.

Cronnell, B. (1985). Language influences in the English writing of third- and sixth-grade Mexican-American students. *Journal of Educational Research, 78*(3), 168–173.

Crystal, D. (1996). *The Cambridge encyclopedia of the English language.* Melbourne, Australia: Cambridge University Press.

Cummins, J. (1976). The influence of bilingualism on cognitive growth: A synthesis of research findings and developmental hypotheses. *Working Papers on Bilingualism, 9,* 1–43.

Cummins, J. (1979). Linguistic interdependence and the educational development of bilingual children. *Review of Educational Research, 49*(2), 222–251.

Cummins, J. (1981). The role of primary language development in promoting educational success for language minority students. In Office of Bilingual Bicultural Education, *Schooling and language minority education: A theoretical framework* (pp. 3–49). Sacramento, CA: State Department of Education.

Cummins, J. (1991). The development of bilingual proficiency from home to school: A longitudinal study of Portuguese-speaking children. *Journal of Education, 173*(2), 85–98.

Cummins, J. (1996). *Negotiating identities: Education for empowerment in a diverse society.* Los Angeles: California Association for Bilingual Education.

Cummins, J. (2003). Reading and the bilingual student: Fact and friction. In G. Garcia (Ed.), *English learners: Reaching the highest level of English literacy* (pp. 2–33). Newark, DE: International Reading Association.

Cummins, J. (2007, April). *Accelerating second language and literacy development.* Presentation made for SDR Associates, Rosemont, IL.

Cummins, J. (2008). *Putting language proficiency in its place: Responding to critiques of the conversational/academic language distinction.* Retrieved May 23, 2008, from *www.iteachilearn.com/cummins/converacademlangdisti.html.*

de Jong, P. F., & van der Leij, A. (2002). Effects of phonological abilities and linguistic comprehension on the development of reading. *Scientific Studies of Reading, 6*(1), 51–77.

Deno, S. L. (1985). Curriculum-based measurement: The emerging alternative. *Exceptional Children, 52,* 219–232.

Deno, S. L., Marston, D., Shinn, M., & Tindal, G. (1983). Oral reading fluency: A simple datum for scaling reading disability. *Topics in Learning and Learning Disabilities, 2,* 53–59.

Deno, S. L., Mirkin, P. K., & Chiang, B. (1982). Identifying valid measures of reading. *Exceptional Children, 49,* 36–45.

De Zutter, H. (1993). *Who said a dog goes bow wow?* New York: Doubleday.

Doughty, C., & Varela, E. (1998). Communicative focus on form. In C. Doughty & J. Williams (Eds.), *Focus on form in classroom second language acquisition* (pp. 114–138). Cambridge, UK: Cambridge University Press.

Doughty, C. J., & Long, M. H. (Eds.). (2003). *The handbook of second language acquisition.* Malden, MA: Blackwell.

Doughty, C. J., & Williams, J. (Eds.). (1998). *Focus on form in classroom second language acquisition.* Cambridge, UK: Cambridge University Press.

Dressler, C., & Kamil, M. (2006). First- and second-language literacy. In D. August & T. Shanahan (Eds.), *Developing literacy in second language learners* (pp. 197–238). Mahwah, NJ: Erlbaum.

Ducate, L. C., & Lomicka, L. L. (2008). Adventures in the blogosphere: From blog readers to blog writers. *Computer Assisted Language Learning Journal, 21*(1), 9–28.

Dulay, H. C., & Burt, M. K. (1974). Natural sequences in child second language acquisition. *Language Learning, 24,* 37–53.

Dulay, H. C., & Burt, M. K. (1977). Remarks on creativity in language acquisition. In M. Burt, H. Dulay, & M. Finocchiaro (Eds.), *Viewpoints on English as a second language* (pp. 95–126). New York: Regents.

Dutro, S., & Moran, C. (2003). Rethinking English language instruction: An architectural approach. In G. G. García (Ed.), *English learners: Reaching the highest level of English literacy* (pp. 227–258). Newark, DE: International Reading Association.

Dymock, S. (1993). Reading but not understanding. *Journal of Reading, 37*(2), 86–91.

Early, M., & Marshall, S. (2008). Adolescent ESL students' interpretation and appreciation of literary texts: A case study of multimodality. *Canadian Modern Language Review, 64*(3), 377–397.

Echevarria, J., Vogt, M. E., & Short, D. J. (2004). *Making content comprehensible for English learners: The SIOP model* (2nd ed.). Boston: Pearson.

Edwards, W., & von Winterfeldt, D. (1986). On cognitive illustrations and their implications. In H. R. Arkes & K. R. Hammond (Eds.), *Judgment and decision making: An interdisciplinary reader* (pp. 642–679). New York: Cambridge University Press.

Ellis, N. (1997). *Second language acquisition.* Oxford, UK: Oxford University Press.

Ellis, N. C., Natsume, M., Stavropoulou, K., Hoxhallari, L., Van Dall, V. H. P., et al. (2004). The effects of orthographic depth on learning to read alphabetic, syllabic and logographic scripts. *Reading Research Quarterly, 39,* 438–468.

Essley, R. (2008). *Visual tools for differentiating reading and writing instruction.* New York: Scholastic.

Fang, Z. (2008). Going beyond the 'Fab Five': Helping students cope with the unique linguistic challenges of expository reading in the middle grades. *Journal of Adolescent and Adult Literacy, 51*(6), 476–487.

Fender, M. (2001). A review of L1 and L2/ESL word integration skills and the nature of L2/ESL word integration development involved in lower-level text processing [Electronic Version]. *Language Learning, 51*(2), 319–96.

Field, J. (2008). Bricks or mortar: Which parts of the input does a second language listener rely on? *TESOL Quarterly, 42* (3), 411–432.

Fitzgerald, J. (1995). English-as-a-second-language reading instruction in the United States: A research review. *Journal of Reading Behavior, 27*(2), 115–152.

Fletcher, R., & Portalupi, J. (1998). *Craft lessons: Teaching writing K–8.* Portland, ME: Stenhouse.

Fletcher, R., & Portalupi, J. (2001). *Writing workshop: The essential guide.* Portsmouth, NH: Heinemann.

Fraser, C. A. (1999). Lexical processing strategy use and vocabulary learning through reading. *Studies in Second Language Acquisition, 21,* 225–241.

Freeman, D. E., & Freeman, Y. S. (1992). Is whole-language teaching compatible with content-based instruction? *CATESOL Journal, 5,* 103–108.

Freeman, D. E., & Freeman, Y. S. (2004). *Essential linguistics: What you need to know to teach reading, ESL, spelling, phonics, grammar.* Portsmouth, NH: Heinemann.

Freeman, Y. S., & Freeman, D. E. (2009). *Academic language for English language learners and struggling readers: How to help students succeed across the content areas.* Portsmouth, NH: Heinemann.

Freire, P. (1970). *Pedagogy of the oppressed.* New York: Continuum.

Fries, C. C. (1945). *Teaching and learning English as a foreign language.* Ann Arbor, MI: University of Michigan.

Fry, E. B. (1980). The new instant word list. *The Reading Teacher, 34,* 284–290.

Fry, E. B., Kress, J. E., & Fountoukidis, D. L. (1993). *The reading teacher's book of lists* (3rd ed.). Englewood Cliffs, NJ: Prentice Hall.

Fuchs, L. S., & Deno, S. L. (1992). Effects of curriculum within curriculum-based measurement. *Exceptional Children, 58,* 232–242.

Fuchs, L. S., Fuchs, D., Hosp, M., & Jenkins, J. R. (2001). Oral reading fluency as an indicator of reading competence: A theoretical, empirical, and historical analysis. *Scientific Studies of Reading, 5*(3), 239–256.

Fuchs, L. S., Fuchs, D., & Maxwell, L. (1988). The validity of informal reading comprehension measures. *Remedial and Special Education, 9*(2), 20–29.

Garcia, G. E. (2000). Bilingual children's reading. In M. Kamil, P. B. Mosenthal, P. D. Pearson, & R. Barr (Eds.), *Handbook of Reading Research* (Vol. 3 pp. 813–834). Mahwah, NJ: Erlbaum.

Gardner, R. C., & Lambert, W. E. (1972). *Attitude and motivation in second language learning*. Rowley, MA: Newbury House.

Genesee, F., Geva, E., Dressler, C., & Kamil, M. (2006). Synthesis: Cross-linguistic relationships. In D. August & T. Shanahan (Eds.), *Developing literacy in second-language learners* (pp. 153–183). Mahwah, NJ: Erlbaum.

German, D., & Newman, R. S. (2007). Oral reading skills of children with oral language (word finding) difficulties. *Reading Psychology, 28*(5), 397–442.

Gersten, R., & Baker, S. K. (2000). *Practices for English-language learners. An overview of instructional practices for English-language learners*. Newton, MA: National Institute for Urban School Development.

Gersten, R., Baker, S. K., Shanahan, T., Linan-Thompson, S., Collins, P., & Scarcella, R. (2007). *Effective literacy and English language instruction for English learners in the elementary grades*. Washington, DC: National Center for Education Evaluation and Regional Assistance.

Geva, E. (2007). Second-language oral proficiency and second-language literacy. In D. August & T. Shanahan (Eds.), *Developing literacy in second-language learners* (pp. 123–139). Mahwah, NJ: Erlbaum.

Gibbons, P. (2002). *Scaffolding language, scaffolding learning*. Portsmouth, NH: Heinemann.

Goodman, K. (1970). Reading: A psycholinguistic guessing game. In D. Gunderson (Ed.), *Language and reading: An interdisciplinary approach* (pp. 107–122). Washington, DC: Center for Applied Linguistics.

Gottlieb, M. (2006). *Assessing English language learners*. Boston: Pearson.

Gottlieb, M., Cranley, E., & Oliver, A. R. (2007). *Writing rubric of the WIDA Consortium grades 1–12. ELP standards and resource guide, 2007 Edition*. The WIDA Consortium. Retrieved August 22, 2008, from *www.wida.us/standards/RG_Speaking%20Writing%20Rubrics.pdf*.

Gottlieb, M., Katz, A., & Ernst-Slavit, G. (2009). *Paper to practice: Using the TESOL English language proficiency standards in pre-K–12 classrooms*. Alexandria, VA: Teachers of English to Speakers of Other Languages.

Gough, P. B., & Tunmer, W. E. (1986). Decoding, reading, and reading disability. *Remedial and Special Education, 7*(1), 6–10.

Grabe, W. (2001). Reading-writing relations: Theoretical perspectives and instructional practices. In D. Belcher & A. Hirvela (Eds.), *Linking literacies: Perspectives on L2 reading-writing connections* (pp. 15–47). Ann Arbor, MI: University of Michigan Press.

Grabe, W., & Stoller, F. (2002). *Teaching and researching reading*. Harlow, UK: Longman & Pearson.

Graves, D. (1973). *Children's writing: Research directions and hypothesis based upon an examination of the writing process of seven-year-old children* (Doctoral dissertation, University of New Hampshire). *Dissertation Abstracts International, 34*, 6255A.

Graves, D. (1983). *Writing: Teachers and children at work*. Portsmouth, NH: Heinemann.

Graves, D., & Hansen, J. (1983). The author's chair. *Language Arts, 60*, 176–183.

Guilloteaux, M. J., & Dornei, Z. (2008). Motivating language learners: A classroom-oriented investigation of the effects of motivational strategies on student motivation. *TESOL Quarterly, 42*(1), 55–78.

Halliday, M. A. K. (1993). Towards a language-based theory of learning. *Linguistics and Education, 5*(2), 93–116.

Hamilton, C., & Shinn, M. R. (2000). *Characteristics of word callers: An investigation of the accuracy of teachers' judgments of reading comprehension and oral reading skills.* Eugene, OR: University of Oregon. Retrieved January 11, 2003, from *www. uoregon.edu/~mshinn/pdfs/wordcallerspr.pdfciera.org/library/reports/inquiry-2/ 2-008/2-008.html.*

Hargis, C. H., Terhaar-Yonkers, M., Williams, P. C., & Reed, M. T. (1988). Repetition requirements for word recognition. *Journal of Reading, 31,* 320–327.

Helman, L. (2005). Spanish speakers learning to read in English: What a large-scale assessment suggests about their progress. In E. Maloch, J. V. Hoffman, D. L. Schallert, C. M. Fairbanks, & J. Worthy (Eds.), *54th Yearbook of the National Reading Conference* (pp. 211–226). Oak Creek, WI: National Reading Conference.

Hiebert, E. H., Brown, Z. A., Taitague, C., Fisher, C. W., & Adler, M. A. (2004). Texts and English language learners: Scaffolding entrée to reading. In F. Boyd, C. Brock, & M. S. Rozendal (Eds.), *Multicultural and multilingual literacy and language* (pp. 32–53). New York: Guilford Press.

Hiebert, E. H., & Fisher, C. W. (2006). Fluency from the first: What works with first graders. In T. Rasinski, C. Blachowicz, & K. Lems (Eds.), *Fluency instruction: Research-based best practices* (pp. 279–294). New York: Guilford Press.

Hiebert, E. H., & Martin, L. A. (2007). Repetition of words: The forgotten variable in texts for beginning and struggling readers. In E. H. Hiebert & M. Sailors (Eds.), *Finding the right texts: What works for beginning and struggling readers* (pp. 47–69). New York: Guilford Press.

Hinkel, E. (Ed.). (2005). *Handbook of research in second language teaching and learning.* Mahwah, NJ: Erlbaum.

Hintze, J., Shapiro, E., & Conte, K. L. (1997). Oral reading fluency and authentic reading material: Criterion validity of the technical features of CBM survey-level assessment. *The School Psychology Review, 26*(4), 535–553.

Hoffman, J. V. (1987). *The oral recitation lesson: A teacher's guide.* Austin, TX: Academic Resource Consultants.

Hoyt, L. (2002). *Make it real: Strategies for success with informational text.* Portsmouth, NH: Heinemann.

Hymes, D. (1971). On communicative competence. In C. J. Brumfit & K. Johnson (Eds.), *The communicative approach to language teaching.* Oxford, UK: Oxford University Press.

Igoa, C. (1995). *The inner world of the immigrant child.* Mahwah, NJ: Erlbaum.

The Internet picture dictionary. (2009). Retrieved Feb. 12, 2009, from *www.pdictionary. com/.*

Jenkins, J. R., & Jewell, M. (1993). Examining the validity of two measures for formative teaching: Reading aloud and maze. *Exceptional Children, 59,* 421–432.

Jimenez, F. (1997). *The circuit: Stories from the life of a migrant child.* Albuquerque, NM: University of New Mexico Press.

Jimenez, R. T., Garcia, G. E., & Pearson, D. P. (1996). The reading strategies of bilingual Latino/a students who are successful English readers: Opportunities and obstacles. *Reading Research Quarterly, 31*(1), 90–112.

Johnson, R., & Moore, R. (1997). A link between reading proficiency and native-like use of pausing in speaking. *Applied Language Learning, 8*(1), 25–42.

Katz, L., & Frost, R. (1992). The reading process is different for different orthographies: The orthographic depth hypothesis. In R. Frost & L. Katz (Eds.), *Orthography, phonology, morphology, and meaning* (pp. 67–84). Amsterdam: Elsevier North Holland Press.

Kieffer, M. J., & Lesaux, N. K. (2008). The role of derivational morphology in the reading comprehension of Spanish-speaking English language learners. *Reading and Writing, 21*(8), 783–804.

Kieffer, M. J., & Lesaux, N. K. (2009). Breaking down to build meaning: Morphology, vocabulary and reading comprehension in the urban classroom. *The Reading Teacher, 61*(2), 134–144.

Kimmel, E. C. (1999). *Balto and the great race.* New York: Random House.

Koda, K. (2005). *Insights into second language reading.* Cambridge, UK: Cambridge University Press.

Koskinen, P. S., Blum, I. H., Tennant, N., Parker, E. M., Straub, M. W., & Curry, C. (1995). Have you heard any good books lately?: Encouraging shared reading at home with books and audiotapes. In L. M. Morrow (Ed.), *Family literacy: Connections in schools and communities* (pp.87–103). Newark, DE: International Reading Association.

Kozub, R. (2000). Reader's theatre and its effect on oral language fluency. *Reading Online.* Retrieved November 1, 2002, from *www.readingonline.org/editorial/august2000/rkrt.htm.*

Krashen, S. (1982). *Principles and practice in second language acquisition.* New York: Pergamon Press.

Krashen, S. (1985). *The input hypothesis.* Beverly Hills: Laredo.

Krashen, S. (1987). Applications of psycholinguistic research to the classroom. In M. H. Long & J. C. Richards (Eds.), *Methodology in TESOL: A book of readings* (pp. 33–44). New York: Newbury House.

Krashen, S. (1992). The effect of formal grammar teaching: Still peripheral. *TESOL Quarterly, 26,* 409–411.

Krashen, S. (2004). *The power of reading: Insights from the research* (2nd ed.). Portsmouth, NH: Heinemann.

Kucer, S. B. (2001). *Dimensions of literacy: A conceptual base for teaching reading and writing in school settings.* Mahwah, NJ: Erlbaum.

Kucer, S. L. (1985). The making of meaning: Reading and writing as parallel processes. *Written Communication, 2*(3), 317–336.

LaBerge, D., & Samuels, S. J. (1974). Toward a theory of automatic information processing in reading. *Cognitive Psychology, 6,* 293–323.

Lado, R. (1977). *Lado English series.* New York: Regents.

Lanauze, M., & Snow, C. E. (1989). The relation between first- and second-language writing skills: Evidence from Puerto Rican elementary school children in bilingual programs. *Linguistics and Education, 1*(4), 323–339.

Lems, K. (2001). An American poetry project for low intermediate ESL adults. *English Teaching Forum, 39*(4), 24–29.

Lems, K. (2002). Music hath charms for literacy . . . in the ESL classroom. *Indiana Reading Journal, 34*(3), 6–12.

Lems, K. (2005). A study of adult ESL oral reading fluency and silent reading comprehension. In E. Maloch, J. V. Hoffman, D. L. Schallert, C. M. Fairbanks, & J. Worthy (Eds.), *54th yearbook of the National Reading Conference* (pp. 240–256). Oak Creek, WI: National Reading Conference.

Lems, K. (2008). *Inverted morphemes pyramid.* Unpublished diagram.

Li, D., & Nes, S. (2001). Using paired reading to help ESL students become fluent and accurate readers. *Reading Improvement, 38*(2), 50–62.

Li, L. (2002). The role of phonology in reading Chinese single characters and two-character words with high, medium and low phonological regularities by Chinese grade 2 and grade 5 students. *Reading Research Quarterly, 37,* 372–374.

List of Grammatical Cases. (2009). Retrieved June 22, 2009, from *en.wikipedia.org/wiki/List of_grammatical cases.*

Long, M. H., & Robinson, P. (1998). Focus on form: Theory, research, and practice. In C. Doughty & J. Williams (Eds.), *Focus on form in classroom second language acquisition* (pp. 15–41). Cambridge: Cambridge University Press.

Longman advanced American dictionary. (2000). Essex, UK: Pearson.

The Longman dictionary of American English (3rd ed.). (2004). Essex, UK: Pearson.

Lyster, R., & Ranta, L. (1997). Corrective feedback and learner uptake: Negotiation of form in communicative classrooms. *Studies in Second Language Acquisition, 19,* 37–61.

The many meanings of get. (1987, January). *English Teaching Forum,* p. 37.

Markell, M. A., & Deno, S. L. (1997). Effects of increasing oral reading: Generalization across reading tasks. *Journal of Special Education, 31,* 233–250.

McCarthey, S. J., Garcia, G. E., Lopez-Velasquez, A. M., & Shumin, G. Y. (2004). Understanding writing contexts for English language learners. *Research in the Teaching of English, 38*(4), 351–394.

McCauley, J. K., & McCauley, D. S. (1992). Using choral reading to promote language learning for ESL students. *The Reading Teacher, 45*(67), 526–533.

McCrum, R., Cran, W., & MacNeil, R. (1986). *The story of English.* New York: Viking.

McGuinness, D. (2004). *Early reading instruction: What science really tells us about how to teach reading.* Cambridge, MA: MIT Press.

McGuinness, D. (2005). *Language development and learning to read: The scientific study of how language development affects reading skill.* Cambridge, MA: MIT Press.

Meyer, B. J. F., Brandt, K. M., & Bluth, G. J. (1980). Use of top-level structure in text: Key for reading comprehension on ninth grade readers. *Reading Research Quarterly, 16,* 72–103.

Mohr, K., & Mohr, E. (2007). Extending English-language learners' classroom interactions using the response protocol. *The Reading Teacher, 60*(5), 440–450.

Moll, L., Estrada, E., Díaz, E., & Lopez, L. (1997). The organization of bilingual lessons: Implications for schooling. In M. Cole, Y. Engeström, & O. Vásquez (Eds.), *Mind, culture, and activity: Seminal papers from the Laboratory of Comparative Human Cognition* (pp. 254–268). Cambridge, UK: Cambridge University Press.

Morris, D. (1993). The relationship between children's concept of word in text and phoneme awareness in learning to read: A longitudinal study. *Research in the teaching of English, 27*(2), 133–154.

Murrow, L. (2008, April 25). The twenty saltiest foods in America. *Men's Health.* Retrieved April 25, 2008, from *www.msnbc.msn.com/id/24313369/.*

Myles, J. (2002). Second language writing and research: The writing process and error analysis in student texts. *TESL-EJ 6*(2). Retrieved March 2, 2009, from *tesl-ej.org/ej22/a1.html.*

Nagy, W. E. (1985). Learning words from context. *Reading Research Quarterly, 20,* 333–353.

Nakamoto, J., Lindsey, K. A., & Manis, F. R. (2007). A longitudinal analysis of English language learners' word decoding and reading comprehension. *Reading and Writing, 20*(7), 691–719.

Nation, I. S. P. (1990). *Teaching and learning vocabulary.* Boston, MA: Heinle and Heinle.

Nation, I. S. P. (2001). *Learning vocabulary in another language.* Cambridge, UK: Cambridge University Press.

National Reading Panel. (2000). *Teaching children to read: An evidence-based assessment of the scientific research literature on reading and its implications for reading instruction.* Washington, DC: National Institute of Child Health and Human Development.

National TESOL Standards. (2008). Retrieved September 1, 2008, from *www.gisd. k12.nm.us/standards/esl/index.html.*

Navaez, D. (2002). Individual differences that influence reading comprehension. In C. C. Block & M. Pressley (Eds.), *Comprehension instruction* (pp. 158–175). New York: Guilford Press.

NIH/National Institute of Child Health and Human Development of the National Institutes of Health. (2004, September 15). Children follow same steps to learn vocabulary, regardless of language spoken. *ScienceDaily.* Retrieved July 11, 2008, from *www.sciencedaily.com /releases/2004/09/040915113243.htm.*

Oded, B., & Walters, J. (2002). Deeper processing for better EFL reading comprehension. *System, 29*(3), 357–370.

Odlin, T. (1989). *Language transfer: Cross-linguistic influences in language learning.* Cambridge, UK: Cambridge University Press.

Odlin, T. (2003). Cross-linguistic influences. In C. J. Doughty & M. H. Long (Eds.), *The handbook of second language acquisition* (pp. 436–486). Malden, MA: Blackwell.

Olson, C. B., & Land, R. (2007). A cognitive strategies approach to reading and writing instruction for English language learners in secondary school. *Research in the Teaching of English, 41*(3), 269–303.

O'Malley, J. M., & Valdez-Pierce, L. (1996). *Authentic assessment for English language learners.* Boston: Addison-Wesley.

Omniglot. (2009). *Omniglot.* Retrieved June 12, 2009, from *www.omniglot.com.*

Online etymology dictionary. (2009). Retrieved February 9, 2009, from *www.etymonline.com/index.php.*

O'Shea, L. J., & Sindelar, P. T. (1983). The effects of segmenting written discourse on the reading comprehension of low- and high-performance readers. *Reading Research Quarterly, 18,* 458–465.

Oxford dictionary of English. (2005). Oxford, UK: Oxford University Press.

Padrón, Y. N., Waxman, H., Brown, A. P., & Powers, R. A. (2000). *Improving classroom instruction and student learning for resilient and non-resilient English language learners.* Santa Cruz, CA: Center for Research on Education, Diversity and Excellence. Retrieved May 23, 2008, from *www.cal.org/crede/pubs/ResBrief7.pdf.*

Pang, E., & Kamil, M. (2003, March). *Cross-linguistic transfer of reading skills in bilingual children.* Paper presented at the meeting of the American Association of Applied Linguistics (AAAL), Arlington, VA.

Parish, H. (1996–2008). *Amelia Bedelia* (series). New York: HarperCollins.

Park, B. (1990–2009). *Junie B. Jones* (series). New York: Random House.

Paulesu, E., McCrory, E., Fazio, F., Menoncello, L., Brunswick, N., Cappa, S. F., et al. (2000). A cultural effect on brain function. *Nature Neuroscience, 3*(1), 91–96.

Pearson, P. D. (2007). An endangered species act for literacy education. *Journal of Literacy Research, 39*(2), 145–162.

Peregoy, S. F., & Boyle, O. F. (2005). *Reading, writing and learning in ESL* (4th ed.). Boston: Pearson.

Phenix, J. (2002). *The writing teacher's handbook.* Portland, ME: Pembroke Publishers.

Pinker, S. (1999). *Words and rules: The ingredients of language.* New York: Basic Books.

Pinker, S. (2000). *The language instinct: How the mind creates language.* New York: Harper.

Pinker, S. (2007). *The language instinct: How the mind creates language.* New York: Harper.

Pluck, M. (2006). "Jonathon is 11 but reads like a struggling 7 year old": Providing assistance for struggling readers with a tape-assisted reading program. In T. Rasinski, C. Blachowicz, & K. Lems (Eds.), *Fluency instruction: Research-based best practices* (pp. 192–208). New York: Guilford Press.

Portalupi, J., & Fletcher, R. (2001). *Nonfiction craft lessons: Teaching information writing, K–8.* Portland, ME: Stenhouse.

Pratt, C., & Grieve, R. (1984). The development of metalinguistic awareness: An introduction. In W. Tunmer, C. Pratt, & M. Herriman (Eds.), *Metalinguistic awareness in children: Theory, research, and implications* (pp. 2–35). New York: Springer-Verlag.

Prince, R. E. C. (2008). *Morphological analysis: New light on a vital reading skill. Usable knowledge.* Cambridge, MA: Harvard Graduate School of Education. Retrieved January 8, 2009, from *www.uknow.gse.harvard.edu/teaching/TC102-407.html.*

Pritchard, R., & O'Hara, S. (2008). Reading in Spanish and English: A comparative study of processing strategies. *Journal of Adolescent and Adult Literacy, 51*(8), 630–638.

Protherough, R. (1993). Three basic questions. In D. Sheridan (Ed.), *Teaching secondary English: Readings and applications* (pp. 124–131). New York: Longman.

Rachlin, H. (1989). *Judgment, decision, and choice: A cognitive/behavioral synthesis.* New York: Freeman.

Ramirez, C. M. (2001). *An investigation of English language and reading skills on read-*

ing comprehension for Spanish-speaking English language learners. Unpublished doctoral dissertation, University of Oregon, Portland.

Rasinski, T. (2000). Speed does matter in reading. *Reading Teacher, 54*(2), 146–151.

Rasinski, T. (2003). *The fluent reader: Oral reading strategies for building word recognition, fluency, and comprehension.* New York: Scholastic Books.

Rasinski, T., Blachowicz, C., & Lems, K. (Eds.). (2006). *Fluency instruction: Research-based best practices.* New York: Guilford Press.

Rasinski, T. V. (1990). Investigating measures of reading fluency. *Educational Research Quarterly, 14*(3), 37–44.

Resource Guide. (2009). *The WIDA performance descriptions.* Retrieved Feb. 6, 2009, from *www.wida.us/standards/RG_Performance%20Definitions.pdf.*

Richard-Amato, P. A. (1988). *Making it happen.* White Plains, NY: Longman.

Richard-Amato, P. A. (2003). *Making it happen* (3rd ed.). White Plains, NY: Longman.

Riedel, B. W. (2007). The relation between DIBELS, reading comprehension, and vocabulary in urban first-grade students. *Reading Research Quarterly, 42*(4), 546–567.

Rivers, W. M. (1981). *Developing foreign-language skills* (2nd ed.). Chicago: University of Chicago Press.

Roberts, T. (2008). Home storybook reading in primary or second language with preschool children: Evidence of equal effectiveness for second-language vocabulary acquisition. *Reading Research Quarterly, 43*(2), 103–130.

Rodriguez, R. (1982). *Hunger of memory: The education of Richard Rodriguez.* Boston: BantamDell.

Rothenberg, C., & Fisher, D. (2007). *Teaching English language learners: A differentiated approach.* Upper Saddle River, NJ: Pearson Merrill Prentice Hall.

Royer, J. M., & Carlo, M. S. (1991). Transfer of comprehension skills from native to second language. *Journal of Reading, 34*(6), 450–455.

Rueda, R., & Garcia, G. (2001). How do I teach reading to ELLs?: Ninth in a series (*Teaching every child to read*). Ann Arbor, MI: Center for the Improvement of Early Reading Achievement.

Rumelhart, D. E. (1980). Toward an interactive model of reading. In R. B. Ruddell, M. R. Ruddell, & H. Singer (Eds.), *Theoretical models and processes of reading* (4th ed.). Hillsdale, NJ: Erlbaum.

Samuels, S. J. (1979). The method of repeated readings. *The Reading Teacher, 32,* 403–408.

Samuels, S. J. (2007). Afterword for B. W. Riedel, The relation between DIBELS, reading comprehension and vocabulary in urban first-grade students. *Reading Research Quarterly, 42*(4), 546–567.

Sasaki, M., & Hirose, K. (1996). Explanatory variables for EFL students' expository writing. *Language Learning, 46,* 137–174.

Saunders, W., & Goldenberg, C. (1999). *The effects of instructional conversations and literature logs on the story comprehension and thematic understanding of English proficient and limited English-proficient students.* Santa Cruz, CA: Center for Research on Education, Diversity & Excellence, University of California.

Savignon, S. (1983). *Communicative competence: Theory and classroom practice: Texts and contexts in second language learning.* Reading, MA: Addison-Wesley.

Scarborough, H. (2001). Connecting early language to later reading (dis)abilities. In S. Neuman & D. Dickensen (Eds.), *Handbook of early literacy research* (pp. 97–110). New York: Guilford Press.

Schmitt, N., & Marsden, R. (2006). *Why is English like that? Historical answers to hard ELT questions.* Ann Arbor: University of Michigan Press.

Schoonen, R., Hulstijn, J., & Bossers, B. (1998). Metacognitive and language-specific knowledge in native and foreign language reading comprehension: An empirical study among Dutch students in grades 6, 8, and 10. *Language Learning, 48,* 71–106.

Shanahan, T., & Beck, I. (2006). Effective literacy teaching for English language learners. In D. August & T. Shanahan (Eds.), *Developing literacy in second-language learners: Report of the National Literacy Panel on language-minority children and youth* (pp. 415–488). Mahwah, NJ: Erlbaum.

Share, D. L., & Stanovich, K. E. (1995). Cognitive processes in early reading development: Accommodating individual differences into a model of acquisition. In J. S. Carlson (Ed.), *Issues in education: Contributions from psychology* (Vol. I, pp. 1–57). Greenwich, CT: J.A.I. Press.

Shinn, M. R., Knutson, N., Good, R. H., Tilly, W. D., & Collins, V. (1992). Curriculum-based measurement of oral reading fluency: A confirmatory analysis of its relation to reading. *School Psychology Review, 21,* 459–479.

Short, D., & Fitzsimmons, S. (2007). *Double the work: Challenges and solutions to acquiring language and academic literacy for adolescent English language learners: A report to Carnegie Corporation of New York.* Washington, DC: Alliance for Excellent Education.

Silva, T. (1993). Toward an understanding of the distinct nature of L2 writing: The ESL research and its implications. *TESOL Quarterly, 27,* 657–677.

Silverstein, S. (1974). *Where the sidewalk ends.* New York: Harper & Row.

Silverstein, S. (1981). *A light in the attic.* New York: Harper & Row.

Skutnabb-Kangas, T., & Toukomaa, P. (1976). *Teaching migrant children's mother tongue and learning the language of the host country in the context of the sociocultural situation of the migrant family.* Helsinki: The Finnish National Commission for UNESCO.

Snow, M. A. (Ed.). (1994). *Project LEAP: Learning English-for-academic-purposes training manual—Yr. 3.* Los Angeles: California State University.

Sobol, D. (1967). *Two minute mysteries.* New York: Apple Paperbacks.

Stahl, S. A., & Kuhn, M. R. (2002). Making it sound like language: Developing fluency. *Reading Teacher, 55*(6), 582–584.

Stanovich, K. (1996). Word recognition: Changing perspectives. In R. Barr, M. Kamil, P. B. Mosenthal, & P. D. Pearson (Eds.), *Handbook of reading research* (Vol. 2, pp. 418–452). Mahwah, NJ: Erlbaum.

Steig, W. (1987). *CDB!* New York: Simon & Schuster.

Steig, W. (2003). *CDC?* New York: Farrar, Straus & Giroux.

Steinman, L. (2005). Writing life 1 in language 2. *McGill Journal of Education, 40*(1), 65–79.

Sticht, T. G., & James, J. H. (1984). Listening and reading. In P. D. Pearson, R. Barr,

M. L. Kamil, & P. Mosenthal (Eds.), *Handbook of reading research* (pp. 293–317). Mahwah, NJ: Erlbaum.

Stoller, F. L., & Grabe, W. (1997). A six T's approach to content-based instruction. In M. A. Snow & D. M. Brinton (Eds.), *The content-based classroom: Perspectives on integrating language and content* (pp. 78–94). White Plains, NY: Longman.

Swain, M. (2000). The output hypothesis and beyond: Mediating acquisition through collaborative dialogue. In J. P. Lantolf (Ed.), *Sociocultural theory and second language learning* (pp. 97–114). Oxford: Oxford University Press.

Swain, M. (2005). The output hypothesis: Theory and research. In E. Hinkel (Ed.), *Handbook of research in second language teaching and learning* (pp. 471–483). Mahwah, NJ: Erlbaum.

Tafa, E., & Manolitsis, G. (2008). A longitudinal literacy profile of Greek precocious readers. *Reading Research Quarterly, 43*(2), 165–185.

Taguchi, E., Takayasu-Maass, M., & Gorsuch, G. J. (2004). Developing reading fluency in EFL: How assisted repeated reading and extensive reading affect fluency development. *Reading in a Foreign Language, 16*(2), 70–96. Retrieved June 24, 2009, from *www.nflrc.hawaii.edu/rfl/October2004/taguchi/taguchi.html*

Taylor, B. P. (1987). Teaching ESL: Incorporating a communicative, student-centered component. In M. H. Long & J. C. Richards (Eds.), *Methodology in TESOL* (pp. 45–60). New York: Newbury House.

Teachers of English to Speakers of Other Languages. (2006). *Pre-K–12 English language proficiency standards. Augmentation of the World-Class Instructional Design and Assessment (WIDA) consortium English language proficiency standards.* Alexandria, VA: Author.

Tellez, K., & Waxman, H. (Eds.). (2006). *Preparing quality educators for English language learners.* Mahwah, NJ: Erlbaum.

Tharp, R. G., Doherty, R. W., Echevarria, J., Estrada, P., Goldenberg, C., Hilberg, R. S., & Saunders, W. M. (2003, March). *Research evidence: Five standards for effective pedagogy and student outcomes. Technical Report No. G1.* Center for Research, Education, Diversity and Excellence. Retrieved May 31, 2008, from *crede.berkeley.edu/research/crede/products/print/occreports/g1.html.*

Thomas, W., & Collier, V. (2002). *A national study of school effectiveness for language minority students' long-term academic achievement.* Technical Report No. 1-1. Center for Research, Education, Diversity and Excellence. Retrieved June 6, 2008, from *crede.berkeley.edu/research/llaa/1.1_final.html.*

Thomas, W. P., & Collier, V. P. (1997). *School effectiveness for language minority students.* Washington, DC: National Clearinghouse for Bilingual Education.

Thorndike, R. L. (1973). *Reading comprehension in fifteen countries.* New York: Wiley.

Tierney, R. J., & Pearson, P. D. (1983). Toward a composing model of reading. *Language Arts, 60,* 568–579.

Tierney, R. J., & Pearson, P. D. (1985). New priorities for teaching reading. *Learning, 13*(8), 14–18.

Tierney, R. J., & Shanahan, T. (1990). Research on the reading–writing relationship: Interactions, transactions, and outcomes. In R. Barr, M. L. Kamil, P. Mosenthal, & P. D. Pearson (Eds.), *Handbook of reading research* (Vol. 2, pp. 246–280). White Plains, NY: Longman.

Torgeson, J. K., & Burgess, S. R. (1998). Consistency of reading-related phonological processes throughout early childhood: Evidence from longitudinal-correlational and instructional studies. In J. L. Metsala & L. C. Ehri (Eds.), *Word recognition in beginning literacy* (pp. 161–188). Mahwah, NJ: Erlbaum.

Tracey, D. H., & Morrow, L. M. (2002). Preparing young learners for successful reading comprehension: Laying the foundation. In C. C. Birch & M. Pressley (Eds.), *Comprehension instruction: Research-based best practices* (pp. 219–233). New York: Guilford Press.

Truss, L. (2003). *Eats, shoots and leaves: The zero tolerance approach to punctuation.* New York: Penguin Books.

University of Chicago Press Journals. (2007, April 27). Non-native kindergarteners learn vocabulary faster than native English-speakers with the right lessons. *ScienceDaily.* Retrieved July 11, 2008, from *www.sciencedaily.com/releases/2007/04/070426110153.htm.*

Van Dijk, T. A., & Kintsch, W. (1983). *Strategies of discourse comprehension.* New York: Academic Press.

Van Gelderen, A., Schoonen, R., De Glopper, K., Hulstijn, J., Simis, A., Snellings, P., et al. (2007). Linguistic knowledge, processing speed, and metacognitive knowledge in first- and second-language reading comprehension: A componential analysis. *Journal of Educational Psychology, 96*(1), 19–30.

Vellutino, F. R., Scanlon, D. M., & Tanzman, M. S. (1994). Components of reading ability: Issues and problems in operationalizing word identification, phonological coding, and orthographic coding. In G. R. Lyon (Ed.), *Frames of reference for the assessment of learning disabilities: New views on measurement issues* (pp. 279–332). Baltimore: Brookes.

Venezky, R. L. (1970). *The structure of English orthography.* The Hague: Mouton.

Vygotsky, L. (1978). *Mind in society.* Cambridge, MA: Harvard University.

Vygotsky, L. (1986). *Thought and language.* Cambridge, MA: MIT Press.

Wagner, R. G., Torgeson, J. K., & Rashotte, C. A. (1994). The development of reading-related phonological processing abilities: New evidence of biodirectional causality from a latent variable longitudinal study. *Developmental Psychology, 30,* 73–87.

Wang, M., & Koda, K. (2007). Commonalities and differences in word identification skills among learners of English as a second language. *Language Learning, 57*(1), 201–222.

Waxman, H. C., & Tellez, K. (2002). *Research synthesis on effective teaching practices for English language learners.* Philadelphia: Temple University, Mid-Atlantic Regional Educational Laboratory, Laboratory for Student Success. (ERIC Document Retrieval No. ED474821).

Whipple, G. (Ed.). (1925). *The twenty-fourth yearbook of the National Society for the Study of Education: Report of the national committee on reading.* Bloomington, IL: Public School Publishing.

White, L. (1991). Adverb placement in second language acquisition: Some effects of positive and negative evidence in the classroom. *Second Language Research, 7,* 133–161.

The WIDA Consortium. (2004). *ACCESS for ELLs.* Oshkosh, WI: Wisconsin Department of Public Instruction.

Williams, J. D., & Snipper, G. C. (1990). *Literacy and bilingualism.* New York: Longman.

Williams, T., Hakuta, K., Haertel, E., et al. (2007). *Similar English learner students, different results: Why do some schools do better? A follow-up analysis, based on a large-scale survey of California elementary schools serving low-income and EL students.* Mountain View, CA: EdSource.

Wittrock, M. C. (1984). Writing and the teaching of reading. In J. M. Jensen (Ed.), *Composing and comprehending* (pp. 77–83). Urbana, IL: National Council of Teachers of English.

Yule, G. (2006). *The study of language* (3rd ed.). Cambridge, UK: Cambridge University Press.

Zipke, M. (2008). Teaching metalinguistic awareness and reading comprehension with riddles. *The Reading Teacher, 62*(2), 128–137.

Zutell, J., & Allen, J. (1988). The English spelling strategies of Spanish-speaking bilingual children. *TESOL Quarterly, 22,* 333–340.

Zutell, J., Donelson, R., Bevans, J., & Todt, P. (2006). Building a focus on oral reading fluency into individual instruction for struggling readers. In T. Rasinski, C. Blachowicz, & K. Lems (Eds.), *Fluency instruction: Research-based best practices* (pp. 265–278). New York: Guilford Press.

Zwiers, J. (2006). Integrating academic language, thinking, and content: Learning scaffolds for non-native speakers in the middle grades. *Journal of English for Academic Purposes, 5*(4), 317–332.

Zwiers, J. (2007). Teacher practices and perspectives for developing academic language. *International Journal of Applied Linguistics, 17*(1), 93–116.

Zwiers, J. (2008). *Building academic language: Essential practices for content classrooms.* Newark, DE: International Reading Association.

Index